Language Acquisition and Contact in the Iberian Peninsula

Studies on Language Acquisition

Edited by
Peter Jordens

Volume 57

Language Acquisition and Contact in the Iberian Peninsula

Edited by
Alejandro Cuza
Pedro Guijarro-Fuentes

DE GRUYTER
MOUTON

ISBN 978-1-5015-1679-5
e-ISBN (PDF) 978-1-5015-0998-8
e-ISBN (EPUB) 978-1-5015-0988-9
ISSN 1861-4248

Bibliographic information published by the Deutsche Nationalbibliothek
The Deutsche Nationalbibliothek lists this publication in the Deutsche Nationalbibliografie;
detailed bibliographic data are available on the Internet at http://dnb.dnb.de.

© 2018 Walter de Gruyter, Inc., Boston/Berlin
Typesetting: Integra Software Services Pvt. Ltd.
Printing and binding: CPI books GmbH, Leck

www.degruyter.com

Contents

Contents

Pedro Guijarro-Fuentes and Alejandro Cuza

Introduction: Language contact and change in the Iberian Peninsula

1 Introduction

The Spanish language is spoken by an estimated 477 million people worldwide. As a consequence, there are many situations in which it comes into contact with other languages. These contact situations include not only uncountable indigenous languages, but also Brazilian Portuguese in Latin America, European Portuguese, Basque, Catalan, Galician, Arabic in Spanish Morocco, English and Philippine dialects in the Philippines, and multiple varieties of American English in the United States and Puerto Rico. Moreover, in other parts of the world, such as the Caribbean Islands, Spanish coexists with French, French Creole, Papiamentu, English, and Dutch. Judeo-Spanish is found in Israel and the Balkans, as well as in other areas of the world where, with some local idiosyncrasies, it has survived for centuries in contact with other languages.

This volume focuses on the contact between Spanish and other language varieties, including Catalan, Portuguese and Galician in the Spanish Peninsula. It is thus important to understand and to know more about the language situation within Spain. *What about the people in the contact situation described herein? How old is the language contact situation?* In Spain, these speech communities are not just in contact, but they are in fact bilingual (e.g., Basque-Spanish, Catalan-Spanish among others). An important factor in understanding the situation in all the bilingual communities of Spain is the process of language shift that has occurred in those communities as a consequence of the political change witnessed during the nineteenth and twentieth centuries. This is particularly relevant nowadays due to the consequences of the ban on all minority languages – including Basque, Galician and Catalan – during the dictatorial regime of Franco which lasted from 1939–1975. Language shift in Basque, Galician and Catalan took place during this time, at least until the introduction of a democratic regime that presaged the passing of the Constitution in 1978. Since the establishment of democracy, access to these minority languages has been increasing through political and socio-cultural activities and through education in particular. Although Basque, Galician and Catalan are considered minority languages, generally

Pedro Guijarro-Fuentes, University of Balearic Islands
Alejandro Cuza, Purdue University

https://doi.org/10.1515/9781501509988-001

speaking, Spanish is not necessarily the dominant language in certain areas due to linguistic and socio-political reasons. Basque, Catalan, and to a lesser extent Galician, have dominant status in certain regions of the country. In this sense, all languages including Spanish can be viewed as having both a dominant or minority status depending on the characteristics of the community.

A number of other issues are also of interest in relation to the recent history and linguistic landscape of the Iberian Peninsula and of Spain in particular. First, all bilingual communities within Spain are more or less diglossic. Second, most minority languages have experienced dialectal diversification, as in the case of Basque, with eight dialects, and of Catalan with four dialects. For that matter, it is notoriously difficult to distinguish between "language" and "dialect". Two distinct linguistic varieties may end up being categorized as dialects or as separate languages depending on whether one uses linguistic, historical, communicative, or political criteria *inter alia*. For instance, by the communicative criterion "mutual intelligibility", the Catalan varieties spoken in Valencia, Mallorca, Catalonia, and Andorra could presumably be categorized as different dialects. This squares with the largely common linguistic properties of these varieties. Yet they are, for past and present political and historical reasons, more commonly thought of as being distinct languages. Most minority languages do not have a very long written tradition, especially considering their dialectal diversification. Thus, either no standard language exists or standardization is currently taking place, as in the case in the Basque country. Because of these specific characteristics, language contact and consequently the acquisition process a speaker is faced with, are unique.

In the present volume, we aim to explore the characteristics of such language contact situations, be it from a structural, developmental, societal or cognitive perspective. In the study of language contact, a significant amount of research has been done on different types of bilingual groups (second language learners, successive bilinguals and heritage speakers), but there is much less research on speakers who have extensive knowledge of two or more typologically proximate languages such as the ones described here. Many, or even most, bilingual speakers grow up speaking a certain variety in their home and community that on one or several levels may differ from other varieties or from the national standard language that is later encountered in school, the media and other situations. Little is known about these speakers' mental representations of a mutually intelligible, closely related spoken variety. Do we observe transfer, attrition and general influence of one variety on the other in bilingual speakers? Is there only a gradual difference, perhaps measurable in terms of typological proximity?

Because language in society is inherently multifaceted and multidisciplinary, the study of such a complex phenomenon as bilingualism (or multilingualism) cannot be justly limited to traditional or purely linguistic approaches, namely to the study of the domains syntax, morphology, phonology, and semantics. Thus, the papers within this volume include not only discussion of languages in contact in the most traditional sense, but also serious explorations of other subfields.

Nevertheless, in spite of all this multidisciplinarianism, we believe the generative tradition embodies the most promise in enlightening us about what happens when two similar or dissimilar languages come into contact with each other. Language contact situations such as the ones described herein can shed new light on the nature of languages in contact in general. We can learn many new aspects about languages when they come into contact, interact, converge and, ultimately, affect each other in a permanent way. Thus, *what happens when two or more languages come into contact? What happens to languages that are used simultaneously in bilingual communities? How is it that languages change substantially and how is it that a new language may develop, over time, from contact situations?*

Much of the existing literature on bilingualism concerns English as one member of the dyad, usually being the more dominant of the two or the majority language. But, what about Spanish or Portuguese as the majority language interacting with minority languages such as Catalan or Galician? Much less has been said about the frequently occurring situations of bilingualism in the Iberian Peninsula. The papers in this collection, prepared for the most part by scholars based in Spain and Portugal, reflect current research interests in bilingualism within formal linguistic theory. Their articles cover a wide range of topics and approaches, but all have in common a contact situation involving Spanish as the dominant or majority language. To help navigate through the volume, in the next section we offer a brief discussion of the papers included.

2 Chapter summaries

The first four contributions focus on Spanish in contact with Catalan. Although there exists a considerable body of work on the acquisition of Catalan, the sociolinguistic context where this acquisition takes place is tacitly assumed to be of no import in the development of mental grammars. Most of the empirical studies conducted on the acquisition of pronominal clitics, for example, have been carried out with children who are mainly exposed to Catalan. In an attempt to break this general trend, Perpiñán (2016) pointed out that, depending on a child's sociolinguistic background, the acquisition of some grammatical structures may be incomplete. She observes a contrast between the judgments and productions of Catalan-dominant and Spanish-dominant speakers of Catalan with respect to the pronominal clitics *en* and *hi*. Departing from Perpiñán's work, the paper by Anna Gavarró (Chapter 1) presents a new grammaticality judgment task and further explores partitivity in the nominal domain (as Noun ellipsis differs between Catalan and Spanish). The results demonstrate differential performance in clitic judgment depending on whether the participants are native speakers of Catalan or Spanish. The paper also reports a correlation between subjects' judgments on partitive clitic production and partitivity in Noun ellipsis. To account for these results, Gavarró argues for the emergence of null pronominals as a result of transfer from Spanish in children with less exposure to Catalan. The null pronominals arise in syntactic contexts where a full pronominal is available in Catalan. On a theoretical level, it seems that the cluster of grammatical properties that characterize the grammar of Spanish-speaking bilinguals of Catalan can be accounted for by the loss of an uninterpretable feature in *v*P and the covert marking of partitivity.

According to Carminati's (2002) *Position of Antecedent Hypothesis* (PAH), Italian null pronouns have antecedents in subject position, while overt pronouns are coreferential with antecedents in object position. PAH's predictions do not extend to all null subject languages (Filiaci, Sorace & Carreiras 2014) or even to different varieties of the same language (Keating, Jegerski, & VanPatten 2016). To date, no studies have assessed the processing of subject pronouns in Catalan or in Spanish bilinguals in contact with Catalan. It has been suggested that systematic and extensive language contact tends to lead to contact varieties in bilingual communities (Perpiñán 2016; Silva-Corvalán 2008) and that the integration of information from the different sources involved in pronominal resolution is challenging for bilingual speakers (Sorace, Serratrice, Filiaci & Baldo 2009).

In this context, the study by Aurora Bel and Estela García-Alcaraz (Chapter 2) aims to compare the interpretation and processing of subject pronouns in Catalan and Spanish on the one hand, and in monolingual and bilingual Spanish in contact with Catalan on the other. In the first experiment, two acceptability judgment tasks, one in Catalan and an equivalent in Spanish, evaluate the strength of three factors in the interpretation of ambiguous subject pronouns within complex sentences. The results from this first experiment show that subordinate clause and main clause orders conform more to the PAH than the reverse, and that null pronouns refer back to subject antecedents in both Catalan and Spanish. However, only Catalan displays the Italian-type division of labor between null and overt pronouns. In the second experiment, the bilingual variety of Spanish/Catalan spoken in Catalonia and monolingual Spanish were contrasted using the same task. The Italian-style division of labor pattern appeared in bilingual Spanish, which suggests crosslinguistic influence from the interpretive biases of Catalan pronoun resolution. The authors also report partial findings from an ongoing and larger self-paced reading study on the integration of syntactic information during temporarily ambiguous pronoun resolution in monolingual and bilingual Spanish in contact with Catalan. The bilinguals' slower reading times at the critical disambiguating region suggest that the bilingual Spanish variety is affected by transfer or, at least, by cross-language activation at the processing level. These findings, together with those of the judgment task, show that the bilingual speakers find it unnatural to form a coreferential chain between an overt pronoun and an antecedent in subject position, which is consistent with Silva-Corvalán's (2008) view that contact situations involve a gradual change of discourse-pragmatic features and processing restrictions.

In Chapter 3, Alejandro Cuza and Pedro Guijarro-Fuentes investigate the distribution of copula *ser* and *estar* (*to be* in English) in the grammars of Catalan/Spanish adult bilinguals born and raised in Mallorca. In Spanish, copula *estar* is required in locative constructions, but in Catalan both copular verbs can be used depending on the animacy features of the subject (Brucart 2012). With stage-level predicates, Spanish also uses *estar* almost categorically, while Catalan is more variable. In both languages, though, *estar* is not allowed with event locatives. No previous work, however, has examined copula use with event locatives among Spanish/Catalan bilinguals, and the role of input frequency in the acquisition of variable contexts. 19 adult bilinguals (age range, 18–27; M=21;4; SD=2.7) born and raised in Mallorca took part in the study. An Elicited Production Task tested the use of *ser* and *estar* in locative constructions with animate and inanimate subjects, in event locative constructions, and in stage-level predicates. For Catalan, the authors predicted the adult bilinguals to show *estar* overextension in locative constructions regardless of animacy features and with stage-level predicates due to the more restricted semantic selection in Spanish. However, the authors did not predict difficulties with event locatives, since both Spanish and Catalan require the use of *ser* in this context. For Spanish, on the other hand, Cuza and Guijarro-Fuentes did not predict any overextension errors of either *ser* or *estar* since Spanish was the dominant language of the participants and the sociopolitical dominant language in Palma de Mallorca. In regard to Catalan, results showed *estar* overuse with both animate and inanimate locative constructions, as expected. With stage-level predicates, participants also preferred *estar* over *ser*, confirming the authors' expectations. With event locatives, the bilingual speakers preferred *ser*, also as expected. Nevertheless, a small number of bilinguals preferred *estar* despite the fact that both Spanish and Catalan do not allow this copula with event nominals. In regard to Spanish, the bilingual speakers preferred *estar* with locatives and stage-level predicates almost categorically, as predicted. With event locatives, the participants overwhelmingly used *ser* rather than *estar*. The findings are discussed along the lines of crosslinguistic influence from Spanish on the Catalan grammar, leading to a more restrictive use of *ser* with adverbial locatives and adjectival predicates.

The linguistic configuration of trilingualism remains understudied today (Hofmann 2001; Montanari 2013; Quay 2011). The comparison of simultaneous trilingual children with bilingual children allows us to evaluate the role of linguistic and non-linguistic factors (e.g., the amount of input) for linguistic development, since trilingual children receive significantly less input in their languages. In Chapter 4, Laia Arnaus Gil, Amelia Jiménez-Gaspar and Natascha Müller examine four trilingual children longitudinally from the age of 1;6 until 5;0, 31 trilingual children and nine multilingual (i.e. more than three languages) children cross-linguistically. For comparison, they also investigate 32 bilingual children. The children were all born in Spain or Germany, and Spanish was one of their three L1s. In the longitudinal study, the trilingual children were exposed to all three languages from birth (Arnaus Gil & Müller 2015). The children were compared on the basis of age, Mean Length of Utterance (MLU) and the results achieved in the Peabody Picture Vocabulary Test (PVT) (Dunn & Dunn 2007). The grammatical domain under study is Spanish copula selection. According to the authors' findings, at a very early stage, monolingual Spanish children show a short, target-deviant stage during which they omit *ser* and overgeneralize *estar* to *ser*-contexts. Bilingual children are qualitatively similar to monolinguals, but their acquisition is delayed (Arnaus Gil 2013). Interestingly, Spanish and Catalan trilinguals outrank bilingual children in Spanish, especially the German-Spanish bilinguals (Arnaus Gil & Müller 2015), even though they have to divide their language exposure time by three. In light of these findings, the authors claim that trilingualism can enhance linguistic development in the absence of the quantity of input that monolingual and bilingual children receive. Furthermore, the early acquisition of a second or third language enables the multilingual child to leave it behind much more quickly than the monolingual or the bilingual child.

The next two papers are concerned with monolingual and heritage speakers of Portuguese, and English-Spanish bilinguals respectively. The study by Pilar Barbosa, Cristina Flores and Cátia Pereira (Chapter 5) investigates the realization of subjects in infinitival complements of causative and perception verbs by adult monolingual and heritage speakers (HSs) of European Portuguese (EP). In EP uninflected infinitival complements of causative and perception verbs take an accusative case marked subject. As for inflected infinitives, standard case theory predicts that the embedded subject should be realized as a nominative pronoun (Raposo 1987). Thirty monolingual Portuguese speakers and 30 HSs of EP living in Germany were asked to complete a Completion task and an Acceptability Judgment task. The authors seek to determine which option (i.e. inflected infinitival complement *versus* uninflected infinitival complement) is more productive in native EP and how each option correlates with the case morphology of the subject of the infinitive (nominative or accusative). Furthermore, they ask whether HSs, who have reduced exposure to EP, show similar preferences as their monolingual peers. The results demonstrate that the performance of both groups is roughly the same. Both groups show a preference for Accusative Case marked subjects. This preference holds also in the case of inflected infinitives, an unexpected result. The authors offer an account of this preference that relies on the particular status of preverbal subjects in a null subject language (NSL) such as EP (Alexiadou & Anagnostopoulou 1998; Barbosa 1995). Unlike monolinguals, heritage speakers show a tendency for using and accepting nominative pronouns even in cases where the infinitive is uninflected. Thus, on par with the raising-to-object option, they allow for the *default* case strategy. A similar behavior has also been reported in early stages of acquisition of the PIC in EP (Santos, Gonçalves & Hyams 2016). In light of these findings, the authors conclude that HSs of EP develop native-like knowledge of these structures but retain features of early stages of acquisition, namely unstable knowledge of the conditions under which the Nominal Case option is blocked.

Even though research on bilingual first language acquisition (2L1) could be conceptualized as monolingual acquisition (L1) of two individual languages, the fact that in 2L1 acquisition there is exposure to input from two languages has consequences in terms of how the two language systems interact in the mind of the bilingual. That is, although it is unquestionable that L1 and 2L1 acquisition share similar mechanisms and processes, there are core issues such as language dominance, crosslinguistic influence and code-switching that are specific to simultaneous bilingual acquisition. Thus, at the core of 2L1 research lies the issue of whether, where, how and when crosslinguistic influence occurs, how language dominance is defined and conceptualized, and whether and how linguistic and psycholinguistic principles constrain code-switching (Döpke 2000; Hulk & Müller 2000; Genesee, Nicoladis & Paradis 1995; Liceras & Fernández Fuertes 2018). Raquel Fernández Fuertes and Juana Liceras examine these issues in Chapter 6. The authors investigate the role of language dominance and crosslinguistic influence in the distribution of sentential subjects and copula predicates *ser* and *estar* among two Spanish/English bilingual twins born and raised in Spain (FerFuLice corpus in CHILDES) as well as code-switching data from the twins and other Spanish-English bilingual children. The authors argue that the occurrence and directionality of crosslanguage interaction is linked to lexical specialization in that, on the one hand, Spanish individual level predicates are realized as copula *ser* while stage level predicates are realized as *estar* and, on the other, Spanish has two sets of overt pronouns (the verbal personal affixes and the overt realization of null subjects). This leads the authors to propose that in the early stages of English-Spanish simultaneous bilingual development, Spanish is the language that constitutes the locus of influence, and that influence has a facilitating effect, evidenced in the early emergence of copula constructions and sentential subjects in English compared to monolingual development. They further argue that the Grammatical Feature Spell-out Hypothesis, a language acquisition constraint on code-switching, provides a language internal account of language dominance which explains the overwhelming preference for the spontaneous production of DP switches where Spanish provides the determiner and English the noun.

The volume ends with a contribution by Francisco Dubert García & Carlos Acuña Fariñas focused on Galician in contact with Spanish (Chapter 7). Galician and Spanish have been in contact since the very origins of both languages. The two languages are structurally, genetically and typologically related. As the intensity of the contact has been growing during the 20th century, more and more grammatical Spanish features have been incorporated into Galician. The authors investigate how the borrowing of Spanish roots that hyper-characterize the expression of various morphosyntactic features of some verbs causes a restructuring of the grammar of an urban variety of Galician. They argue that the incorporation of Spanish borrowings seems to lead to increased complexity of Galician's grammar. However, what seems to be a complexification of the actual grammar might in fact be a simplification process from the bilingual speaker's point of view.

3 Conclusion

As outlined in the introductory section, it is clear that there are considerable differences among the variety of languages spoken in the Iberian Peninsula. These differences ultimately mirror the differences existing in adult and children's bilingual mental grammar. As such, bilingual children may or may not converge on the same grammar of the standard variety. Thus, the extent of the cross-linguistic differences and the individual differences in the rate of acquisition observed in some of the studies included herein are only indications that languages are learned differently given the different internal and external circumstances. As languages change fast, creating new hybrid languages, divergence in the rate and in the style of acquisition of different linguistic domains is simply due to the unstable and diverse environment in which bilingual language acquisition is operating.

We hope that these articles serve as a springboard for discussion and an inspiration for further study both by seasoned researchers and younger scholars who might work on structural and developmental aspects of bilingualism involving closely related linguistic varieties. We also hope that interdisciplinary trends develop further, with a view to better integrating the knowledge and understanding of bilingual individuals in society. We wish to give our deepest thanks to the contributors for their excellent work and dedication to the present volume. We are also deeply indebted to the external reviewers who made this research endeavour possible. Last but not least, we express sincere appreciation to Peter Jordens of Amsterdam VU University for his help and guidance in organizing this volume, and to Lara Wysong of De Gruyter Mouton Press for her commitment, expertise and courtesy.

References

Alexiadou, A. & Anagnostopoulou, E. 1998. Parametrizing AGR: Word order, V-movement, and EPP-checking. *Natural Language and Linguistic Theory* 16. 491–540.

Arnaus Gil, L. 2013. *La selección copulativa y auxiliar: las lenguas romances (español – italiano – catalán – francés) y el alemán en contacto. Su adquisición en niños bilingües y trilingües*. Tübingen: Narr.

Arnaus Gil, L. & N. Müller. 2015. The acquisition of Spanish in a bilingual and in a trilingual setting: Combining Spanish with German, French and Catalan. In T. Judy & S. Perpiñán (eds.), *The acquisition of Spanish in understudied language pairings*, 135–168. Amsterdam: Benjamins.

Barbosa, P. 1995. *Null Subjects*. Cambridge, MA: MIT PhD dissertation.

Batllori, M. & F. Roca.2011. The grammaticalization of ser and estar in Romance. In Dianne Jonas, John Whitman & Andrew Garrett (eds.), *Grammatical change: origins, nature, outcomes*. Oxford: Oxford University Press.

Bel, A. 2003. The syntax of subjects in the acquisition of Spanish and Catalan. *Probus* 15. 1–26.

Brucart, J. M. 2012. Copular alternation in Spanish and Catalan attributive sentences. *Revista de Estudos Linguísticos da Universidade do Porto* 7. 9–43.

Döpke, S. 2000. Generation of and retraction from crosslinguistically motivated structures in bilingual first language acquisition. *Bilingualism: Language and Cognition* 3(3). 209–226.

Dunn, L. M., D. M. Dunn, A. Lenhard, W. Lenhard, R. Segerer & S. Suggate. 1986. *Peabody (Peabody Picture Vocabulary Test)*. Diablo: Pearson.

Filiaci, F., A. Sorace & M. Carreiras. 2014. Anaphoric biases of null and overt subjects in Italian and Spanish: a cross-linguistic comparison. *Language and Cognitive Processes* 29(7). 825–843.

Genesee, F., E. Nicoladis, & J. Paradis. 1995. Language differentiation in early bilingual development. *Journal of Child Language* 22(3). 611–631.

Hulk, A. & Müller, N. 2000. Bilingual first language acquisition at the interface between syntax and pragmatics. *Bilingualism: Language and Cognition* 3(3). 227–244.

Keating, G., J. Jegerski & B. VanPatten. 2016. Online processing of subject pronouns in monolingual and heritage bilingual speakers of Mexican Spanish. *Bilingualism: Language and Cognition* 19(1). 36–49.

Liceras, J. M. & R. Fernández Fuertes. 2018. Subject omission/production in child bilingual English and child bilingual Spanish: The view from linguistic theory. *Probus* 29(1).

Montanari, S. 2013. Productive trilingualism in infancy: What makes it possible? *World Journal of English Language* 3(1). 62–77.

Perpiñán, S. 2016. Catalan-Spanish bilingualism continuum: The expression of adverbial clitics in different types of early bilinguals. *Linguistic Approaches to Bilingualism*. doi 10.1075/lab.15004.

Perpiñán, S. 2014. Locatives and existentials in L2 Spanish: the acquisition of the semantic contrasts between ser, estar and haber. *Second Language Research* 30(4). 485–514.

Quay, S. 2011. Trilingual toddlers at daycare centers: the role of caregivers and peers in language development. *International Journal of Multilingualism* 8 (1). 22–41.

Raposo, E. 1987. Case theory and infl-to-comp: The inflected infinitive in European Portuguese. *LI* 18. 85–109.

Santos, A. L., A. Gonçalves & N. Hyams. 2016. Aspects of the acquisition of object control and ECM-type verbs in European Portuguese. *Language Acquisition* 23(3). 199–233.

Silva-Corvalán, C. 2008. The limits of convergence in language contact. *Journal of language contact* 2(1). 213–224.

Sorace, A., L. Serratrice, F. Filiaci & M. Baldo. 2009. Discourse conditions on subject pronoun realization: Testing the linguistic intuitions of older bilingual children. *Lingua* 119. 460–477.

Anna Gavarró
Language acquisition and change: The acquisition of the Catalan partitive and locative clitics

Abstract: Although there exists a considerable body of work on the acquisition of Catalan, the sociolinguistic context in which this acquisition takes place is tacitly assumed to be of no import in the development of mental grammars. Most of the experimental studies conducted on the acquisition of pronominal clitics have been carried out with children who are mainly exposed to Catalan. In a break from this general trend, Perpiñan (2016) stressed that, depending on a child's sociolinguistic background, the acquisition of some grammatical structures may be incomplete, as exemplified by a contrast between the judgments and productions of Catalan-dominant and Spanish-dominant speakers of Catalan with the pronoun clitics *en* and *hi*. Extending on Perpiñan's work, I present a new grammaticality judgment task and further explore partitivity in the nominal domain (as Noun ellipsis differs between Catalan and Spanish). The results show a differentiated performance in clitic judgment depending on whether the participants are native speakers of Catalan or Spanish, and a correlation between their judgments on partitive clitic production and partitivity in Noun ellipsis. To account for these results, I hypothesize the emergence of null pronominals as a result of transfer from Spanish in children less exposed to Catalan, in syntactic contexts in which a full pronominal is available in Catalan. The cluster of grammatical properties that characterize Spanish native speakers of Catalan can be accounted for by the loss of an uninterpretable feature in vP and covert marking of partitivity.

1 Introduction

Partitive and locative pronouns are found in only a subset of the contemporary Romance languages, although it is known that they were part of the pronominal inventory of e.g. Old Portuguese and Old Spanish, exemplified in (1) and (2) respectively (examples taken from Martins 2001).

Anna Gavarró, Universitat Autònoma de Barcelona

https://doi.org/10.1515/9781501509988-002

(1) das ditas herdades e quintãa e Casal dela (...)
     of-the above-mentioned lands and farm and house of-it (...)

     que daqui adeãte o ouusse o dito Monsteiro liuremete
     that from-now on it should-own the above-mentioned monastery freely

     e e paz e fezesse **ende** o.que lhj aprouuesse sem ebargo seu nehuu.
     and in peace and should-do of-it whatever itself wished without
     constraint of-him none

'that from now on the monastery owns the lands and the farm with its house
without any constraints, using them freely in any manner that the monastery may
wish' (Old Portuguese, 1383)

(2) Aves torpes nin roncas **hi** non se acostavan.
     birds injured nor snorty there not themselves would lie
     'Injured birds or snorty birds would not be able to sleep there.'

(Old Spanish)

While these pronouns disappeared from Old Portuguese and Old Spanish in the
15th century (and may have been weak pronouns, as opposed to clitics, as argued
by Martins 2001), they have persisted as pronominal clitics in e.g. contemporary
Catalan, French and Italian. Example (3) illustrates partitive clitics and example
(4) locative clitics in Catalan.

(3) De cafè, no **n'**he pres.
     of coffee NEG part-cl have had
     'Coffee, I haven't had any.'

(4) A la biblioteca, no **hi** vaig mai.
     to the library NEG loc-cl go never
     'To the library, I never go.'

The acquisition of these clitics is relatively understudied; in this paper I extend
former work on the acquisition of these two types of clitics by Catalan native
speaking children and adult Spanish-Catalan bilingual speakers (drawing from
Gavarró et al. 2011 and Perpiñán 2016) and hypothesize on the course of language
change in Catalan. The paper is organized as follows. In section 2 I summarize
the findings in the acquisition literature. In section 3 I focus on the grammar of
partitive clitics, and hypothesize on the features that are lost in a new system akin
to that of modern Spanish and Portuguese. In section 4 I present a grammaticality

judgment task the results of which are complementary to those of Perpiñan (2016). Conclusions are drawn in section 5.[1]

2 Background

A first study on the acquisition of the partitive clitic *en* of Catalan was conducted by Gavarró, Mata and Ribera (2006). It involved the analysis of the spontaneous productions of three children from the CHILDES database, Gisela (age range 1;10,7–4;2,3, 20 files analyzed), Guillem (age range 1;1,29–4;0; 33 files) and Josep (1;1,28–4;0; 31 files). First occurrence of *en* varied in age depending on the child, but happened around MLU 1.5. *En* was produced from early on, but also optionally omitted for a period of time; Table 1 gives the absolute number and percentage of production and omission of partitive clitics in obligatory contexts in six MLU periods.

Table 1: Partitive clitic production and omission (from Gavarró et al. 2006).

MLU	clitic production	clitic omission	total clitic contexts
<1.5	3 (50%)	3 (50%)	6
<2	5 (71.4%)	2 (28.6%)	7
<2.5	42 (87.5%)	6 (12.5%)	48
<3	61 (83.3%)	14 (18.6%)	75
<3.5	49 (79%)	13 (21%)	62
>3.5	51 (83.6%)	10 (16.4%)	61
Total	211 (81.5%)	48 (18.5%)	259

In a second study on partitive clitic development, Gavarró, Guasti, Tuller, Prévost, Belletti, Cilibrasi, Delage and Vernice (2011) considered Catalan, French, and Italian clitics by means of an elicitation task in 5-year-old children. Some differences emerged in the production of the clitic between the languages, as seen in Figure 1, probably due to differences in the administration of the task, and can be regarded as spurious. However, it could be established

---

1 I would like to acknowledge the students at the Universitat Autònoma de Barcelona who took part in the experiment reported. Acknowledgments are also due to two anonymous reviewers for their detailed comments, Silvia Perpiñan for sharing her work with me, Anna Bartra for discussion, and Lena Morrill for carrying out the statistical analyses. Any remaining errors are my own. This work has been supported by projects FFI2014-56968-C4-1-P and FFI2017-87699-P.

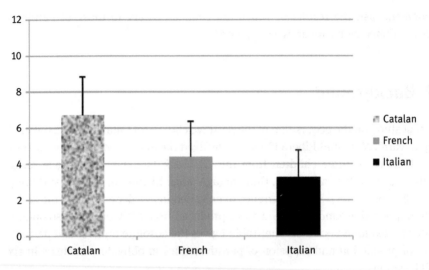

Figure 1: Mean number of responses (/12) with a partitive clitic.

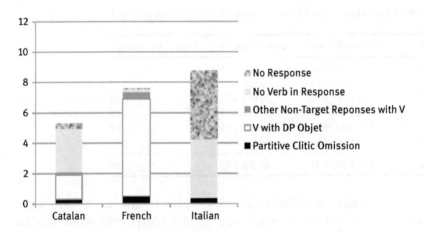

Figure 2: Mean number of responses not containing a partitive clitic (/12).

for all three languages that levels of partitive omission were very low at age 5, as shown in Figure 2.

The path of development in typically developing children can be accounted for under the Unique Checking Constraint (Gavarró, Torrens and Wexler 2010, after Wexler 1998). In that account clitic derivations that involve participle agreement are maturationally delayed, and this explains the optional omission of third person object clitics in the languages with participle agreement (Catalan, French, Italian). For the same reason, partitive clitics are expected to be optionally omitted since they trigger participle agreement in Catalan (exemplified in (5)), French and Italian. Participle agreement varies in realization in these languages: in French it is subject to phonological erosion, in Catalan it is mostly visible with feminine objects, not so much with masculine objects, still it remains a feature of these three contemporary varieties.

(5) De pel.lícules de Fassbinder, **n**'he vistes moltes.
     of films-f-pl of Fassbinder PARTcl have.1s seen-f-pl many
     'Films by Fassbinder, I have seen many.'

Under this account, the maturational effect of the UCC disappears by age 4, and so is not expected to have any effect in healthy individuals after that age.[2]

Perpiñan (2016) examined *en* and *hi* clitics in adult speakers of Catalan with varying degrees of early exposure to Catalan; of the 57 participants in her study, 22 were Catalan-dominant, 15 were balanced Catalan-Spanish bilinguals and 20 were Spanish-dominant bilinguals. She ran both a grammaticality judgment task and an elicited production task. In the elicited production task she asked questions the answer to which required the production of a locative, partitive or oblique clitic; in the grammaticality judgment task she asked for judgments where a lead-in sentence was followed by the experimental item; the experimental items included (i) a full DP (6); (ii) a target clitic (7); (iii) ungrammatical clitic omission (8); and (iv) ungrammatical doubling (9).

(6) a. Els nens passegen per la platja. Passegen per la platja cada tarda.
         the children walk-3pl on the beach walk-3pl on the beach
         every afternoon
     b. Els bebès sempre tenen gana. El meu sempre té gana!
         the babies always have-3pl hunger the mine always has hunger

(7) a. Els nens passegen per la platja. Hi passegen cada tarda.
         the children walk-3pl on the beach CLloc walk every afternoon

---

2 I refer the reader to Gavarró et al. (2010) for details on how the UCC operates. Basically, clitic omission is one way of avoiding a UCC violation (while ClP fails to be projected); clitic production implies a violation of the UCC but is on target with respect to ClP projection. Both are 'minimal violators' and are thus found optionally.

b. Els bebès sempre tenen gana. El meu sempre en té!
the babies always have-3pl hunger the mine always CLpart has

(8) a. Els nens passegen per la platja. Passegen cada tarda.
the children walk-3pl on the beach walk-3pl every afternoon
b. Els bebès sempre tenen gana. El meu sempre té!
the babies always have-3pl hunger the mine always has

(9) a. Els nens passegen per la platja. Hi passegen per la platja cada tarda.
the children walk-3pl on the beach CLloc walk-3pl on the beach
every afternoon
b. Els bebès sempre tenen gana. El meu sempre en té gana!
the babies always have-3pl hunger the mine always CLpart has
hunger

((6) to (9) exemplify the locative and partitive uses of *hi* and *en* only; the experiment by Perpiñan included the same number of items with oblique *hi* and oblique *en*, which I do not reproduce for reasons of space. They correspond to PP complements introduced by prepositions *a* and *de*, respectively.) The results of the production task are reproduced in Table 2 and show clear discrepancies in performance amongst the three groups, with clitic production being very high amongst the Catalan-dominant speakers, very low amongst the Spanish dominant speakers, and somewhere in between for the balanced Catalan-Spanish bilinguals. The one case in which Catalan-dominant speakers did not produce the clitic consistently was that of locative *hi*, and that is not surprising given that the resulting sentence is grammatical, unlike what happens when *en* is omitted (cf. (8a) and (8b)).

In the grammaticality judgment task, the Catalan-dominant group produced judgments that were statistically different from those of the Spanish-dominant group (in that the Spanish-dominant participants accepted both clitic omissions and ungrammatical clitic doubling). The balanced Catalan-Spanish bilinguals generally patterned with the Catalan-dominant group (the differences between the two groups not being statistically significant), but in the case of clitic *en* ungrammatical productions (omission in particular) were accepted by the balanced bilinguals more often than by the Catalan-dominant speakers.

To sum up, the Spanish-dominant group showed robust differences with respect to the Catalan-dominant in both grammaticality judgment and production, especially in the ungrammatical conditions. The balanced bilinguals were closer to the Catalan-dominant participants in grammaticality judgement, but closer to

Table 2: Mean percentages of correct answers (from Perpiñan 2016: 24).

clitic	group	target clitic	omission	full DP	other clitic	other structure
obliq.*en*	Catalan	90.5%	4.8%	.9%	1.9%	1.9%
	bilingual	61.3%	14.7%	20%	4%	0
	Spanish	42.1%	21.05%	24.2%	10%	0
partit. *en*	Catalan	96.2%	0	3.8%	0	0
	bilingual	72%	14.7%	12%	0	1.3%
	Spanish	69.5%	20%	8.4%	0	0
num. *en*	Catalan	87.6%	1.9%	8.6%	0	0
	bilingual	52%	28%	16%	0	0
	Spanish	48.4%	41.1%	6.3%	1%	1%
obliq. *hi*	Catalan	91.4%	5.7%	0	2.9%	0
	bilingual	38.6%	36%	9.3%	14.7%	0
	Spanish	22.1%	45.3%	12.6%	17.9%	0
loc. *hi*	Catalan	34.3%	63.8%	0	1.9%	0
	bilingual	13.3%	84%	1.3%	0	1.3%
	Spanish	6.3%	80%	3.2%	9.5%	0

the Spanish-dominant when we turn to production (see Table 2). The conclusion drawn by Perpiñan (2016) was that time of onset of acquisition cannot be the sole determining factor in the levels of performance attained (since all the participants had been exposed to Catalan at the age of 0–3 years), and that quantity and quality of input also have to be taken into account to explain acquisition path and attainment.

3 On the adult grammar of partitivity in Romance

Let us now consider the grammar underlying the performance by the adult participants seen above. In Gavarró, Torrens and Wexler (2010) it was noted that participle agreement triggered by third person object clitics is found with a cluster of grammatical properties. First, adjacency between the verb and the object is required in the languages with participle agreement, but not in those without it. Compare Catalan VOS and the ban on VSO (10) with the availability of both in Spanish (11) (Catalan examples taken from Solà 1992)

(10) a. *Avui comprarà en Joan menjar.
today will-buy D Joan food

    b. Avui comprarà menjar en Joan.
       today will-buy food D Joan
       'Today Joan will buy food.'

(11) a. Hoy comprará Juan comida.
       today will-buy Juan food
       'Today Juan will buy food.'
    b. Hoy comprará comida Juan.
       today will-buy food Juan
       'Today Juan will buy food.'

Spanish behaves the same as e.g. Portuguese, Romanian and Greek in this respect, all languages without participle agreement (see Ordóñez 2007, Tsakali and Wexler 2004), while Italian patterns with Catalan; French being a non-null subject language, it does not allow postverbal subjects and so the contrast in (10) cannot be reproduced for independent reasons.

Second, for direct objects, clitic doubling appears not to be an option in the Catalan/Italian language type (12), while it is possible in Greek and some American varieties of Spanish (13) (see Torrego 1998, Tsakali and Wexler 2004). (Clitic doubling is possible in Catalan with indirect object clitics, see Martin 2012.)

(12) *El Joan la va visitar a l'àvia.
     the Joan cl-f PAST visit to the grandmother

(13) Juan la visitó a la abuela.
     Juan cl-f visited to the grandmother
     'Juan visited the grandmother.'

Let us consider the analysis of these phenomena. Belletti (2004) argued that the word order in (11) is possible because the object remains in a low VP position, instead of raising to a VP-external position where it would be Case-assigned; (10) would then result from obligatory raising to the Case-position. Gavarró et al. (2010) hypothesized that object raising was due to a [−interpretable] feature in *v*P, the very same feature that triggered overt participle agreement. Case assignment would take place by Agree when the derivation involved no object raising (as in (11a)). Tsakali and Wexler (2004) argued that "a language is a clitic-doubling language if and only if it does not have agreement with the participle, assuming the appropriate morphology exists"; in their analysis, if the feature in *v*P is [+interpretable] (and lack of participle agreement follows), the clitic coexists with an object in its base position (feature checking taking place by Agree, without overt raising); clitic doubling results from having an overt DP in that position, rather than *pro*. The derivation is represented in (14).

(14) CIP[Cl ... vP[vP vP[... V *pro*/DP]]]

Gavarró et al. (2010) argued that the effects of the feature value of vP extended beyond third person (definite) object clitics. Partitives are a case in point: as illustrated above, they trigger past participle agreement in Catalan, French and Italian (although only optionally in Catalan – but that is also the case for third person object clitics) and, therefore, under the analysis proposed, v bears a [–interpretable] feature in their derivation.[3] Participle agreement is only attested when there is an associate of the clitic moving through Spec, vP – not with a full DP object (as in Kayne 1977). Hence I hypothesize that the [–interpretable] feature in vP is responsible for obligatory object raising resulting in VOS/*VSO and for participle agreement, with both direct objects and partitives.

Assuming this analysis for Catalan, the hypothesis in this paper is that the grammar of (a subset of) Spanish-dominant speakers of Catalan does not involve a [–interpretable] feature in vP, just like the grammar of adult Spanish. The inventory of clitics would possibly include a null partitive pronoun, as in adult Spanish, as well as a null locative/oblique pronoun. (The motivation for such null pronouns would lie in the need for thematically selected arguments to be syntactically present.) As a consequence, the productions of these speakers would (i) allow null pronominals where *hi* and *en* are found in Catalan, (ii) allow word order patterns that depart from those of Catalan, in particular VSO, and (iii) be less restrictive with clitic doubling. The question remains as to what is the relation between the interpretability of the feature in vP and the presence of null pronominals in the inventory: the observed facts of contemporary Romance suggest that overt partitive pronominals are only found in languages with a [– interpretable] feature in vP.

---

3 An anonymous reviewer points out that the clitic *en* only triggers past participle agreement in French if it stands for the whole object, as in (i), not if it pronominalises only a part of the object, as in (ii).

(i) Jean a écrit beaucoup de lettres. Regarde ces lettres – J' en ai prises.
   Jean has written many of letters Look-at these letters I cl-part have taken-f.pl
(ii) Jean a écrit beaucoup de romans. Regarde ces romans – J' en ai lu(*s) certains.
   Jean has written many of novels Look-at these novels I cl-part have read(*pl) some

Although relevant for the characterization of partitivity, this is a difference I do not consider further in this paper.

In the nominal domain, we also find variation within Romance, in particular with partitive NPs in elliptical contexts. Consider the examples in (15)–(16) and (17)–(18) for Catalan and Spanish (the first two examples come from Brucart and Gràcia 1986).

(15) No vull la faldilla negra, vull la vermella.   (Catalan)
      NEG want-1s the skirt black want-1s the red
      'I don't want the black skirt, I want the red one.'

(16) No quiero la falda negra, quiero la roja.   (Spanish)
      NEG want-1s the skirt black want-1s the red
      'I don't want the black skirt, I want the red one'

(17) He trencat una tassa blava i una *(de) blanca.   (Catalan)
      have-1s broken a cup blue and a of white
      'I broke a blue cup and a white one'

(18) He roto una taza azul y una (*de) blanca.   (Spanish)
      have-1s broken a cup blue and a white
      'I broke a blue cup and a white one'

While definite Noun ellipsis follows the same pattern in the two languages (15)–(16), for indefinites a contrast emerges: Catalan requires *de* 'of' to introduce the AP, Spanish not only does not require it, but bans it (17)–(18). Indefinites other than *un* 'one', such as *algun* 'some', or *molt* 'much, many', and numerals, also require *de* in Catalan; indefinites without an overt quantifier behave identically; see (19)–(22), all examples taken from Martí (1995).

(19) alguna *(de) buida
      some of empty 'some empty one'

(20) molts *(de) diferents
      many of different 'many different ones'

(21) tres *(de) barats
      three of cheap 'three cheap ones'

(22) N'he comprat *(de) blaus i *(de) blancs.
      CLpart have bought of blue-pl and of white-pl
      'I have bought some blue ones and some white ones.'

De is not inserted when the N is overt, as shown in (23).

(23) *He trencat un plat de blanc.
      have-1s broken a plate of white
      'I have broken a white plate.'

The obligatoriness of *de* holds for nominal ellipsis with a postnominal AP; *de* does not appear when the noun is followed by a PP or a relative clause, as illustrated in (24) and (25).

(24) un (*de) amb taques
      one of with stains
      'one with stains'

(25) uns (*de) que tenen taques
      some of that have-3pl stains
      'some that are stained'

The asymmetry between APs, on the one hand, and PPs and relatives clauses, on the other, is what motivated the analysis of Martí (1995) according to which *de* is a partitive Case marker: prepositions are Case markers, and do not receive Case, nor do CPs. The structure adopted for nominals by Martí is essentially the one proposed by Giusti (1992), where a QuantifierP dominates a CaseP (KP), as in (26). KP assigns partitive Case if Q is indefinite.

(26) $_{QP}[Q$ $_{KP}[$ $_K[de]$ $_{NumP}[AP$ $_{NumP}[Num ... $_{NP}[$ $_N[e]]]]]]$

Martí further argues that partitive Case marking occurs in the same way with clitic *en* in dislocation, exemplified in (27), and in (5) above.

(27) De llibres, en té molts.
      of books CLpart has many
      'Books, s/he has many.'

Spanish avoids *de* in dislocations as well (28).

(28) (*De) libros, tengo muchos.
      of books have-1s many
      'Books, I have many.'

Under her analysis, what distinguishes Catalan from Spanish is that partitive Case marking in Catalan must be overt (or, to be exact, that K must be visible): when the N raises to K, as in (29), K is overt; when it does not, *de* must overtly appear to mark partitive K.

(29) $_{QP}[Q[un]\ _{KP}[_K[gat]_{NumP}[\ _{AP}[petit]\ _{NumP}[\ _{Num}[\overline{gat}]\ ...\ _{NP}[_N[\overline{gat}]]]]]]$
        a cat small

As noted by Bernstein (1993), Spanish Noun ellipsis is also morphosyntactically marked; compare (30a) and (30b):

(30) a. **Un** libro rojo está encima de la mesa.
          a book red is on of the table
          'There is a red book on the table.'
      b. **Uno** rojo está encima de la mesa.
          a-ms red is on of the table
          'There is a red one on the table.'

The indefinite *un* in (30a) alternates with *uno* in (30b); *-o* is according to Bernstein (1993) a functional head "able to license an NP lacking lexical content", i.e. it licenses ellipsis. An NP lacking an adjectival complement would likewise be preceded by *uno* (*Uno está encima de la mesa* 'One (of them) is on the table'). Briefly, Catalan and Spanish impose different restrictions on NP ellipsis that follow partly from differences in partitive Case marking. Additional differences have been shown above, regarding word order and partitive cliticization. However, the two phenomena cannot be unified, as a scrutiny of other Romance varieties shows.

Italian patterns with Catalan in partitive cliticization (31), and in the presence of a preposition in dislocations (32), but with nominal ellipsis it behaves like Spanish (with the morpheme – *o* licencing ellipsis), rather than Catalan – see (33).[4] (Example (32) is from Benincà et al. 1988, (33) is from Bernstein (1996).)

(31) Ne ho viste.
        CLpart have-1s seen-f.pl
        'I have seen (some of) them.'

---

4 *Di* is possible in nominal ellipsis in Italian, but renders a different interpretation, not equivalent to Catalan *de* nominal ellipsis.

(32) Di sedie, ne abbiamo portate molte nel magazzino.
　　 of chairs CLpart have-1pl brought many in-the store
　　 'Chairs, we have taken many to the store.'

(33) Ne ho visto uno rosso.
　　 CLpart have-1s one-m red-m
　　 'I have seen a red one.'

Italian also demonstrates that *di* in dislocations is associated with partitive Case: when the object cliticizes in an Accusative clitic, *di* is omitted (34) (example from Benincà et al. 1988).

(34) (*Di) riso di questa qualità, lo mangiamo spesso.
　　 of rice of this quality CLacc eat-1pl often
　　 'Rice of this quality, we often eat.'

In French, nominal ellipsis contexts do not require (or allow) the preposition *de* as Case licenser, nor do we find a morphological marker licensing ellipsis (35) (example from Kayne 1977). French, however, like Catalan and Italian, introduces dislocated partitive complements with *de* (as in *de maison* in (35)).

(35) Vous en avez vraiment **une petite**, de maison.
　　 you CLpart have-2s really a little of house
　　 'You really have a LITTLE house.'

The implication of the Italian and French patterns is that there is no intrinsic link between the presence of the partitive clitic and the partitive marker in nominal elliptical constructions, as it is possible to have one without the other. French and Italian exemplify varieties intermediate between Spanish (with no overt partitive marking) and Catalan (where partitive marking appears consistently – see also Martí 2010, where the constructions discussed here appear under the name of false partitives). The facts observed are summarized in Table 3.

Table 3: Partitive grammatical marking and VSO.

	ne/en partitive clitic	dislocation partitive P	nominal partitive P	VSO
Catalan	+	+	+	–
Italian	+	+	–	–
French	+	+	–	–
Spanish	–	–	–	+

In the first part of this section I hypothesized that partitive clitic production follows from the same parameter setting that gives rise to the ban on VSO; now I have shown that, even though it belongs to the grammar of partitivity in adult Catalan, partitive marking in elliptical nominals cannot be part of the very same parameter (under the assumption that we want to account for the facts of Romance in a homogeneous way). This implies that the two phenomena may occur independently of each other in an individual. On the other hand, the prediction of the analysis put forward is that *en* cliticization and the ban on VSO are strongly associated because they are parametrically related. Experimentally, if we have varying exposure to Catalan, we may expect, at one end of the spectrum, native speakers of Catalan whose judgments are the ones described above; at the other end, we may expect to find Spanish-dominant speakers whose judgments regarding partitive and locative clitics are closer to those of Spanish speakers (allowing a null pronoun, etc.). Crucially, we do not expect any speaker to accept VSO and have a target grammar of partitive clitics.

4 A grammaticality judgment task

In order to test the link between clitic omission and the loss of other grammatical properties in the grammar of Catalan (specifically concerning the partitive clitic), I designed a grammaticality judgment task. The task included the following experimental conditions: (i) grammatical *hi* (locative or oblique) clitic production; (ii) ungrammatical *hi* omission; (iii) ungrammatical *hi* doubling; (iv) grammatical partitive *en* clitic production; (v) ungrammatical *en* omission; (vi) ungrammatical *en* doubling; (vii) grammatical nominal partitive constructions; (viii) ungrammatical nominal partitive constructions (with *de* omission); (ix) ungrammatical VSO. Conditions (i) to (vi) constituted Perpiñan's (2016) experiment detailed above and partially replicated it.

The control items included grammatical and ungrammatical sentences involving third person object clitics (third person object clitic production, omission and doubling) and the distractors were grammatical sentences of various types, amongst them canonical SVO sentences.

The experimental conditions are exemplified here, and the remaining items appear in the Appendix.

(36) Què poses als torrons? jo hi poso ou, ametlla i sucre.   (*hi* production)
    what put-2s in-the nougat? I CL put egg, almond and sugar

(37) Què poses al farcit? jo poso panses i pinyons.   (*hi omission)
    what put-2s in the stuffing? I put raisins and pinenuts

(38) Hi poso mel al iogurt.   (*_hi_ doubling)
      CLloc put-1s honey in.the yoghurt

(39) La Maria, de carn, no en menja mai.   (_en_ production)
      the Maria of meat NEG CLpart eats never

(40) El Dr. Turró, de medicina, sabia molta.   (*_en_ omission)
      the Dr Turró of medicine knew much

(41) No en beu vi perquè és abstemi.   (*_en_ doubling)
      NEG CLpart drinks wine because is abstemious

(42) La mare porta una maleta gran i una de petita.   (partitive NP)
      the mother carries a suitcase big and one of small

(43) He comprat tres llibres vells i tres nous.   (*partitive NP)
      hve-1s bought three books old and three new

(44) Ha triat vostè benzina sense plom.   (*VSO)
      have chosen you petrol without lead

Since no pictures accompanied the written sentences, to provide a context some sentences with(out) a clitic were preceded by a question that rendered the production of the clitic necessary (see, for example, (36) and (37) above).

Each experimental condition was represented by four tokens; the control items included four third person object clitics and six ungrammatical sentences with third person object clitic omission or doubling, plus 14 grammatical sentences corresponding to distractors. This amounted to a total of 60 items, counterbalanced for grammaticality. They were presented in pseudorandom order.

Participants

Thirty-three undergraduate students (age range 19–34) at the Universitat Autònoma de Barcelona in Bellaterra took part in the experiment. They were asked to indicate their mother tongue, and most of them identified themselves as being native speakers of Catalan (n = 20), or Spanish (n = 10); one participant identified her/himself as a Catalan/Spanish native, and there were also one native speaker of Polish and one of Arabic. I labelled the two groups for which there was more than one participant "Catalan-native" and "Spanish-native", as opposed to the terms "Catalan-dominant" and "Spanish-dominant" used by Perpiñan (2016), since I did not carry out any test or administer any questionnaire to determine dominance, instead leaving it to the participant to name their mother tongue.

Procedure

The grammaticality judgment task was administered online, and therefore participants judged the written version of the sentences (this may be of some import, since dislocations are marked by punctuation, while doubling is simply indicated by the absence of a comma). The instructions that preceded the task asked the participants to rate each sentence on a 4-point scale, indicating whether they thought they sounded 'very good' (1), 'quite good' (2), 'quite bad' (3) or 'very bad' (4). In cases where the experimental item was preceded by a question (e.g. (36) above), participants were asked to judge the second sentence in the context introduced by the first.

Coding and statistical analysis

For the purposes of the statistical analysis, unless otherwise indicated, judgments that rated a sentence as 'very good' and 'quite good' were taken together as indicating that the participant found them well-formed, and judgments as 'quite bad' and 'very bad' as indicating that the participant found them ill-formed. The statistical analyses were carried out using R base packages, R version 3.3.1 (R Development Core Team 2016), and the MASS package.

Results

The results of the task for all participants together appear in Table 4.

In Table 5 the results are broken down according to the native language of the participants. (Since there was only one bilingual Catalan/Spanish speaker, one native speaker of Polish and one native speaker of Arabic, I omit their results hereafter, unless otherwise indicated.)

These percentages show that control items (third person object clitics) are on target for Catalan and Spanish speakers alike, both in judging grammatical production and omission; however, doubling yielded lower performance for all participants – an issue to which we return. For the experimental conditions, there are differences between the two groups (Catalan natives and Spanish natives), especially with the partitive clitic *en*, VSO and nominal ellipsis. These

Table 4: Percentage correct answers, all participants.

	condition	percentage correct
3rd p obj clitic (controls)	production	81.06%
	*omission	97.96%
	*doubling	53.54%
hi clitic	production	78.79%
	*omission	56.57%
	*doubling	33.85%
en clitic	production	86.36%
	*omission	79.55%
	*doubling	66.67%
partitive NP	+de	90.8%
	*–de	29.55%
*VSO		69.47%
fillers		91.54%

Table 5: Percentage correct answers, all participants, by native language.

native language	Catalan native-speakers	Spanish native-speakers
3rd obj clitic	81.25%	80%
*3rd omission	100%	96.55%
*3rd doubling	55%	53.33%
hi production	83.75%	72.5%
hi omiss	61.66%	50%
hi doubling	39.24%	23.07%
en production	92.5%	82.5%
en omission	92.5%	55%
en doubling	78.75%	45%
part NP	90%	89.58%
*part NP	42.5%	10%
*VSO	77.5%	56.41%
fillers	91.39%	91.42%

differences emerge in the ungrammatical conditions more than in the grammatical.

The answers in their raw format (1, 2, 3 or 4) have been analyzed using Principal Component Analysis (PCA) including data only from individuals who answered all items. The results can be seen in figure 3. This two-dimensional plot shows the first two principal components, which explain 37.1% of the overall

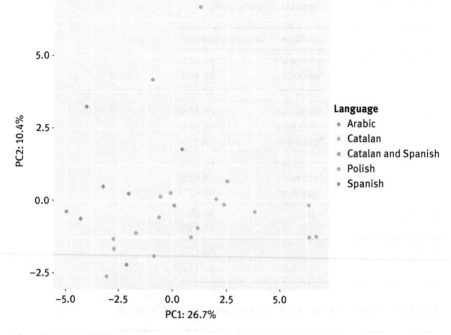

Figure 3: PCA, individual performance.

variance; each dot represents a participant. Differences amongst native speakers of Catalan are largely represented by PC1, whereas the variance corresponding to the variability between speakers of other languages is captured in PC2. The differences in PC1 are found in items with doubling with *hi*, *hi* omission and nominal ellipsis without *de* – meaning that variation in these sentence types is emerging even amongst native speakers of Catalan. The differences in PC2 are given by variation in *hi* and *en* cliticization (i.e. target production). Overall we find a differentiated performance as a function of native language.

We performed Fisher's exact test to compare the two main groups of speakers, native Catalan and native Spanish speakers, by condition. No difference emerged in the control third person object clitic conditions (production, omission, doubling). There were statistically significant differences between the two groups of speakers in *en* clitic doubling (p-value = 0.0003617, odds ratio 4.464231), *en* clitic omission (p-value = 3.445e-06, odds ratio 9.848027), VSO (p-value = 0.03097, odds ratio 2.637846) and P omission in nominal ellipsis (p-value = 0.0003127, odds ratio 6.559851). If we consider conditions in groups, the results are as follows. Performance with *en* clitics (production, omission and doubling) is statistically different between the two groups (p-value = 8.775e-09, odds ratio 4.661063), as is performance with clitic *hi* (again production, omission and doubling) (p-value = 0.03268, odds ratio 1.695359) and nominal ellipsis (p-value = 0.01513, odds ratio 1.926694).

Next, we sought to determine if there were any correlations between sentence types (taking into account all participants). Figures 4 and 5 are scatterplots of the absolute number of correct answers for each of the participants; for the *en* clitic along the x axis and for partitives and VSO respectively along the y axis. The size of the points represents the number of individuals with the same number of correct answers in both items. There is a positive trend in both, namely, individuals who perform well with *en* clitic sentences generally do so also with VSO and NP ellipsis.

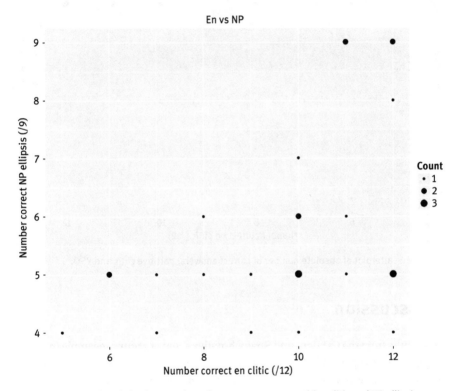

Figure 4: Scatterplot of absolute number of correct answers, partitive clitic and NP ellipsis.

The statistical associations were determined using a Chi-square test. We established a threshold of correct answers of 90% to consider that a participant had command of a given structure, and found that knowledge of *en* cliticization (production, omission, doubling) indeed correlated with knowledge of the conditions on nominal ellipsis (p-value = 0.01982); by contrast, no correlation was found between knowledge of *en* cliticization and VSO. Given the low number of VSO items (only 3 items in the whole experiment), a broader study would give more statistical power to understand this latter correlation.

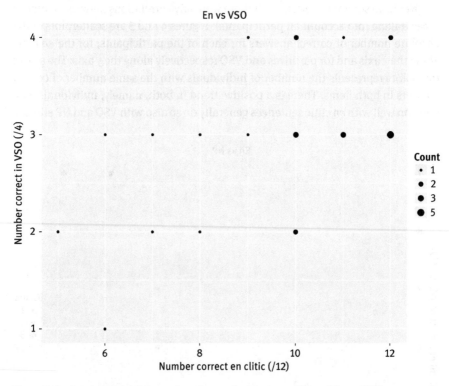

Figure 5: Scatterplot of absolute number of correct answers, partitive clitic and VSO.

5 Discussion

The results from the Catalan- and Spanish-native speaker groups resemble in many respects those reported in Perpiñan (2016). To summarize: she found that the Catalan-dominant group did not allow omission, and *en* omission least of all, as has been found here; the Spanish-dominant group accepted *en* omission most of the time, and accepted clitic doubling more than any other group; again the findings here are consistent with Perpiñan's; the omission of clitic *hi* was accepted much more often than the omission of clitic *en*, and this too was found to be the case here. These results may indicate a higher resilience of the partitive system when compared to the clitic *hi*, but other factors may also be relevant. As noted above, especially with locative *hi*, it is difficult to find a context that absolutely requires it; for example, if you take (45), *hi* in the second clause appears to be optional because the second sentence may introduce either a paraphrase of the first (in which case the clitic is required) or a generalization of the first (children walk every afternoon, somewhere or other). Although contexts such as these were avoided in the experiment reported here, sentences with *hi* often have a grammatical counterpart without *hi*, and this may impact performance in the experimental setting.

(45) Els nens passegen per la platja. (Hi) passegen cada tarda.
      the children walk on the beach CLloc walk every afternoon
      (=(7) above)

Second, the doubling condition may also misrepresent the grammar of the participants who took part in the experiment. Doubling was rejected by Catalan-native speakers at rates of 55% (with third person object clitics), 39.24% (*hi*) and 78.75% (*en*); by Spanish-native speakers, at rates of 53.33% (third person object clitics), 23.07% (*hi*) and 45% (*en*). There is a difference as a function of group, with Spanish native speakers being more likely to accept doubling, but doubling is also accepted by Catalan native speakers at unexpected high rates with third person object clitics and *hi*. As pointed out, clitic left dislocation (CLLD) allows in one single sentence the clitic and the full DP in a dislocated position, as exemplified in (46); the intonational contour of CLLD is solely indicated by a comma in the conventional writing system. There is the possibility that speakers have judged the sentences with doubling as cases of CLLD, which are grammatical. (If this is the case, then the question remains as to why they did this more often with *hi* and third person object clitics than with partitive *en*.) The only way to resolve this potential confound would be to run the experiment with prerecorded sentences, where the intonational pattern could not be ignored. This remains for future research.

(46) A la biblioteca, hi aniré demà.
      to the library CLloc go-FUT-1s tomorrow
      'Tomorrow I will go to the library'

The results obtained in the conditions that were introduced in the new grammaticality judgment task show that Catalan-native and Spanish-native speakers produce different judgments regarding the VSO order (banned in Catalan, allowed in Spanish) and nominal ellipsis (which requires a partitive marker *de* in Catalan and disallows it in Spanish). Furthermore, they show that knowledge of the conditions governing nominal ellipsis in Catalan correlates with knowledge of partitive cliticization. This favours the claim in Martí (1995) that Catalan requires overt partitive marking in all its partitive constructions, unlike Spanish, and also unlike other Romance varieties which mark partitivity some of the time. On the other hand, a correlation between *en* cliticization and avoidance of VSO could not be demonstrated in this grammaticality judgment task; further testing remains for the future.

The association between *en* cliticization, lack of *en* omission and the ban on VSO is characteristic of the grammar of Catalan; however, we also saw that children acquiring Catalan, omit *en* clitics (as well as third person object clitics) at the ages of 2 and 3. In work on word order, Gavarró and Cabré-Sans (2009) carried out a study of the spontaneous productions of three Catalan-speaking children up to the age of 3 (ages: 1;2,3–3;0,27, 1;2,28–3;0,13 and 1;7,20–3;0,2) and found that VSO was completely absent from their productions; in fact, these very young children produced the word order patterns in the same proportions as adults from MLU 2.5. Even though there is an apparent coincidence between the performance of the young Catalan-speaking children and the Spanish-dominant bilinguals, the underlying mechanisms explaining one and the other are divergent. While child production is deviant for maturational reasons, as argued in Gavarró et al. (2010), adult Spanish-dominant bilinguals have mature grammars, albeit different from those of Catalan-dominant bilinguals. By hypothesis, they are no longer subject to the constraint that forces overt partitive Case marking, and do not have a [–interpretable] feature in *v*P banning VSO. Loss of this feature value in *v*P constitutes a parametric change.

Little space has been devoted here to the analysis of *hi*; as with *en*, the grammar of Catalan (and other varieties in which an analogous clitic is part of the repertoire) does not allow doubling, nor omission when the locative/PP is selected by the verb. For the speakers who allowed doubling and omission, the parametric change may involve the appearance of a null locative/PP. How to formulate the link between *hi* and *en* in the grammatical system remains for future research.

The picture that emerges from the current study is one where the grammars of Catalan-native and Spanish-native speakers are quite distinct, with different requirements regarding, for example, the expression of partitivity – i.e. individual performance shows that differences follow a pattern that can be accounted for in terms of parameters. The loss of syntactic partitivity that was illustrated in the introduction with Spanish and Portuguese is also illustrated to a certain extent with contemporary Catalan as spoken by Spanish-dominant speakers and may affect the path of language change.

References

Belletti, Adriana. 2004. Aspects of the low IP area. In L. Rizzi (ed.), *The structure of IP and CP. The cartography of syntactic structures*, vol. 2, 16–51. Oxford/New York: Oxford University Press.

Beninca, Paola, Gianpaolo Salvi & Lorenza Frison. 1988. L'ordine degli elementi della frase e le construzioni marcate. In L: Renzi (ed.), *Grande grammatica italiana di consultazione. I. La frase. I sintagmi nominale e preposizionale*. Bologna: Il Mulino.

Bernstein, Judy B. 1993. *Topics in the syntax of nominal structure across Romance*. New York: City University of New York doctoral dissertation.

Bernstein, Judy B. 1996. Pure and hybrid adjectives. Talk presented at the Universitat Autònoma de Barcelona.

Brucart, José M. & Lluïsa Gràcia. 1986. I sintagmi nominali senza testa: uno studio comparato. *Rivista di Grammatica Generativa* 11. 3–32.

Gavarró, Anna & Yolanda Cabré-Sans. 2009. Subjects, verb classes and word order in child Catalan. In J. Grinstead (ed.), *Perspectives on typical and atypical Hispanic language development*, 175–194. Amsterdam/Philadelphia: John Benjamins.

Gavarró, Anna, Maria Teresa Guasti, Laurie Tuller, Philippe Prévost, Adriana Belletti, Luca Cilibrasi, Hélène Delage & Mirta Vernice. 2011. The acquisition of partitive clitics in Romance five-year-olds. *Iberia* 3(2). 1–19.

Gavarró, Anna, Meritxell Mata & Eulàlia Ribera. 2006. L'omissió dels clítics d'objecte i partitius en el català infantil: dades espontànies. In C. Pusch (ed.), *Zeitschrift für Katalanistik*. Special volume, *La gramàtica pronominal del català – Variació, evolució, funció/The grammar of Catalan pronouns – Variation, evolution, function*, 27–46. Aachen: Shaker.

Gavarró, Anna, Vicenç Torrens & Ken Wexler. 2010. Object clitic omission: two language types. *Language Acquisition* 17(4). 192–219.

Kayne, Richard. 1977. *Syntaxe du français. Le cycle transformationel*. Paris: Éditions du Seuil.

Martí, Núria. 1995. *De* in Catalan elliptical nominals: a partitive Case marker. *Catalan Working Papers in Linguistics* 4(2). 243–265.

Martí, Núria. 2010. *The syntax of partitives*. Bellaterra: Universitat Autònoma de Barcelona doctoral dissertation.

Martin, T. 2012. *Deconstructing Catalan object clitics*. New York: New York University doctoral dissertation.

Martins, Ana Maria. 2001. Deficient pronouns and linguistic change in Portuguese and Spanish. In J. Quer, J. Schroten, M. Scorretti, P. Sleeman & E. Verheugd (eds.), *Romance languages and linguistic theory 2001*, 213–230. Amsterdam/Philadelphia: John Benjamins.

Ordoñez, Francisco. 2007. Two specs for postverbal subjects: Evidence from Spanish and Catalan. In S. Baauw, F. Drijkoningen & M. Pinto (eds.), *Romance languages and linguistic theory 2005*. Amsterdam/Philadelphia: John Benjamins.

Perpiñán, Silvia. 2016. Catalan-Spanish bilingualism continuum: The expression of adverbial clitics in different types of early bilinguals. *Linguistic Approaches to Bilingualism*. doi 10.1075/lab.15004.per

R Development Core Team. 2016. *R: A language environment for statistical computing*. R Foundation for Statistical Computing, Vienna. URL http://www.R-project.org.

Solà, Jaume. 1992. *Agreement and subjects*. Bellaterra: Universitat Autònoma de Barcelona doctoral dissertation.

Torrego, Esther. 1998. *The dependencies of objects*. Cambridge, MA: MIT Press.

Tsakali, Vina & Kenneth Wexler. 2004. Why children omit clitics in some languages, but not in others: New evidence from Greek. In J. van Kampen & S. Baauw (eds.), *Proceedings of GALA 2003*, Volume 2, 493–504. Utrecht: LOT.

Venables, W. N. & B. D. Ripley. 2002. *Modern applied statistics with S*. Fourth Edition. New York: Springer.

Wexler, Kenneth. 1998. Very early parameter setting and the unique checking constraint: A new explanation of the optional infinitive stage. *Lingua* 106. 23–79.

Appendix

Experimental items (excluding the ones in the body of the paper), control items and distractors

1. Han cantat tots els estudiants.
   have sung all the students
2. Aquest llibre? No he llegit.
   this book? NEG have-1s read
3. Qui contribueix a la ciència? Contribueixen les investigadores.
   who contributes to science? contribute the researchers
4. Aquest pastís, quantes espelmes té?
   this cake how many candles have-3s
5. De llet, no pren mai perquè té intolerància.
   of milk NEG have never because has-3s intolerance
6. A les escoles, fan activitats i tothom participa.
   in the schools make-3p activities and everybody participates
7. D'hamburgueses, els americans mengen moltes.
   of hamburgers the Americans eat-3pl many
8. A l'obra, mengen els paletes una barra de pa.
   at the plot eat the bricklayers a loaf of bread
9. Els nens fan els deures a casa.
   the children make-3pl the homework at home
10. El Dr. Turró era un expert en medicina: en sabia molta de medicina.
    the Dr Turró was an expert in medicine CLpart knew much of medicine
11. En vull un de vermell.
    CLpart want-1s one of red
12. Els bebès sempre en tenen gana.
    the babies always CLpart have-3pl hunger
13. Vostè ha triat gasoil.
    you have chosen gasoil
14. En posa quatre espelmes.
    CLpart puts four candles
15. Toquen els violinistes el violí al segon moviment.
    play the vilinists the violin in.the second movement
16. Quin llibre vols, tu? jo en vull un curt.
    which book want-2s you I CLpart want-1s one short
17. De pastes, en fan de dolces i de salades.
    of pastries CLpart make-3pl of sweet and of salty

18. Els adolescents pensen en els amics: pensen molt.
    the adolescents think in the friends think-3pl much
19. Tinc dos ordinadors: un de taula i un de portàtil.
    have-1s two computers one of desk and one of portable
20. Els adolescents es preocupen pel futur: hi pensen molt.
    the adolescents REFL worry-3pl for.the future CLhi think-3pl much
21. Els bebès tenen molta gana: el meu sempre en té molta.
    the babies have much hunger the mine always CLpart has much
22. Llegeix cada dia el meu pare el diari.
    reads each day the my father the newspaper
23. En tinc dos: un de nou i un de vell.
    CLpart have-1s two one of new and one of old
24. Cada dia llegeix tres diaris.
    every day reads three newspapers
25. Els estudiants hi pensen molt en l'examen.
    the students CLhi think much in the exam
26. Què penja a la paret? hi penja un pòster.
    what hangs in the wall CLloc hangs a poster
27. Els nens passegen per la platja: hi passegen cada tarda.
    the children walk through the beach CLloc walk each afternoon
28. El Dr. Turró era un expert en medicina: en sabia molt.
    the Dr Turró was an expert in medicine CLpart knew much
29. Els nens sempre tenen gana: el meu sempre té.
    the children always have hunger the mine always has
30. La Maria ha arribat tard.
    the Maria has arrived late
31. La Maria ha cantat la cançó.
    the Maria has sung the song
32. Aquesta pel.lícula? la vaig veure l'any passat.
    this film   it PAST-1s see the year last
33. Pensen en totes les conseqüències.
    think-3pl in all the consequences
34. No m'hi poso sucre al cafè.
    NEG REFL CL-loc put-1s sugar in.the coffee
35. No la recordo.
    NEG it remember-1s
36. No el recordo el dia de Nadal.
    NEG it remember-1s the day of Christmas
37. Recordo l'últim dia de classe.
    remember-1s the last day of class

38. Hi posa l'oli al pa.
    CLloc puts the oil in.the bread
39. El Tibidabo, el veig des de la finestra.
    the Tibidabo it see-1s from the window
40. El veig el quadre de Picasso.
    it see-1s the painting of Picasso
41. Les vacances? recordo molt.
    the holidays   remember-1s much
42. Les recordo molt les vacances d'estiu.
    them remember-1s much the holidays of summer
43. De claus, n'he perdut moltes.
    of keys CLpart have-1s lost many
44. L'examen? ja he fet.
    the exam already have-1s done
45. Tinc unes ulleres platejades i unes negres.
    have-1s some glasses silver and some black
46. Busco unes arracades platejades i unes daurades.
    look-1s some earrings silver and some golden
47. Cada dia faig un sudoku.
    every day make-1s a sudoku
48. Han vingut els Reis d'Orient.
    have-3pl come the kings of Orient
49. Hem anat a la platja.
    have-1pl gone to the beach
50. Posarem olives a l'amanida.
    put-FUT-3pl olives in the salad
51. Han posat quatre espelmes al pastís.
    have-3pl put four candles in.the cake

Aurora Bel and Estela García-Alcaraz

Pronoun interpretation and processing in Catalan and Spanish bilingual and monolingual speakers

Abstract: In the current study the interpretation and processing of subject pronouns in Catalan and Spanish, on the one hand, and in monolingual and in bilingual Spanish in contact with Catalan, on the other, are compared in order to assess whether systematic and extensive language contact leads to a bilingual contact variety impacted by cross-linguistic influence. First, two equivalent acceptability judgment tasks were conducted by Catalan and Spanish speakers showing that null pronouns pick up subject antecedents both in Catalan and Spanish, but only Catalan displays an Italian-type division of labor between null and overt pronouns. Second, the Spanish version of the task was performed by monolinguals and bilingual speakers of the Spanish variety spoken in Catalonia and a division of labor pattern of the Italian type appeared in bilingual Spanish, indicating an effect of cross-linguistic influence from interpretive biases of Catalan pronouns. Third, this latter interpretive trend was also confirmed in an online self-paced reading task since Catalan-Spanish bilinguals displayed more biased preferences: faster reading times for null pronouns linked to subjects and overt pronouns to objects than monolinguals. These findings, which can be explained resorting to transfer, are also consistent with the view that contact-induced changes can enhance choices that are present, even to a lesser degree, in the non-contact variety.

1 Introduction

There has been much interest surrounding the issue of how anaphoric reference involving null and overt subject pronouns in null-subject languages is retrieved and processed in real time. Psycholinguistic research on anaphora resolution, such as the influential Position of Antecedent Hypothesis (henceforth PAH), has shown that, in Italian subordinate-main anaphora, null pronouns prefer to

Aurora Bel and Estela García-Alcaraz, Universitat Pompeu Fabra and University of Ottawa

https://doi.org/10.1515/9781501509988-003

pick up antecedents in subject position, which is structurally more prominent, and overt pronouns prefer antecedents in object position, which is less prominent. The predictions of the PAH hold for Italian but have not been borne out in all studies addressing different null subject languages (see Filiaci, Sorace and Carreiras 2014 for differences between Italian and Spanish) or even different varieties of the same language (Keating, VanPatten and Jegerski 2016 observed different patterns in Mexican Spanish from those attested in Iberian Spanish by Alonso-Ovalle et al. 2002 or Filiaci, Sorace and Carreiras 2014). In Catalan, which is also a null subject language, research on subject pronouns points at the existence of interpretive biases of the Italian type (Mayol 2010; Bel, Perera and Salas 2010). In addition, it is known that the properties involved in pronominal resolution are composed by fine-grained operations and are dependent on the efficient integration of information of different sources (structural, pragmatic, etc.); the solving strategies involved in real-time resolution seem to be affected in bilinguals leading to the well-known overextension strategy of overt pronouns (Sorace 2011). Moreover, it is widely accepted that systematic and extensive language contact tends to lead to contact varieties in bilingual communities (Silva-Corvalán 2008 or de Prada Pérez 2009 for Spanish subject pronouns usage; Perpiñan 2017 for Catalan clitics). This is the particular case of Catalonia where, albeit often to a different extent, children grow up with two languages (Catalan and Spanish) that are, in addition, very close typologically and display similarities in pronoun distribution that may result in cross-linguistic influence, stressing the overlapping options.

In this context, the present study aims to compare the interpretation and processing of both null and overt subject pronouns in bilingual Spanish in contact with Catalan against monolingual Spanish. To efficiently contrast these two varieties, it is necessary to previously address the processing patterns of Catalan and Spanish languages. To date, no studies have assessed the processing of subject pronouns in Catalan or in bilingual Spanish in contact with Catalan; this is a novelty of the present study. Moreover, the particular sociolinguistic context addressed here offers a unique opportunity to corroborate previously reported findings among bilinguals in the specific domain of pronoun interpretation and to test whether the impact of bilingual experience is more evident in cases in which the interpretation and processing of non-categorical linguistic structures involving multiple cues are at stake, as it is in our case (see Holler and Suckow 2015 for an overview on the role of a variety of linguistic and cognitive factors involved in pronoun resolution). In this piece of research, we restricted ourselves to considering only the set of factors derived from the PAH.

Individual and societal bilingualism: The case of language contact in Catalonia

In the bilingualism field, it is common to distinguish individual and societal bilingualism. From the individual perspective, it is fairly uncontroversial to refer to simultaneous bilingualism (2L2, or two languages from birth) and to sequential bilingualism (or child L2) (Meisel 2011, Montrul 2008). There is empirical evidence suggesting that the age of first bilingual exposure matters and that before age 4 the developmental pattern of acquisition of these so-called early sequential bilinguals, particularly that of inflectional morphology and syntax, is comparable to that of simultaneous bilinguals. On the other hand, late sequential bilinguals, i.e. children exposed to the other language after the age of 6, develop specific aspects of grammatical knowledge in a fashion similar to that of adult L2 learners since crucial changes seem to happen around the age of onset to the L2 at age 6 or 7 (Meisel 2011). There is no consensus among researches regarding what happens when the language exposure begins at ages 5–6: whereas authors like Meisel consider that the linguistic development resembles the adult L2 learning process, other authors claim that it rather mirrors simultaneous bilinguals – the learner is not an adult (Schwartz 2004). Still, other authors argue that age 4 may be not relevant to some aspects of (second) language acquisition that are acquired after this age or to errors that can be best explained resorting to cross-linguistic influence from the child's other language (Unsworth 2013) or to limited amount of language input (Unsworth 2016). From this rapid review it is clear that the field is far from reaching consensus on this debate; therefore, to reduce variability we were conservative and only speakers exposed to both languages before age of 3–4 years were assigned to our bilingual group.

A distinction between categorical and non-categorical linguistic phenomena involving preferences regarding pragmatic felicity has been made to explain why pronominal reference is acquired rather later in development. There is evidence showing that it takes a lot of time, even for monolingual children, to fine-tune the division of the referential space to interpret and produce the appropriate referring expressions: Shin & Cairns (2012) and Bel & Albert (2016) found that Spanish children as old as 12–13 still do not manage to correctly use overt subject pronouns. For bilinguals, this task is more taxing as it requires a more demanding matching assignment to determine which specific form corresponds to a specific function in both languages which, in addition, can display overlapping options (Serratrice and Hervé 2015). To do that, cognitive language-external resources involved in executive functions are required and these processes are more taxed in bilinguals, who seem to be more sensitive to cognitive complexity: "Competition for resources and cognitive load are in fact critical factors in the coordination of constantly changing pronoun-context mappings in the real-time use of anaphoric expressions" (Sorace 2016). In other words, we are facing a complex aspect of language, both from the perspective of language development and cognitive skills.

In Spain, the case of Catalonia is a perfect laboratory to explore the effects of language contact given that it is a historically bilingual community where both languages, Catalan and Spanish, are co-official and used in everyday communication interactions (see Boix and Sanz, 2008, for an overview of the sociolinguistic, cultural and political features of the Catalan society). Literature on language contact argues that systematic and prolonged language interaction in bilingual social contexts can alter specific linguistic features generating contact varieties that may, ultimately, induce language change (Silva-Corvalán 2008). In this sense, it has been noted for a long time, mainly from descriptive perspective (Sinner 2004), that a specific variety of Spanish is spoken in Catalonia; more recently this variety has attracted the attention of researchers who work in the generative framework. To mention a couple of examples, Perpiñán (2015) showed how the overlapping of copular verbs in Spanish and Catalan leads to a redistribution of use rates and values in contact Spanish so that *ser* is overused to the detriment of *estar* in locative contexts and Guijarro-Fuentes and Marinis (2009) reported an overuse of the personal object marker *a* in the Spanish of Catalan-Spanish bilinguals.

Interface phenomena have been hypothesized to be affected by cross-linguistic influence. Together with semantic features, which are involved in the two examples above, pragmatic features seem to be prone to cross-linguistic influence and this is consistent with Silva-Corvalán's (2008) view that contact situations involve the gradual change of discourse-pragmatic features. The topic addressed here, that of the choice of referential forms, concerns a syntax-pragmatics interface phenomenon, which entails the integration of lexical, structural and discourse information and can be a potential locus for transfer/change. A robust finding regarding the interpretation of pronominal subjects in bilinguals is that of variability that is manifested in the overextension of the scope of overt pronouns in contexts where null pronouns would be more natural for native speakers (Sorace 2011). Different explanations beyond cross-linguistic influence have been offered and a number of them have focused on the bilingual experience itself. Recently, in a comprehensive paper, Sorace (2016) focuses on the asymmetrical findings regarding executive functions in bilingualism: while some components of the executive functioning appear to be enhanced by the bilingual experience (for example, inhibitory control skills), some disadvantages related to processing restrictions are also reported. Thus, if the processing resources of bilingual speakers are more taxed, the efficient integration and coordination in real-time processing of lexical, grammatical and pragmatic information required to exclude inconsistent antecedent choices in pronoun resolution may lead bilinguals to rely on an unmarked form, as Sorace (2011) suggested, or on a learner's default form, as Tsimpli (2011) claimed, which in both cases coincides with the overt pronoun.

To sum up, there is accumulating evidence that individual and societal bilingualism may lead to convergence of the two language systems involved thus triggering changes in the variety spoken by functional bilinguals. The main candidates for such changes are particular constructions where conflicting or uneven evidence is at stake, and this is more evident in interface constructions than in narrow grammatical domains.

The position of Antecedent Hypothesis in Spanish and Catalan

In the last fifteen years, significant numbers of studies have been conducted to investigate the interpretive properties of null and overt third person subject pronouns and have revealed that their antecedent choices exhibit complementary preferences (see Sorace 2011 for a detailed review). This fruitful line of research was initiated by Carminati (2002) and her 'Position of Antecedent Hypothesis' (PAH), a processing strategy that accounted for the interpretation of Italian null and overt pronouns in ambiguous intra-sentential main-subordinate contexts. According to the PAH, null pronouns tend to establish interpretive dependencies with antecedents that occupy prominent subject positions whereas overt pronouns tend to solve their dependencies with antecedents in non-prominent object positions. From a discourse perspective, these findings might be reinterpreted in terms of the [±Topic Shift] feature, so that null pronouns would express topic continuity in retrieving subject antecedents from a previous clause and overt pronouns would convey a change of topic in referring back to object antecedents, which are not topical elements. It is worth noting that the PAH, interpreted either in syntactic or discourse terms, expresses interpretation preferences rather than categorical grammatical options.

The PAH's predictions in Spanish were first tested by Alonso-Ovalle, Fernández-Solera, Frazier and Clifton (2002). The authors investigated null and overt subject pronouns' co-reference resolution patterns in inter-sentential contexts. The findings were that while null pronouns clearly retrieve subject antecedents, overt pronouns do not show a clear-cut preference for object over subject antecedents. Thus, Alonso-Ovalle et al.'s (2002) results do not reveal a division of labor between pronouns in Spanish in the way predicted by the PAH. Similar co-reference preferences are also found in more recent studies in Spanish intra-sentential contexts using online (Filiaci 2011; Filiaci et al. 2014) and offline interpretation data techniques (Jegerski, VanPatten and Keating 2011; Keating, VanPatten and Jegerski 2011). In addition, the study of null and overt pronouns' interpretative biases in longer texts shows similar results: clear biases with null pronouns, uneven flexible tendencies with overt pronouns (Domínguez 2013, Lozano 2016).

Of special interest is the study by Filiaci (2011) on the co-referential properties of null and overt pronouns in embedded clauses using a clause-by-clause self-paced reading task. For the first time, two different clause orders were contrasted: main-subordinate vs. subordinate-main. The results evinced a clear bias in linking null pronouns to prominent subject antecedents, mainly in subordinate-main order, but a flexible behavior in linking overt pronouns to subject and object antecedents in both clause orders. A recent study by Chamorro, Sorace and Sturt (2016) using eyetracking techniques on main-subordinate temporal anaphora revealed that the control Spanish group had a clear bias towards the object as the antecedent for the overt pronoun whereas the bias towards either antecedent with the null pronoun was unclear. These preferences were consistent with those from Filiaci (2011) for Spanish in main-subordinate contexts and from Carminati (2002) for Italian in the same clause order. Bel and García-Alcaraz (2015) also investigated the effect of clause order, but differently from previous studies, including that of Filiaci, the authors controlled for the implicit causality of the first-clause verb to avoid any semantic bias towards the subject or the object. Their results showed that in completely ambiguous contexts with no other clues than the syntactic ones, speakers had no other option than to resort to the PAH to resolve the anaphora, chiefly in subordinate-main contexts. Bel, Sagarra, Comínguez & García-Alcaraz (2016) found similar results when investigating null and overt pronouns' interpretative biases in partially ambiguous intrasentential contexts (main-subordinate clause order) by a self-paced reading task. Thus, according to recent offline and online studies, Spanish does not seem to differ from Italian when ambiguity is not at stake.

While the testing of the PAH in Spanish has been quite productive, there have been very few studies covering the analysis of pronominal anaphora resolution in Catalan. Mayol & Clark (2010) tested the PAH in inter-sentential contexts such as in (1) below:

(1)   La Marta escrivia sovint a la Raquel. pro/ella vivia als Estats Units.
      'Marta wrote frequently to Raquel. pro/she lived in the United States.'

The authors found that Catalan obeys the biases encoded by the PAH since null pronouns' proportion recovering subject antecedents was 70.3% and the proportion for overt pronouns referring back to object antecedents was 64.5%. In an additional self-paced reading experiment similar outcomes were found, which were also compatible with PAH predictions.

Bel, Perera and Salas (2010) looked at the production of null and overt pronouns in Catalan narratives. After isolating all third-person pronouns in subject position, the morphosyntactic form and the syntactic function of the antecedent, among other variables, were codified. Their results revealed that, like in comprehension data, null pronouns were mainly found to refer back to subject antecedents while overt pronouns were more flexible and retrieved either subject or object antecedents. However, due to the low number of overt pronouns, which is common in production data, the results did not allow the authors to draw conclusions but to point at behavior tendencies. In this sense, our study can contribute to further understanding of intra-sentential overt pronouns' interpretive biases.

From a variationist viewpoint, de Prada Pérez (2009) studied pronoun expression in oral production by Spanish-Catalan bilingual speakers from Menorca (where the Balearic variety of Catalan is spoken). The results provided a similar number of overt pronouns in L1 Spanish speakers (29.3%), L1 Catalan speakers (28%), Spanish dominant-Catalan bilinguals (29.9%) and Spanish-Catalan dominant bilinguals (29.2%). A detailed analysis of the co-reference variable, which is defined by the author in terms of [± maintenance] of the subject across clauses, showed that the four aforementioned groups used null pronouns to maintain the subject from one clause to another and overt subjects (Determiner Phrases and overt pronouns) were preferred to express a change of referent.

The present study aims at further exploring interpretive choices of subject pronouns providing new empirical data from unexplored Spanish contact varieties (the Spanish spoken in Catalonia), and from Catalan, which has received little attention. These contexts introduce a novelty with respect to previous studies. Also, it is our goal to analyze whether contact language situations favor convergent outcomes, as Silva-Corvalán (2008) and de Prada Pérez (2009) suggested for the specific topic addressed here. Given that, as previously highlighted, slight differences between the two pronoun resolution systems are restricted to overt pronouns, a coincidence in null pronoun resolution is anticipated and a possible effect of Catalan overt pronoun choices onto the Spanish system of bilinguals is expected. If, on the other hand, as some authors have suggested (Tsimpli 2011), bilinguals resort to the learner's default form, the one which is typically overused – i.e. the overt pronoun-, an overextension of the scope of the overt pronouns would be expected – i.e. freely interpreted overt pronouns; it is worth noting that it has been proposed that the linguistic default form is the null pronoun (Sorace 2011). This outcome would additionally converge with the monolingual Spanish overt pronoun resolution patterns. Before addressing these predictions, we need to find out what the resolution patterns in Catalan and Spanish are and we address this issue in experiment 1, section 3.

2 Research questions

In this study, we aim to better understand the interpretation and processing of subject pronouns in Spanish and Catalan, on the one hand, and in monolingual and in bilingual Spanish in contact with Catalan, on the other, by means of both offline and online tools. Being more specific, we want to investigate the following questions:

1. What are the interpretative biases of null and overt third person subject pronouns in both Catalan and Spanish? Are they equivalent and guided by the same properties in both languages? In other words, is the PAH operative in both languages?
2. Does the contact variety of Spanish spoken in Catalonia differ from monolingual Spanish regarding the properties that modulate the offline comprehension of null and overt pronouns? Provided that is the case, what factors appear to be more problematic or more likely to be shaped by cross-linguistic influence?
3. Do Catalan-Spanish bilinguals differ from Spanish monolinguals in online processing of null and overt pronouns? In case they do, are there any factors contributing to more cognitively demanding processing that impact bilingual pronominal resolution?

Experiment 1 specifically addresses question 1 and experiment 2 focuses on question 2. To address question 3, we provide preliminary data of an online experiment on pronoun processing.

3 Comprehension judgment data

Experiment 1. Comparing Catalan and Spanish

Participants

Forty Catalan speakers of the central variety and 48 monolingual Spanish speakers voluntarily participated in experiment 1. All the participants completed a language background questionnaire in which they provided linguistic and socio-linguistic background information.

Catalan speakers were recruited from the university and were born and raised in Catalonia. They all recognized Catalan as their dominant language and as their main language of communication on a daily basis. All the participants started their contact with Catalan earlier than with Spanish and in all cases before the age of 3. Participants primarily came from Catalan dominant families: 53.5% declared Catalan as their home language, 14.3 % Spanish and 32.2 % confirmed a bilingual home situation. In the latter two cases, only those with an excellent self-reported level of Catalan and those who self-identified themselves as Catalan-dominant were included. Thus, we can consider all of them as Catalan speakers although they are, in fact, functional bilinguals (as the self-reported knowledge of lan-guages in Table 1 reveals), which represents the sociolinguistic reality of Cata-lonia. Spanish dominant speakers, as well as speakers from Spanish dominant families, were excluded from the study.

Table 1: Catalan speakers' sociolinguistic background.

Speakers information	Mean	SD
Age (years)	20.52	1.29
Onset age of exposure to oral Catalan (mean in years)	0.45	0.99
Onset age of exposure to oral Spanish (mean in years)	2.89	2.10
Self-reported Catalan level (out of 4)	3.99	0.06
Self-reported Spanish level (out of 4)	3.98	0.06
Average daily use of Catalan in childhood (out of 6)*	4.57	0.99
Average daily use of Catalan in puberty (out of 6)*	4.44	1.02
Average daily use of Catalan in adulthood (out of 6)*	4.35	0.95

Note: * From 1 to 6 (1=only Spanish; 6=only Catalan)

Spanish speakers were university students born and raised in Valladolid (mean age=22.16; SD=2.49), a monolingual region in Spain.

Materials

To determine pronoun resolution preferences in ambiguous contexts in Spanish and Catalan, two equivalent untimed acceptability judgment tasks (AJT) were designed. The test items included two clauses: in the first one, two characters of the same gender were introduced by a proper name; in the second either a null or overt pronoun appeared in subject position. For each item, a continuation sentence was introduced to provide an interpretation that favored either the subject or the object character. Participants were requested to rate the acceptability of the continuation sentence on a four-value Likert scale (1=totally unacceptable, 4= perfectly acceptable). The experimental sentences were completely ambiguous with no semantic cues that disambiguated the pronoun; to this end, the verbs included in the first clause were not semantically biased towards the character in subject or object position: all Spanish verbs had neutral implicit causality (from Goikoetxea, Pascual and Acha, 2008). For Catalan, translated equivalents were used; we assumed that the effect of implicit causality across languages is similar, particularly in such closely related languages (Rudolph & Försterling, 1997).

Three conditions, with two levels each, were tested: type of pronoun (null vs. overt), position of the antecedent (subject vs. object) and clause order (main-subordinate clause vs. subordinate-main clause). Subordinates were temporal adjunct clauses introduced by *cuando/quan*, 'when', and *mientras/mentre*, 'while'. A total of 64 experimental items (8 per condition level) and 80 fillers were included in each language test. All items were counterbalanced and randomized across two lists and participants were randomly assigned to one list. Examples for each condition are provided in (2) and (3) below, one for each language:

(2) Main-subordinate order (example from the Spanish AJT)
     Irene saludó a Catalina cuando pro/ella entró en la tienda.
     a. Irene entró en la tienda. (Subject interpretation)
     b. Catalina entró en la tienda. (Object interpretation)
     'Irene greeted Catalina when pro /she entered the store'
     'Irene entered the store' vs. 'Catalina entered the store'

(3) Subordinate-main order (example from the Catalan AJT)
     Mentre en Cèsar desmentia en Joaquim, pro/ell es va posar vermell.
     a. En Cèsar es va posar vermell. (Subject interpretation)
     b. En Joaquim es va posar vermell. (Object interpretation)
     'While Cèsar refuted Joaquim, pro/he turned red.'
     'Cèsar turned red' vs. 'Joaquim turned red'

If the PAH is operative in Catalan and Spanish, we expect that subject interpretation will be favored in the null pronoun condition (*pro*) whereas object interpretation will be preferred in the overt pronoun condition (*él/ell*). Additionally, more clear biases are predicted in subordinate-main than in main-subordinate order (Filiaci 2011).

Results

Table 2 shows the descriptive statistics by Language (Spanish and Catalan); results are displayed respectively for each sentence relationship.

Table 2: Descriptive statistics of acceptability preference of pronouns in Spanish and Catalan.

Clause order		Main-subordinate			
Pronoun		Null pronoun		Overt pronoun	
Antecedent		Subject	Object	Subject	Object
Spanish	Mean	2.80	2.82	2.32	2.90
	SD	0.51	0.59	0.71	0.69
Catalan	Mean	2.79	3.04	2.28	3.26
	SD	0.37	0.45	0.39	0.38

Clause order		Subordinate-main			
Pronoun		Null pronoun		Overt pronoun	
Antecedent		Subject	Object	Subject	Object
Spanish	Mean	3.64	2.13	2.56	2.88
	SD	0.37	0.60	0.66	0.68
Catalan	Mean	3.50	2.03	2.46	3.09
	SD	0.38	0.52	0.58	0.41

Repeated measures ANOVAs were performed on all within-subjects variables (Sentence order, Pronoun and Antecedent) and Language as between-subjects factor. A nearly significant main effect of Pronoun ($F(1, 42) = 3.881$, $p = .055$) and the following significant interactions were observed: Clause order*Antecedent ($F(1, 42) = 153.261$, $p = .001$), Pronoun*Antecedent ($F(1, 42) = 118.050$, $p = .001$), Clause order*Pronoun*Antecedent ($F(1, 42) = 79.648$, $p = .001$). The effect of Language alone was not found to be significant but the interaction Antecedent*-Language almost reached statistical significance ($F(1, 42) = 3.084$, $p = .086$). In short, these results suggest that the interaction between Pronoun and Antecedent indicates an overall division of labor between overt and null pronouns.

Given the triple interaction and based on previous findings that clause order plays a role in anaphora resolution biases, we conducted separate tests for each clause order relationship: Figures 1 and 2 visually display different configuration patterns: overt pronouns exhibit a noticeably steady pattern across clause orders

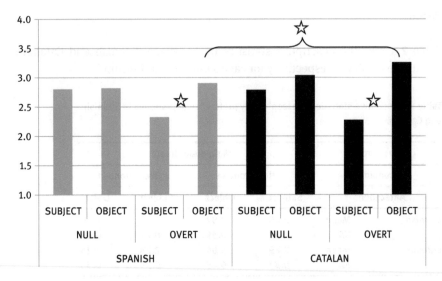

Figure 1: Main-subordinate clause order. Pronoun-antecedent choices.

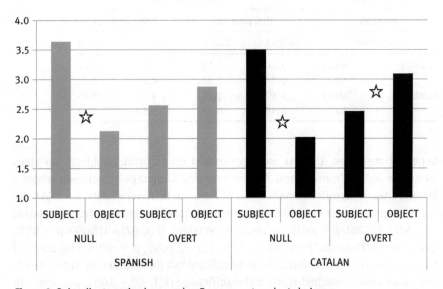

Figure 2: Subordinate-main clause order. Pronoun-antecedent choices.

while null pronouns seem sensitive to different clause orders in both languages. For main-subordinate order, the repeated measures ANOVA revealed a main effect of Pronoun ($F(1, 42) = 6.012$, $p = .018$) and Antecedent ($F(1, 42) = 29.166$, $p = .001$). There were also a significant Pronoun*Antecedent interaction ($F(1, 42) = 25.641$,

p = .001) and a borderline significant one between Pronoun*Antecedent*Language (F(1, 42) = 3.616 , p = .064). Bonferroni adjusted pairwise tests derived from the three-way interaction analysis indicated that Spanish and Catalan differed in the overt pronoun object antecedent condition (p = .041): overt pronouns in Catalan were more clearly biased in selecting antecedents in object position than in Spanish, which points to an Italian-type of overt pronoun resolution in Catalan. However, although a parallelism can be found in both languages in that null pronouns are significantly biased to co-refer with antecedents in subject position (p = .001 for Spanish and p = .002 for Catalan) in comparison with overt pronouns, differences between both antecedents in null pronouns achieved no significance in Spanish and only marginal significance in Catalan (p = .089); on the other hand, Spanish and Catalan overt pronouns displayed a significant difference in antecedent choice (both p = .001) showing preference towards object antecedents. In sum, as known from previous research, the PAH strategy barely emerges in main-subordinate clause order.

As for subordinate-main order, the repeated measures ANOVA yielded a main effect of Antecedent alone (F(1, 42) = 43.108, p = .001) and a significant interaction of Pronoun*Antecedent (F(1, 42) = 165.156, p = .001). Although no significant effect was attested neither for Language alone nor for the interaction, from the perspective of antecedent choice it was very revealing that Bonferroni-corrected post hoc tests gave significant differences between pairs of pronouns within the antecedent condition; that is, both pronouns displayed significant preferences for one antecedent over the other with subtle divergences between languages. More concretely, in Spanish and Catalan null pronouns clearly picked up antecedents in subject position (both p = .001); however whereas in Catalan overt pronouns unequivocally were biased towards object antecedents (p = .001), this pattern appeared rather attenuated in Spanish (only marginal significance was observed, p = .055). Briefly, the subordinate-main order gives rise to the PAH effect and this effect is much more pronounced in Catalan displaying an Italian-type division of labor between null and overt pronouns, consistent with findings from Mayol and Clark (2010).

Experiment 2. Comparing monolingual and bilingual Spanish

Participants

Seventy Spanish-Catalan bilingual speakers and 48 monolingual Spanish speakers participated voluntarily in experiment 2. As in experiment 1, all the participants completed a language background questionnaire.

Spanish speakers were those of experiment 1 (university students from Valladolid). Spanish-Catalan bilingual speakers were university students born and raised in Catalonia. They identified themselves as balanced bilinguals and admitted feeling as comfortable in Spanish as in Catalan. Participants mainly belonged to bilingual families: 41.6 % acknowledged a bilingual home situation, 38.9% declared Catalan as their home language and 19.4 % Spanish. In the few cases in which the family language was one of the two languages, only those participants with an excellent knowledge and broad usage of both languages were included in the study. In any case, all participants started continuous and extensive exposure to both languages before preschool level. It should be noted that the average daily usage of Catalan is slightly higher than Spanish in childhood, puberty and adulthood (Table 3). It is also worth remembering that our participants were university students and Catalan is the main language of instruction at different educational levels. The values for usage in Table 3 include the more proximal contexts of home and school as well as leisure spaces; however, the calculation of the average usage in social leisure environments during puberty and adulthood decreases to a mean value of 3.76. This is an indication of the existent alternation between languages in these contexts.

Table 3: Bilingual speakers' sociolinguistic background.

Speakers information	Mean	SD
Age (years)	20.91	1.82
Onset age of exposure to oral Catalan (mean in years)	1.62	1.39
Onset age of exposure to oral Spanish (mean in years)	2.15	1.89
Self-reported Catalan level (out of 4)	3.98	0.06
Self-reported Spanish level (out of 4)	3.95	0.11
Average daily use of Catalan in childhood (out of 6)*	4.30	1.13
Average daily use of Catalan in puberty (out of 6)*	4.33	1.06
Average daily use of Catalan in adulthood (out of 6)*	4.38	0.98

Note: *From 1 to 6 (1=only Spanish; 6=only Catalan)

Materials

The task administered in experiment 2 was the Spanish version of the AJT described in page 45 above. If cross-linguistic influence is at stake, slightly different biases will be expected in bilingual and monolingual Spanish. This would be particularly evident in overt pronouns, the pronoun form without obvious and definite biases (Sorace 2016).

Results

The average acceptability rates for condition and group are shown in Table 4 separately for each clause order. At first glance, the comparison of data from experiments 1 and 2 (Table 2 and 4) reveals a parallelism in acceptance ratings between Catalan speakers and bilingual Spanish.

Table 4: Descriptive statistics of acceptability preference of pronouns in monolingual and bilingual Spanish.

Clause order		Main-subordinate			
Pronoun		Null pronoun		Overt pronoun	
Antecedent		Subject	Object	Subject	Object
Monolingual	Mean	2.80	2.82	2.32	2.90
Spanish	SD	0.51	0.59	0.71	0.69
Bilingual	Mean	2.80	2.96	2.30	3.14
Spanish	SD	0.34	0.52	0.53	0.45

Clause order		Subordinate-main			
Pronoun		Null pronoun		Overt pronoun	
Antecedent		Subject	Object	Subject	Object
Monolingual	Mean	3.64	2.13	2.56	2.88
Spanish	SD	0.37	0.60	0.66	0.68
Bilingual	Mean	3.48	2.21	2.39	3.20
Spanish	SD	0.50	0.59	0.44	0.49

A repeated measures ANOVA with the same within-subject factors as in Experiment 1 and Group as between-subjects factor was conducted. Significant main effect for Pronoun ($F(1, 57) = 8.384$, $p = .005$) was found. Interactions between Clause order*Antecedent ($F(1, 57) = 143.325$, $p = .001$), Antecedent *Group ($F(1, 57) = 4.805$, $p = .032$), Pronoun*Antecedent ($F(1, 57) = 132.007$, $p = .001$) and Clause order*Pronoun*Antecedent ($F(1, 57) = 108.144$, $p = .001$) were found.

To further interpret these results, separated analyses for each clause order were conducted. Starting with main-subordinate order, the following effects were revealed: a main effect of Pronoun ($F(1, 57) = 9.303$, $p = .003$), Antecedent ($F(1, 57) = 31.147$, $p = .001$) and the interaction Pronoun*Antecedent ($F(1, 57) = 27.073$, $p = .001$). However, this interaction does not indicate a PAH effect since pronoun interpretation biases go in the opposite way as the one derived from the PAH (see Figure 3). These

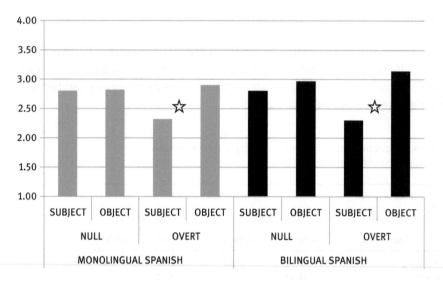

Figure 3: Main-subordinate clause order. Pronoun-antecedent choices.

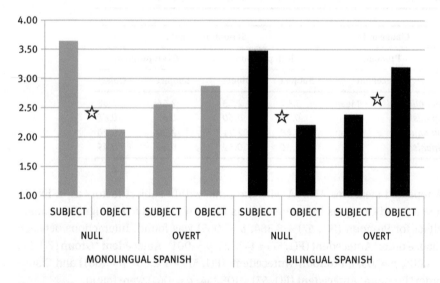

Figure 4: Subordinate-main clause order. Pronoun-antecedent choices.

results are expected since, as in experiment 1 and in previous research addressing the role of clause order, the PAH's effect did not arise for main-subordinate clause order; Filiaci (2011) refers to this result as a weakening of the null-subject bias. No effect of Group, alone or in interaction, was found so both groups perform similarly.

Regarding sentences with subordinate-main order (see Figure 4), the ANOVA generated the following significant values: a main effect of Antecedent (F(1, 57) = 29.196, p = .001) the interaction Pronoun*Antecedent (F(1, 57) = 199.836 , p = .001) and the interaction Antecedent*Group (F(1, 57) = 5.016 , p = .018). The Bonferroni post-hoc pairwise comparison result obtained in the latter interaction showed that the bilingual group rated both null and overt pronouns together linked to subject antecedents (p = .052) significantly lower than monolinguals; in other words the Subject preference attested in varied studies (Serratrice and Hervé 2015) is not particularly strong among bilinguals. This result becomes more evident in the three-way interaction: although this interaction did not achieve significance as a whole, the post-hoc pairwise comparison revealed that both null and overt pronouns were significantly biased to subject and object antecedents respectively (both p = .001) among bilinguals whereas the null pronoun clearly showed a bias to subject antecedents (p = .001) and the overt pronoun had no bias, or almost no bias (p = .070) among monolinguals. Previous findings in Spanish also report the flexibility showed by overt pronouns (Filiaci 2011, Filiaci et al. 2014).

4 Online data

To determine whether there are particular biases in pronoun antecedent choice, preliminary data comparing the processing of subject pronouns by Spanish monolingual speakers (N=49; mean age 23.5) and bilingual speakers (N=32; mean age 22.7) of the same origin as those of experiment 2 are reported. Four conditions were tested: pronoun (null and overt) and antecedent (subject and object position). The task was a word-by-word self-paced reading task that consisted of 24 experimental sentences (6 per condition) and 84 fillers; all sentences were followed by a comprehension question. The experimental sentences consisted of a main-subordinate temporal clause; the (null or overt) pronoun was placed in the second clause and two competing potential antecedents in the first clause, either in subject or object position. The matrix verbs were semantically unbiased –i.e. implicit causality was controlled– making the sentences temporally ambiguous until the disambiguating element, i.e. the object of the subordinate clause, was read. Example (4) illustrates a test trial for the four conditions tested:

(4) El profesor sorprende al alumno mientras pro / él lee un cómic/manual en la clase.
The teacher surprises the student while pro/he is reading a comic/ handbook in class.

Online processing was evaluated with reading time (RT) data for each word region. However, analyses were run from the word from which the interpretation is disambiguated, i.e. the noun head of the object NP. If participants display higher RTs in a particular condition that promotes an interpretation linked to a specific antecedent, this would be a symptom of interpretation difficulties on that condition. Figure 5 shows RT data for each word from the verb of the subordinate clause. Four GLMMs (Generalized Linear Mixed Models) were conducted, one for each dependent variable (RTs for each word from the disambiguating object head noun), and had Group, Pronoun and Antecedent as fixed factors and Subject and Item as random factors. No effects were revealed at the head object (*'comic'*) – the processing load associated with disambiguation appears later on- or at the Determiner (*'la'*) of the subsequent PP. The most interesting effects emerged at the Preposition (*'en'*), which immediately followed the disambiguating region, and the final Noun of the PP (*'clase'*), where increased processing on the sentence-final word emerged as a result of wrap-up effects.

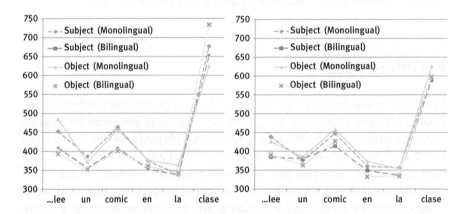

Figure 5: Reading Times (in ms) in each word region by antecedent and type of pronoun in monolingual and bilingual Spanish.

As for RTs at the preposition (*'en'*), a main effect of Pronoun (F(1, 316) = 7.703, *p* = .006) – i.e., null pronouns were read slower than overt pronouns- and an interaction of Group*Pronoun*Antecedent (F(1, 316) = 4.056, *p* = .045) were found to be significant. This three way interaction showed that clauses with null pronouns were read slower than clauses with overt pronouns when the antecedent was the subject (*p* = .062) but not when the antecedent was the object (*p*= .696) among monolinguals; the opposite was obtained for bilinguals: clauses with null pronouns were read slower than clauses with overt pronouns when the antecedent was the object (*p*= .006) but not when the antecedent was the subject (*p*= .705). From the perspective of Group this pattern became more visible: bilinguals processed more rapidly overt pronouns linked to object antecedents than monolinguals (*p*= .014) suggesting a strong bias of overt pronouns towards antecedent in object position among this group. This, together with the strong preference of null pronouns to be interpreted as correferent with subjects, points to a division of labor of pronouns in the Spanish of our bilinguals, close to the pattern found in their other language, Catalan (see the results from Experiment 1). Nevertheless, at this region a processing penalty associated with the less reasonable object antecedent for a null pronoun does not appear.

Parallel effects were observed at the sentence-final noun ('*clase*') but with increased RTs due to wrap-up effects typical of final integration of information at this region (see the high values in the last region; Figure 5); according to Jegersky (2014) a reading time effect linked to a specific condition can appear even during sentence wrap-up. An effect of Pronoun (F(1, 316) = 13.833, *p* = .001) and a three-way interaction of Group*Pronoun*Antecedent (F(1, 316) = 4.077, *p* = .044) were observed. Post-hoc pairwise comparisons revealed that monolinguals processed null pronouns slower than overt pronouns (*p*= .006) with object antecedents and bilinguals processed faster overt pronouns than null pronouns (*p*= .002) with object antecedents. Interestingly, the bilingual group showed a processing penalty when they had to solve null pronouns correferent with the less reasonable, or unnatural, antecedent since they significantly read slower object antecedents than subject antecedents (*p*= .051). Overall, these findings suggest that bilinguals have a bit more polarized system of pronoun resolution that discriminates more reliably between null and overt pronouns. Is this a response to the burden that bilingualism itself produces to the speakers when they face the task of integrating structural and pragmatic information to interpret pronouns (observe that, in general, bilinguals show slower reading times than monolinguals) or, alternatively (or, in addition) are our bilinguals experiencing some influence from the other language?

5 General discussion and conclusion

The present study examines the interpretive and processing properties of null and overt pronouns in Catalan and Spanish, on the one hand, and monolingual and bilingual Spanish, in contact with Catalan, on the other. Besides the type of pronoun and the syntactic function of antecedent as constituent elements of the Position of Antecedent Hypothesis (PAH), whose predictions we test in the present piece of research, we also wanted to ascertain whether relative clause order is a key factor affecting pronoun resolution. Indeed, our results reveal the validity of our predictions given that clause order impacts the referential choices of pronominal anaphors: main-subordinate clause order is less PAH-constrained, particularly as to what null pronouns are concerned, than subordinate-main clause order, where a clear PAH effect arises. This can be well explained in parsing terms since, in the latter contexts, more memory resources are involved waiting for a second clause whose existence is indicated by the (temporal) conjunction that initiates the preceding subordinate clause and acts as a cue for the syntactic parser (Garnham, Oakhill and Cain, 1998); as a result, both potential antecedents are active and accessible in memory and, when the subject pronoun is encountered in the following matrix clause, its reference can be easily recovered resorting to the strategy put forth by the PAH. This effect was also observed in previous studies (Carminati 2002, Bel and García-Alcaraz 2015). There is still an issue that remains open for debate and further investigation: why are null pronouns more impacted than overt pronouns in main-subordinate contexts? Maybe it can be related to differing discourse expectations regarding topic continuity and change that null and overt pronouns, on the one hand, and main-subordinate relative clause order, on the other, entail. Summarizing, the analysis of our data has attested differences between Catalan and Spanish pronominal systems showing that these two languages are not equally sensitive to structural prominence; possibly Spanish relies more on the linear distance of the antecedent than on its syntactic function, as suggested by Filiaci et al. (2014).

Regarding our first research question, i.e. the operativeness of the PAH, although both languages have an equivalent set of pronominal forms, they do not match perfectly in preference choices: parallel interpretive biases in null pronouns, which solve anaphoric dependencies with antecedents in a previous subject position, but small divergences in the resolution of overt pronouns have been attested (i.e. Catalan overt pronouns more strongly object-biased than Spanish ones). In other words, the predictions of Carminati's (2002) PAH are borne out at the interpretive level in Catalan but not in Spanish. These findings for Spanish are consistent with previous results in Peninsular Spanish mainly for subordinate-main anaphora: null pronouns refer back to subject antecedents whereas overt pronouns do not show a clear-cut bias towards object over subject antecedents (Alonso-Ovalle et al. 2002, even at the intersentential level, Filiaci 2011 and Filiaci et al. 2014); unlike Spanish, Catalan does follow the PAH's sanctioned route (Mayor and Clark, 2010), similarly to Italian.

With regard to whether cross-linguistic influence modulates the interpretive and parsing patterns of intrasentential subject anaphora resolution in the bilingual variety, results clearly display the existence of an effect at both interpretive and processing levels. Looking first at interpretative judgment data, mainly in subordinate-main clause order in which more evident PAH's effects arise, the near significant triple interaction of pronoun, antecedent and group when comparing monolingual and bilingual Spanish, suggests that bilinguals interpret anaphoras in accordance with their L1 biases. This pattern becomes more obvious in contrasting the bar charts in Figures 2 and 4, where landscapes with notably analogous profiles are revealed in the Catalan pronoun choices and in the bilingual variety of Spanish spoken in Catalonia; to be more precise, the flexibility – or insensitiveness towards a specific antecedent- showed by Spanish overt pronouns in our data, as well as in previous data (see previous paragraph), is not reproduced in the Spanish contact variety tested here. On the other hand, interpretive preferences regarding null pronouns remain stable across different null-subject languages (Catalan, Spanish, Italian, Croatian, Greek, etc.) and across different varieties within the same language (Peninsular, Mexican or Argentinean Spanish) as it is in our case (monolingual and bilingual Spanish): the strong sensitivity to syntactic prominence that null pronouns displays goes beyond specific characteristics of languages/varieties so that the interpretation patterns remain unmovable and always converge.

From the processing angle, although both groups, monolinguals and bilinguals, exhibited a processing penalty when establishing co-reference in the most unnatural conditions – i.e., between null pronouns and matrix objects and between overt pronouns and matrix subjects-, the three-way interaction between group, pronoun and antecedent can be taken as a first piece of evidence that bilinguals in this study follow the PAH in a similar way that Catalan speakers do: their shorter RTs in conditions sanctioned by the PAH – i.e., null pronouns linked to subjects and overt pronouns to objects- compared to monolinguals, who reveal the opposite pattern, point to the influence of Catalan biases and not to an overextension of overt pronouns due to a lack of detailed, or superficial, processing of this interface phenomenon that has been reported for bilinguals (Sorace 2016). Given that our sentence stimuli are completely ambiguous until the point where the object disambiguating region is reached and that other cues were absent (recall that we carefully controlled for the implicit causality of the first verb), our bilinguals do not resort to a universal strategy such as subject preference (Serratrice and Hervé 2015) to solve the referential dependencies, but to the referential choices of the other language giving rise to some traces of cross-linguistic influence.

As indicated in the introduction, prior work on anaphora resolution has shown that bilinguals overextend the scope of the overt subject pronouns to the scope of the null subject pronouns (Sorace 2011) whereas the conditions of interpretability of null pronouns become restricted and steady; in other words, overt pronouns appear to be underspecified regarding their interpretive preferences. This indeterminate –i.e. unbiased- character of overt pronouns that has been attributed to bilingualism itself is not revealed by our experimental data but an effect of cross-linguistic influence that gives rise to pronominal patterns close to Catalan and consistent with the PAH; in other words, bilingual speakers assign null pronouns to subject antecedents and overt pronouns to object antecedents

The explanation from the transfer angle we have just mentioned is not incompatible with that of convergence between the bilingual and the monolingual Spanish varieties that is promoted in language contact situations (Silva-Corvalan 2008). As stated earlier, there is contradicting evidence concerning the compliance of the PAH in Spanish; for example, Keating et al. (2016) and Bel and García Alcaraz (2015) observed that monolingual speakers of Mexican Spanish and Peninsular Spanish, respectively, exhibited comprehension biases of the Italian type in solving null pronouns with subject antecedents and overt pronouns with object antecedents; particularly, Keating et al. (2016) noticed faster RTs in sentences complying with the predictions of the PAH. These results are somewhat in contrast with those by Filiaci et al. (2014) and the ones discussed here for monolingual Spanish. Nevertheless, and broadly speaking, it could be presumed that, even though they did not reach significance as they did in other studies, the monolingual tendencies attested in the current work regarding overt pronouns (Figure 4) are reinforced by transfer of the stronger biases displayed by Catalan overt pronouns, thus creating a convergent solution in bilingual interpretation.

Our study results also reveal another interesting pattern: sentences with overt pronouns display faster reading times in the final region, whereas sentences with null pronouns exhibit processing penalty effects, even in contexts that favor a subject antecedent (see Figure 5). These results suggest that null pronouns are, in general, more costly to process than overt pronouns, which is in line with findings from other data sources (Filiaci et al. 2014, Bel et al. 2016). There is experimental evidence that empty categories involve more effortful processing than overt categories (Yamashita et al. 1993).

There are still a couple of questions that need answers. Regarding specifically overt subject pronouns, it should be noted that the greater variability that seems to go along with the overextension of overt pronouns among bilinguals (Sorace 2011) is not present in our bilingual data nor can it be seen as the learner's default (Tsimpli (2011) as a solution to compensate for inconsistent efficiency in mapping pronoun forms and pragmatic functions. Contrary to what was expected, bilinguals do not seem to be cognitively taxed in pronoun resolution processing since they spend less time than monolinguals in all regions under different conditions, except for null pronouns referring back to object antecedents (see Figure 5). In the latter condition bilinguals showed a clear processing penalty at the wrap-up final region thus indicating that this option actually embodies a coerced reading and, as such, the cognitive load increases; it is worth remembering that the default and less problematic mapping for a null pronoun is maintaining reference by being linked to a preceding subject.

It could well be that the problem we are facing is much broader that typically assumed and that there is a confluence of features, both internal and external, that reinforce an already attested trend in a particular direction. Contact-induced changes can be favored by the retention of variants that are present, even to a lesser extent, in non-contact varieties. Concentrating again on overt pronouns, which are placed in the center of the controversy, it can be said that the internal transfer solution that the bilinguals we analyzed would be adopting, that is, associating overt pronouns mainly to object antecedents, might be pressed and reinforced by external data from Spanish input compatible with the option selected. At this stage, our results are well-matched with the idea of functional convergence as defended by Sánchez (2015); according to her proposal, a fusion of functional features from the two languages is observed when a set of features little activated (or not at all) in language A is frequently activated by input of language B in the bilingual mind. In our particular case, we are concerned with pragmatic features which seem even more malleable and propitious to mutation so that it is feasible that significant or subtle trends in overt pronoun resolution is Spanish (see Figure 4 and the description above where the availability of Spanish overt pronouns linked to object antecedents is actually an option) could be enhanced by the particular overlapping solutions of the Catalan overt pronouns system.

From these findings, it is not easy to predict whether language change in the Spanish contact variety scrutinized could be induced in the lines observed here or whether language change is already a reality in the context of Catalonia. The differences observed can be more apparent than realistic as they involve changes in the frequency of use. As reported, divergent frequencies and patterns are also attested in different varieties of Spanish. Moreover, by borrowing ideas from Meisel (2011), the bilingual Spanish-Catalan system reported constitutes the input for different generations of bilingual speakers. Children growing up in this linguistic environment are exposed to that variety of Spanish and, then, their options show the ones present in the input they receive. To what extent the Spanish system addressed here is a reflection of the 'steady' language contact variety, slightly different from other varieties, or the result of a bilingual system impacted by cross-linguistic influence from Catalan cannot be answered unequivocally in a single study and remains open to further inquiry.

Our study also shows inconclusive results with regards to the alleged bilingual disadvantage in specific linguistic domains such as the interface phenomena. The hypothesis that cognitive functions and less automatic processing are factors that characterize difficulties or uneven patterns of pronoun resolution in bilinguals (Serratrice and Hervé 2015, Sorace 2016) does not seem to fit very well in our case: bilingual processing does not appear to be less automatic compared to monolingual processing. Findings in L2 pronoun resolution processing indicate that it is modulated by language proficiency (Bel et al. 2016). In this study, we have been very selective in selecting bilinguals with full competence in both languages; they are, in addition, university students that have achieved fine language and communication skills and are continuously exposed to their two languages in the same and varied sociolinguistic contexts and engaged in bilingual conversations; also the early age of onset to bilingualism has also been controlled for; as a consequence, we have a group of very balanced, highly competent and functional bilinguals. Since these factors have been demonstrated to play an important role in executive functioning in bilinguals (Costa, Santesteban and Ivanova 2006), it is possible that cognitive control responsible for the interpretation and processing of anaphors could be higher among functional bilinguals than among other types of unbalanced bilinguals. In this sense, isolating different groupings of bilinguals (Catalan-dominant bilinguals, Spanish-dominant bilinguals, etc.), as Perpiñan (2017) does in her study of Catalan clitics, could open promising avenues of research related to the potential explanatory role of this set of factors.

Acknowledgments: This research has been supported by two grants from Spain's Ministry of Economy, Industry and Competitiveness (FFI2012-35058 and FFI2016-75082-P).

References

Alonso-Ovalle, L., S. Fernández-Solera, L. Frazier & C. Clifton. 2002. Null vs. overt pronouns and the topic-focus articulation in Spanish. *Rivista di Linguistica* 14. 151–169.
Bel, A. & M. Albert. 2016. The development of referential choice in Spanish narratives among school-age children and adolescents. In J. Perera, M.Aparici, E. Rosado & N. Salas (eds.), *Written and spoken language development across the lifespan*, 251–269. Frankfurt: Springer.
Bel, A. & E. García-Alcaraz. 2015. Subject pronouns in the L2 Spanish of Moroccan Arabic speakers. In T. Judy & S. Perpiñán (eds.), *Acquisition of Spanish in understudied language pairings*, 201–232. Amsterdam: John Benjamins.
Bel, A., J. Perera & N. Salas. 2010. Anaphoric devices in written and spoken narrative discourse: Data from Catalan. *Written Language and Literacy* 13(2). 236–259.
Bel, A., N. Sagarra, J. P. Comínguez & E. García-Alcaraz. 2016. Transfer and proficiency effects in L2 processing of subject anaphora. *Lingua* 184. 134–159.
Boix, E.J. & C. Sanz. 2008. Language and identity in Catalonia. In J. Rothman & M.M Nino-Murcia (eds.), *Language and identity*, 87–108. Philadelphia: Benjamins.

Carminati, M.N. 2002. *Processing of Italian subject pronouns*. University of Massachusetts at Amherst PhD dissertation.

Chamorro, G., A. Sorace & P. Sturt. 2016. What is the source of L1 attrition? The effect of recent L1 reexposure on Spanish speakers under L1 attrition. *Bilingualism: Language and Cognition* 19. 520–532.

Costa, A., M. Santesteban & I. Ivanova. 2006. How do highly proficient bilinguals control their lexicalization process? Inhibitory and language-specific selection mechanisms are both functional. *Journal of Experimental Psychology Learning Memory and Cognition* 32(5). 1057–1074.

de Prada Pérez, A. 2009. *Subject expression in Minorcan Spanish: Consequences of contact with Catalan*. The Pennsylvania State University PhD dissertation.

Domínguez, L. 2013. *Understanding interfaces: Second language acquisition and native language attrition of Spanish subject realization and word order variation*. Amsterdam: John Benjamins.

Filiaci, F. 2011. *Anaphoric preferences of null and overt subjects in Italian and Spanish: a cross-linguistic comparison*. University of Edinburgh Ph.D. dissertation.

Filiaci, F., A. Sorace & M. Carreiras. 2014. Anaphoric biases of null and overt subjects in Italian and Spanish: a cross-linguistic comparison. *Language and Cognitive Processes* 29(7). 825–843.

Garnham, A., J. V. Oakhill, K. Cain. 1998. Selective retention of information about the superficial form of text: Ellipses with antecedents in main and subordinate clauses. *The Quarterly Journal of Experimental Psychology* 51A. 19–39.

Goikoetxea, E., G. Pascual & J. Acha. 2008. Normative study of the implicit causality of 100 interpersonal verbs in Spanish. *Behavior Research Methods* 40(3). 760–772.

Guijarro-Fuentes P. & T. Marinis. 2009. The acquisition of personal preposition a by Catalan–Spanish and English–Spanish bilinguals. In J. Collentine, M. García, B. Lafford & F. Marcos Marín (eds.), *Selected proceedings of the 11th Hispanic Linguistics Symposium*, 81–92. Somerville: Cascadilla Press.

Holler, A. & K. Suckow (eds.). 2015. *Empirical perspectives on anaphora resolution*. Berlin/ Boston: Walter de Gruyter.

Jegerski, J. 2014. Self-paced reading. In J. Jegerski & B. VanPatten (eds.), *Research methods in second language psycholinguistics*, 20–49. New York: Routledge.

Jegerski, J., B. VanPatten, & G. Keating. 2011. Cross-linguistic variation and the acquisition of pronominal reference in L2 Spanish. *Second Language Research* 27(4). 481–507.

Keating, G., J. Jegerski & B. VanPatten. 2016. Online processing of subject pronouns in monolingual and heritage bilingual speakers of Mexican Spanish. *Bilingualism: Language and Cognition* 19(1). 36–49.

Keating, G., B. VanPatten & J. Jegerski. 2011. Who was walking on the beach? Anaphora resolution in Spanish heritage speakers and adult second language learners. *Studies in Second Language Acquisition* 33. 193–221.

Lozano, C. 2016. Pragmatic principles in anaphora resolution at the syntax-discourse interface: advanced English learners of Spanish in the CEDEL2 corpus. In M. Alonso Ramos (ed.), *Spanish learner corpus research: state of the art and perspectives*, 236–265. Amsterdam: John Benjamins.

Meisel, J.M. 2011. *First and second language acquisition: parallels and differences*. Cambridge: Cambridge University Press.

Mayol, L. & R. Clark. 2010. Pronouns in Catalan: Games of partial information and the use of linguistic resources. *Journal of Pragmatics* 42. 781–799.

Montrul, S. 2008 *Incomplete acquisition in bilingualism: re-examining the age factor*. Amsterdam: John Benjamins.

Perpiñan, S. 2015. The locative paradigm in the L2 Spanish of Catalan native speakers. In T. Judy & S. Perpiñán (eds.), *The acquisition of spanish in understudied language pairings*, 105–132. Amsterdam: John Benjamins.

Perpiñan, S. 2017. Catalan-Spanish bilingualism continuum: The expression of non-personal Catalan clitics in the adult grammar of early bilinguals. *Linguistic Approaches to Bilingualism* 7:5. 477–513.

Rudolph, U. & F. Försterling. 1997. The psychological causality implicit in verbs: A review. *Psychological Bulletin* 121. 192–218.

Sánchez, L. 2015. Crosslinguistic influences, functional interference, feature reassembly and functional convergence in Quecha-Spanish bilingualism. In S. Perpiñan and T. Judy (eds.), *The acquisition of Spanish as a second language: data from understudied language pairings*, 19–48. Amsterdam: John Benjamins.

Schwartz, B. D. 2004. Why child L2 acquisition? In J. Van Kampen & S. Baauw (eds.), *Proceedings of generative approaches to language acquisition 2003*, 47–66. Utrecht: LOT Occasional Series.

Serratrice, L. & C. Hervé. 2015. Referential expressions in bilingual acquisition. In L. Serratrice & S. E.M. Allen (eds.), *The acquisition of reference*, 311–333. Amsterdam: John Benjamins.

Shin, N. & H. Cairns. 2012. The development of NP selection in school-age children: Reference and Spanish subject pronouns. *Language Acquisition* 19(1). 3–38.

Silva-Corvalán, C. 2008. The limits of convergence in language contact. *Journal of language contact* 2(1). 213–224.

Sinner, C. 2004. *El castellano de Cataluña*. Tübingen: Niemeyer.

Sorace, A. 2011. Pinning down the concept of "interface" in bilingualism. *Linguistic Approaches to Bilingualism* 1. 1–33.

Sorace, A. 2016. Referring expressions and executive functions in bilingualism. *Linguistic Approaches to Bilingualism* 6(5). 669–684.

Tsimpli, I.M. 2011. External interfaces and the notion of "default". *Linguistic Approaches to Bilingualism* 1. 101–103.

Unsworth, S. 2013. Assessing age of onset effects in (early) child L2 acquisition. *Language Acquisition* 20. 74–92.

Unsworth, S. 2016. Early child L2 acquisition: Age or input effects? Neither, or both? *Journal of Child Language* 43. 603–634.

Yamashita, H., L. Stowe, & M. Nakayama. 1993. Processing of Japanese relative clause constructions. In P. Clancy (ed.), *Japanese/Korean linguistics: II,* 248–263. Stanford: CSLI.

Alejandro Cuza and Pedro Guijarro-Fuentes

The distribution of copulas *ser* and *estar* in Spanish/Catalan bilinguals

Abstract: The present study investigates the distribution of copula verbs *ser* and *estar* in Spanish and Catalan among nineteen (n=19) adult bilinguals born and raised in Palma de Mallorca, Spain. An elicited production task tested the participants' patterns of use of both copula verbs in three contexts: with adverbial locatives, stage-level adjectives and event locatives. Catalan and Spanish diverge in copular use with adverbial locatives and adjectives but behave similarly in their exclusive use of *ser* with event locatives. As predicted, results showed a marked overextension of *estar* in Catalan locatives and adjectival predicates, supporting previous work. Although some participants alternated both copulas with locatives in Catalan, the use of *estar* was clearly preferred at the individual level. In regard to event locatives, the participants behaved target-like in their restrictive use of *ser*. There were no difficulties in Spanish, where *estar* is obligatory with adverbial locatives and adjectives and *ser* with event locatives. We argue that the overextension of *estar* in Catalan stems from crosslinguistic influence from Spanish and structural overlap. Spanish copular *estar* appears to be substituting the semantic scope of *ser* use in Catalan but only in areas where the two languages diverge.

1 Introduction

The present study examines the knowledge of the distribution of copula verbs *ser* and *estar* in Spanish and *éssere* and *estar* in Catalan ('to be' in English) among Catalan/Spanish adult bilinguals. Although copula distribution in Spanish has been extensively examined among English-speaking L2 learners of Spanish (Bruhn de Garavito & Valenzuela 2008; Geeslin 2002, 2003; Geeslin & Guijarro Fuentes 2006, 2007; VanPatten 1985), the acquisition of copulas *ser* and *estar*

Note: Address of Correspondence: Alejandro Cuza. School of Languages and Cultures. Department of Spanish and Portuguese. Purdue University. 640 Oval Drive. Stanley Coulter Hall. West Lafayette, IN. 47907. Email: acuza@purdue.edu

Alejandro Cuza, Purdue University
Pedro Guijarro-Fuentes, University of Balearic Islands

https://doi.org/10.1515/9781501509988-004

in Catalan/Spanish bilinguals remains underexplored (Perpiñán 2015; Sanz & González 1995). We aim to fill this gap in the literature by examining the bidirectional distribution of these two copula verbs in Spanish/Catalan adult bilinguals born and raised in Palma de Mallorca, Spain. Specifically, we examine the development of copula distinctions in the following contexts: locative adverbs with animate (1a–1b) and inanimate (2a, 2b) subjects, stage-level adjectives (3a–3b) and event locatives (4a–4b):

(1) animate locatives
   a. SPAN: El perro **está/*es** debajo del escritorio.
   b. CATA: El gos **és/està** sota la l'escriptori.
            "The dog is under the desk."

(2) inanimate locatives
   a. SPAN: La peluquería **está/*es** detrás del hotel.
   b. CATA: La perruqueria **és/està** darrera de l'hotel.
            "The hair salon is behind the hotel."

(3) stage-level adjectives
   a. SPAN: El café **está /*es** frío.
   b. CATA: El café **és/està** fred.
            "The coffee is cold."

(4) event locatives
   a. SPAN: El festival **es/*está** en la Plaza Mayor
   b. CATA: El festival **és/*està** en la Plaça Major.
            "The festival is at the Plaza Mayor"

Copula distribution in Catalan is interesting to examine for two main reasons. First, although Spanish and Catalan are typologically similar, the distribution of copulas *éssere/ser* and *estar* is similar in some contexts but quite different in others (Brucart 2012; Camacho 2012; Solà 1987). For example, both *éssere* and *estar* are possible in Catalan with adverbial locatives (1b, 2b) and stage-level predicates (3b), while Spanish usually allows only *estar* in these contexts (1a, 2a, 3a). However, both languages behave similarly in their required use of *éssere* with event locatives (4a and 4b). The structural overlap in the use of *estar* with locatives and adjectives as in (1) to (3) above might favor an overextension of *estar* in Catalan, as we will discuss shortly. On the other hand, both languages require copular *ser* with event locatives, which might mitigate any processing constraints the learner faces with copular distribution in this context. The learner must process both the semantic properties of the eventive subject [-animate] as well as the semantic extensions of the locative predicate. Thus, it is interesting to examine the extent to which bilingual speakers of these two languages are affected by bilingualism effects. Following existing literature in bilingual development (Pérez-Leroux, Pirvulescu & Roberge 2009; Meisel 2007), we consider the notion of bilingualism effects as a type of language interdependence evidenced by crosslinguistic influence from one grammar into the other due to several interrelated internal and external factors, including structural overlap (Müller & Hulk 2001), language dominance (Argiri & Sorace 2007; Montrul & Ionin 2012; Silva-Corvalán & Treffers-Daller 2015; Unsworth 2015; Montrul 2015), and language exposure and use (Montrul 2008; Unsworth 2013). Structural overlap refers to those instances where one language (Language A) allows more than one option for a specific structure, and the other language (Language B) overlaps with one of those options leading to unidirectional transfer from Language B into Language A (Hulk & Müller 2000). This is relevant to our study in the case of adjectival or locative contexts where Catalan (Language A) allows both *ser* and *estar* but Spanish (Language B) only allows *estar*. Therefore, we would expect unidirectional transfer from Spanish into Catalan evidenced in an overextension of copula *estar*.[1] We define language dominance as the language in which the bilingual speaker feels more comfortable with in his day-to-day interactions in a bilingual context.[2] Research with early and late bilingual development has demonstrated a significant role for language dominance in bilingual development reflected in unidirectional transfer from the stronger language to the weaker language (Montrul & Ionin 2012; Paradis & Genesee 1996). However, this has not always been the case, and internal factors like structural overlap seem to play a more decisive role in the selectivity of transfer.

Second, this language pair is interesting to examine because most of bilingualism research has been conducted in contexts where one language is a minority or heritage language, as is the case of Spanish in the U.S. (Cuza & Pérez-Tattam 2016; Montrul 2004; Montrul & Sánchez Walker 2013; Polinsky 2011; Sorace 2005; Putnam & Sánchez 2013; Silva-Corvalán 1986, 1994). However, the Spanish/Catalan bilingual situation is different in Mallorca as both languages have

---

1 For Hulk & Müller (2000), in addition to structural overlap considerations, the structure in question must be part of the syntax/pragmatics interface (C-Domain) for crosslinguistic influence to occur. However, we believe that structural overlap considerations represent an optimal explanation even for cases where the syntax interfaces with other domains like semantics.
2 This concept involves other essential dimensions including linguistic proficiency, processing ability, fluency, frequency of language exposure and use, as well as identity and cultural identification issues (see Gertken, Amengual, & Birsong for recent analysis 2014).

equal official status in the Balearic Islands (Blass-Arroyo 2007). However, attitudes towards language and bilingualism are not always positive (Pieras-Guasp 2002). Research in this bilingual community adds to current research in assessing important issues including the role of cross-linguistic influence, patterns of language exposure and use and community characteristics. As argued by Baker (1996) and others, bilingualism is a social phenomenon that exists and develops not only in the mind of the speaker but also in the context in which he lives. In this respect, both Catalan and Spanish are part of the fabric of the bilingual community of Palma de Mallorca, and both languages have a high degree of ethnolinguistic vitality (Pieras-Guasp 2002). Ethnolinguistic vitality refers to the beliefs that a community has towards any specific language that cause a specific ethnolinguistic group to remain distinct, and to behave as an active collective entity in intergroup relations (e.g., Bourhis Giles & Rosenthal 1981; Pérez-Leroux, Cuza & Thomas 2011). As we will discuss shortly, Pieras-Guasp (2002) found that young Spanish/Catalan adults living in Palma de Mallorca value Catalan for instrumental purposes; however, Spanish is the language that they value the most for social interactions and peer relationships. In addition to these two main contributions, our study also adds to current research by examining copula use with event locatives among Spanish/Catalan bilinguals, an area of research so far underexplored.

In what follows, we provide a background on the existing distinctions between Catalan and Spanish in regard to copula use and distribution, followed by previous research in the acquisition of *ser* and *estar* in adult bilinguals. We then present our experiment, the participants and the results of the study. The discussion and conclusions appear in section 5.

2 Copula distribution in Spanish and Catalan

The use of copula verbs *ser* and *estar* in Spanish has often been discussed in relation to individual-level vs. stage-level predicates, reflecting permanent (e.g., Rosa es estudiante "Rose is a student"), and circumstantial properties of the subject (e.g., Miguel está cansado "Michael is tired") respectively (e.g., Camacho 2012; Demonte & Masullo 1999; Diesing 1992; Fernández-Leborans 1995, 1999). For Spanish-English bilinguals, the acquisition of these distinctions has been found to be problematic given the fact that English does not make this distinction (e.g., Geeslin 2002, 2003; Geeslin & Guijarro Fuentes 2006, 2007; Silva-Corvalán 1986; VanPatten 1985). In English, both aspectual meanings are expressed by the verb 'to be'. Furthermore, acquisitional delays are also motivated by frequency effects, and variability in the input with respect to the *ser* and *estar* alternation in Spanish. For example, there are cases where copular *estar* is used to refer to an irreversible characterization of the subject (e.g., Napoleón Bonaparte está muerto "Napoleon Bonaporte is dead"). It is also possible for circumstantial character-izations to occur with copula *ser* (Juan *es* muy popular "John is very popular") (Zagona 2013). In the latter example, John might be very popular at the moment but this is likely to change. The interval in which the categorization occurs is temporally delimited, but *ser* is still required. This variability in *ser* and *estar* alternation with adjectival predicates in Spanish creates fuzziness in the input, leading to learnability issues, including *ser* overextension to contexts where *estar* is required or vice versa.

Previous research combines the strengths of a stage-level vs. individu-al-level analysis with the view that copula distinctions are aspectual in nature (e.g., Camacho 2012; Fernández-Leborans 1995, 1999; Gallego & Uriagereka 2009; Schmitt, Holtheuer & Miller 2004). This approach accounts for *ser* and *estar* alter-nation with adjectives (Juan es alto vs. Juan está alto "John is tall"), the use of *estar* with adverbial locatives (e.g., La Biblioteca Nacional está/*es en Madrid "The National Library is in Madrid")[3] and the categorical use of *ser* with event locatives (El concierto es/*está en la plaza "The concert is at the plaza").

In this regard, Zagona (2013) argues that *ser* and *estar* alternation stems from the presence of an uninterpretable feature [uP] (perfective/imperfective aspect) regulating the complements of *estar* but not those of *ser*. Within this approach, copula selection is determined by the syntactic properties of the predicate (p. 305). The formal feature [uP] determines the complements of copula *estar* (*estar*: [v [uP]...]). With adjectives, the complements of *estar* would include a beginning and an endpoint, while the complements of *ser* do not, as represented (5a) and (5b):

(5) a. Mi mamá *está* joven   (*estar*, $+uP$)
         "My mom is young"
     b. Mi mamá *es* joven   (*ser*, $-uP$)
         "My mom is young"

In (5a), the sentence can be interpreted as either 'My mother looks young' or 'My mother is young'. However, in (5b) only a more permanent interpretation is possi-ble ('My mother is young') since the complement of the copula does not take an *uP*.

---

3 The use of copular *ser* in this context can be grammatical in Colombian Spanish; the subject might be unique in the discourse and perhaps have a topic interpretation (José Camacho, per-sonal communication).

For locative constructions, Zagona argues that the stative uP of *estar* has to be checked by a stative preposition (e.g., *en* 'in') expressing a single location (6a). If the copula *estar* takes a preposition denoting direction or path (e.g., *a* 'to', *hacia* 'toward'), which does not have a stative interpretation, the derivation crashes (6b):

(6) a. Dora [$_v$ [$_{uP}$ *está* [$_P$ location *en* [$_{DP}$ la playa]]]]
"Dora is at the beach."
b. *Dora [$_v$ [$_{uP}$ está_[$_{P\_path}$ *a* [$_{DP}$ la playa]]]]
"Dora is at the beach."

The reason why the derivation crashes in (6b) is because the verb and its complement (PP) do not share the same aspectual properties (stative for the copula and path for the PP).[4] This proposal also accounts for the ungrammaticality of e*star* with an event locative as a complement, as in (7) below:

(7) * La fiesta [$_v$ [$_{uP}$ está [$_{P\_path}$ en [$_{DP}$ el rancho]
"The party is at the farm"

The prepositional phrase in this case has an eventive aspectual meaning (+Theme) provided by the determiner phrase, which contains a path component. This causes a clash with the stative interpretable features intrinsic to the copula *estar* (Zagona 2013: 317). The stative uP of *estar* has to be checked with those of its complement or the derivation crashes.

In regard to Catalan, copulas *ser* and *estar* have also been analyzed in terms of permanent vs. circumstantial properties of the subject (e.g., Brucart 2012; Falk 1979). However, in contrast with Spanish, Catalan is quite variable, as native speakers often use either copula indiscriminately with stage-level adjectives (8a) and locatives (8b):

(8) a. L'aigua és/està bruta   (adjectival predicate)
"The water is dirty"
b. Les sabates estan/són sota el llit   (adverbial locative)
"The shoes are under the bed"

---

4 Although Zagona's proposal is quite optimal in accounting for *ser* and *estar* alternation in Spanish, it does not completely capture cases where *estar* can have a stative interpretation with a preposition that usually encodes *path* or *direction*. For example, in Cuban Spanish, it is not ungrammatical to say *Ellos **están hacia** la playa,* meaning that they are at the beach. Although this can also mean path/direction (They are on their way to the beach), a stative meaning is also available.

Researchers have argued that the selection of one copula over the other with adverbial locatives as in (8b) is somehow constrained by the animacy features of the subject (e.g., Brucart 2012; Perpiñán 2015; Sanz & Gonzáles 1995). This, however, has not been completely demonstrated. Others have argued that in standard Catalan, only *ser* is allowed in locative constructions, and that the use of *estar* is the result of contact with Spanish and internal language change (e.g., Sanz & González 1995; Solà 1987). This prescriptive argument has not been supported empirically, as Catalan has always been in contact with Spanish, and both languages have co-official status.[5] Therefore, the existence of a standard variety (non-contact variety for many) is difficult to determine. However, it is the case that the Eastern Catalan variety spoken in Catalonia (provinces of Barcelona, Tarragona, Girona and Lleida) is considered more formal than other varieties (e.g., Balearic, Valencian), and is the variety often used in written registers, TV and radio.

In what follows, we discuss previous work on the acquisition of copula distribution in Spanish and Catalan and pose the research questions and hypotheses that guide the present study.

3 Previous research with Catalan/Spanish bilinguals

There is no doubt that the acquisition of the *ser* and *estar* distribution is a challenging process, just like the acquisition of the subjunctive mood or past tense aspectual interpretations in Spanish. Difficulties and delays have been amply observed in different populations and with different language pairs, including Spanish monolingual children (e.g., Holtheuer 2011; Schmitt et al. 2004; Schmitt & Miller 2007; Sera 1992), Catalan/Spanish bilingual children (Cuza & Guijarro-Fuentes 2017; Arnaus-Gil & Müller 2015), Spanish-English bilingual children (e.g., Cuza, Reyes & Lustres 2017; Liceras, Fernández Fuertes & Alba de la Fuente 2012; Silva-Corvalán 1994; Silva-Corvalán & Montanari 2008), and in English-speaking L2 learners (Bruhn de Garavito & Valenzuela 2008; Geeslin 2002, 2006; Pérez-Leroux, Álvarez & Battersby 2010). However, research on the patterns of *ser* and *estar* use in Catalan/Spanish bilinguals remains underexplored, except

---

5 We acknowledge that that there are some communities in Catalonia and in the Balearic Islands where Catalan is the stronger/dominant language. However, this does not mean that Spanish is not spoken or that a contact situation does not exist. It is safe to say that, overall, this is not the linguistic reality of Catalonia or the Balearic Islands. Both regions are extremely bilingual, and both languages enjoy co-official status.

for a few studies (e.g., Geeslin & Guijarro Fuentes 2008; Perpiñán 2015; Sanz & González 1995).

In regard to Spanish monolingual children, Sera (1992) found *estar* over-extension to contexts where *ser* should be used, including event locatives. The author argues that the use of *estar* with event locatives stems from the incorrect interpretation of the event as an object by the child, given the extended use of *estar* with spatial locations in the input (Sera 2008). Cuza, Reyes & Lustres (2017), however, counter this view by documenting *estar* overextension with event locatives in Spanish/English bilingual children born and raised in the US, even though they seem to distinguish events from spatial locations in comprehension. The authors argue that rather than interpreting events as objects, difficulties with this domain are better explained in terms of frequency effects associated with this particular "subclass" of copula use in Spanish, which lead to inevitable developmental delays. In their seminal study with a Spanish/English bilingual child, Silva-Corvalán and Montenari (2008) found only one instance of event locatives out of 696 tokens produced by a Spanish-English bilingual child (e.g., Mi cumpleaños está en mayo "My birthday is in May"), and three instances out of 510 tokens produced by the adult caregiver. This supports the view that the use of copulas *ser* and *estar* with event locatives is less frequent in the input. In addition to low frequency effects, Spanish allows for other competing forms to express the same eventive meaning (e.g., *tendrá lugar* "it will take place"), which further increases the ambiguity of the input. These competing forms for *ser* in eventive locatives are also available in Catalan and other Romance languages (*tindrà lloc* "it will take pace").

In regard to adult Catalan/Spanish bilinguals, research has documented overextension of *estar* in Catalan (Sanz & González 1995) as well *estar* underuse in Spanish (Perpiñán 2015; Geeslin & Guijarro-Fuentes 2008). In their investigation with Catalan/Spanish bilinguals from the region of Tortosí in Catalonia, Sanz & González (1995) found *estar* overuse, crucially with animate subject references and with adjectives denoting physical conditions. Inanimate subjects were affected in a lesser degree. However, some adjectives appeared in contrast or in free variation with *ser* (e.g., *gord* "fat"). The authors argue that it is in these particular cases where individual differences like age play a role in the degree of *estar* overextension. For example, they found that younger speakers showed a clear preference towards *estar* over *ser*, and used *estar* in their speech in cases that the older informants considered ungrammatical (La revista està molt bonica "The magazine is very pretty") (Sanz & González 1995 : 5). The authors conclude that the internal change in progress taking place in Catalan towards a preference to *estar* is accelerated by contact with Spanish, where *estar* is required with locatives and adjectives (e.g., Gutiérrez 1992; Silva-Corvalán 1994).

The idea of an acceleration of language change in a language contact situation was examined by Geeslin & Guijarro-Fuentes' (2008) study. They investigated *estar* and *ser* distribution in Spanish among bilingual speakers in contact with Galician, Catalan and Basque. The authors compared the frequency of copula use between and within groups and aimed to identify factors that favored the use of one copula over the other. Crucially, they investigated whether contact with another language necessarily leads to more frequent selection of *estar* in Spanish. Geeslin & Guijarro-Fuentes found that the degree of *estar* selection diverged across bilingual groups, and that some predictors for *estar* use were actually common to all groups. Results showed that all groups behaved significantly differently from monolinguals and demonstrated significant variation in copula selection. However, the direction of the differences diverged across groups. While Spanish/Catalan and Spanish/Valencian bilinguals showed lower rates of *estar* selection, the Basque/Spanish and the Galician/Spanish speakers showed higher rates of *estar* use compared to Spanish monolingual speakers. Therefore, bilingualism by itself is not deterministically related to *estar* selection or the simplification of the copular system in Spanish. This is the case among languages in contact with similar copular systems (Spanish and Catalan) but also among languages in contact where the copular systems diverge (Spanish and Basque). In contrast to Silva-Corvalán's (1994) proposal, the overextension of *estar* was not directly related to contact with other languages or the lack of access to a formal written variety of Spanish.

Perpiñán (2015) investigated the distribution of copulas *ser* and *estar* as well as indefinite *haber* in the L2 Spanish grammar of Catalan speakers via an acceptability judgement task and an oral production task. Results from the production task showed underuse of *estar* with locatives in Spanish among the Catalan speakers. This suggests transfer effects from Catalan L1, where *estar* is restricted to locate objects (Solà 1987: 126). However, in contrast with previous work, Perpiñan did not find overproduction of *ser* in Spanish but rather higher use of *haber* ("to have") and *llevar* ("to carry"). Regarding intuition, the author found that the Catalan speakers accepted *ser* to locate objects in Spanish, in contrast to the Spanish monolinguals. It appears then as if the familiarity with Catalan leads to *estar* reduction in Spanish locative constructions. Perpiñán also found that all participants recognized that *ser* must be used with events (La reunión es en el hotel "The meeting is at the hotel"), and correctly rejected *estar* in those contexts. The author argues that the reduced use of *estar* with locatives in Spanish might stem from the frequent use of *ser* in Catalan, which instead could activate the necessary uninterpretable feature needed in Spanish to yield a locative interpretation for *ser* (Perpiñán 2015: 127). Although this is a possibility, the nature of the production task could have also conflated the results, leading to *estar* underuse in production. The participants might have underused *estar* not because it is underspecified in their L2 system but simply because they had other lexical options they could have used (El libro está en la mesa vs. Hay un libro en la mesa "There is a book on the table"). The lower rate of *estar* production could have been a task effect, not necessarily a developmental issue; this is also conflated in the monolingual norm, where the use of *estar* vs. *haber* in this context might be constrained by dialectal issues. As for the acceptance of *ser* with locative constructions in Spanish (AJT), this is something that calls for an item analysis. The use of *estar* with adverbial locatives in Spanish is not categorical; the input does provide ambiguous evidence (El baño está/es a la izquierda "The bathroom is to the left") (See Camacho 2012 for discussion).

Following previous work as well as the existing differences between Spanish and Catalan as far as copular distribution is concerned, we examine the following research questions:

RQ1: Do Spanish/Catalan adult bilinguals show target distribution of copular *ser* and *estar* in both languages? If not,

RQ2: Are the difficulties with copular distribution more pronounced in the use of *estar* with adjectives and locatives in Catalan than in Spanish stemming from structural overlap effects?

RQ3: What is the role of language dominance in this process? That is, is the degree of target behavior in copula distribution in each language correlated with language dominance?

We follow Hulk & Müler's (2000) structural overlap hypothesis in predicting unidirectional transfer from Spanish into Catalan as evidenced in a higher use of copular *estar*. Catalan (Language A) allows both *ser* and *estar* with locatives and adjectives; Spanish (Language B) overlaps with Catalan in allowing only *estar*. Therefore, we expect overextension of *estar* in Catalan stemming from crosslinguistic influence from Spanish. However, we do not expect transfer effects from Catalan into Spanish evidenced by an overextension of *ser* with Spanish locatives or adjectives since that option is not available in Spanish (as far as the contexts under investigation are concerned). As mentioned earlier, Hulk & Müller's (2000) proposal for crosslinguistic influence implies (1) that there is a structural overlap between the two languages, and (2) that the structure under consideration lies at the syntax-pragmatics interface. However, we argue that structural overlap as a condition for transfer can also be applied to syntax-semantics interface structures or even the narrow syntax. This is in light of research documenting transfer effects in contexts where the two languages overlap in a specific structure (e.g., clitic climbing in Spanish but not in English) with no pragmatic extensions (Pérez-Leroux, Cuza & Thomas 2011).[6] Furthermore, we don't expect overextension of copula *estar* with event locatives in either language; this option is ungrammatical in both Spanish and Catalan. We also don't predict overextension of *ser* to stage-level predicates or locatives in Spanish where *estar* is required. The use of *estar* in locatives and with stage-level predicates is very categorical in Spanish and quite salient in the input. All of the participants have native-like proficiency in Spanish and therefore we would not expect this type of error (e.g., *El agua es sucia "The water is dirty" or *Dora es en la playa "Dora is at the beach"). We hypothesize the following:

H1: The bilingual speakers will overextend copular *estar* to (a) Catalan locatives (e.g., El gos **està** sota la l'escriptori "The dog is under the desk.") and (b) in Catalan adjectival contexts (e.g., La sopa **està** calenta "The soup is hot"). In these two contexts copula *ser* is also possible in Catalan, leaving one overlapping structure with Spanish (*estar*).

H2: The participants will not overextend copular *estar* to event locatives in Catalan where *ser* is required. Both languages behave the same way in this context (e.g., El festival és a la Plaça Major; El festival **es** en la Plaza Mayor "The festival is at the Plaza Mayor").

H3: The participants will not show (a) overextension of *ser* in contexts where *estar* is required in Spanish (adverbial locatives or stage-level predicates) or (b) overextension of *estar* with event locatives where *ser* is obligatory (e.g., La fiesta **es** en casa de María "The house is at Mary's house.").

In what follows we present the experiment and the results.

---

6 Pérez-Leroux et al. (2011) found that Spanish/English bilingual children prefer post-verbal clitic placement in reconstruction environments in Spanish (Mara quiere ver**lo**), an option not attested in monolingual children, who prefer preverbal placement (Maria **lo** quiere ver). The authors argue for crosslinguistic effects from English despite no pragmatic extensions in Spanish reconstruction contexts.

4 The experiment

Community characteristics

The present study took place in Palma de Mallorca, the capital city of the Autonomous Community of Balearic Islands in Spain. Catalan and Spanish are the
co-official languages of the Balearic Islands, as per the Linguistic Normalization
Law of 1986, and both languages are widely spoken in Mallorca (Blass-Arroyo
2007). The specific dialect of the Catalan spoken in Mallorca is *Mallorquín*, which
goes back to the thirteenth century, but nowadays most people refer to it as simply
Catalan. *Mallorquín* is often used as the ethnic identification, and is independent
of language use or competence in Catalan (Melià 1997; Siguan 1999).[7]

Catalan is compulsory in Mallorca's public-school system, and most residents (around 73%) speak Catalan with different degrees of bilingual ability. In
Palma, specifically, most of its residents have native-like linguistic competence
in Spanish. Spanish is preferred over Catalan among the younger generation for
peer-interaction, as they do not relate language dominance with ethnic identity (Melià 1997). Although Mallorcan residents are schooled almost entirely in
Catalan depending on the type of school (public vs. private) and region, Spanish
remains the main language for social interaction and intergroup relationships
among the youth. In this regard, Pieras-Guasp (2002) argues that Spanish has
a higher instrumental value than Catalan in Palma, and it is the language preferred by the younger generation for social mobility and power. Thus, it is safe
to argue that in Palma, Spanish is the dominant language for most of its residents. This is also emphasized by the large number of non-Catalan residents who
have immigrated to Palma from other regions of Spain, and the region's massive
tourist industry. However, both Spanish and Catalan have equal official status,
and neither of the two languages can be considered as a minority/heritage language at the individual or societal level. This is a situation similar to the current
linguistic diversity of Montreal (Quebec, Canada), where both English and French
are widely spoken. This linguistic integration is optimal for bilingual development, although the patterns of use of one language vs. the other do diverge, as is
common in most bilingual communities. English is also widely spoken as *lingua
franca* due the enormous impact of the tourist industry in the Bay of Palma and

---

7 Despite several morphosyntactic and lexical dialectal differences between Balearic and
Mainland Catalan dialects, there are no reported dialectal differences to our knowledge in the
use of *ser* and *estar*.

the large number of business and commerce between the Balearic Islands and the UK (Bruyèl-Olmedo & Juan-Garau 2010; 2015).

Participants

Nineteen (*n*=19) Catalan-Spanish sequential bilinguals, born and raised in Palma de Mallorca, were recruited for the study via word of mouth. Their age range was 18–27 years of age (*M*=22; *SD*=3.1). The participants were exposed to Spanish and/ or Catalan at home before the age of 5;0 in different degrees depending on the linguistic background of their parents. However, all of them were exposed to Catalan at the time of school immersion. All of the participants except one were university students at a major research university in Palma de Mallorca. They completed a detailed language background questionnaire (adapted from Cuza 2013) which elicited information regarding age, formal education, employment, parents' primary languages, patterns of language use and exposure in different contexts as well as a self-proficiency measure.

In regard to their language background, 50% of the participants indicated having Catalan as their home language during early childhood, 22% indicated having Spanish, and 27% indicated having both. In regard to their patterns language use at school, 59% indicated that they spoke mostly Catalan or a little more Catalan than Spanish; 12% indicated that they spoke mostly Spanish and 29% that they spoke both. Similar patterns of use were reported at home where 61% of the participants indicated that they spoke either only Catalan or mostly Catalan. In social situations, their patterns of language used changed drastically: 39% reported speaking a little more Spanish than Catalan or only Spanish; 33% indicated speaking both, and only 27% indicated speaking only Catalan. This reflects the bilingual situation in Palma where Spanish is highly spoken in social situations, even though most young bilinguals have been educated and raised primarily in Catalan. When we asked the participants which language they felt more comfortable with, 44% indicated Catalan, 22% indicated Spanish and 33% indicated both. It is clear from this information that most of the participants were Catalan dominant, but they all had excellent knowledge of Spanish as well, and used it more than Catalan in social situation with friends. Table 1 summarizes this information:

Structures under analysis and tasks

As discussed earlier, the goal of our study was to examine the distribution of copula verbs *ser* and *estar* in Catalan and Spanish in four contexts: animate and inanimate locatives where *estar* is obligatory in Spanish but not in Catalan, stage-level adjectives

Table 1: Participants' linguistic background.

	Adult Bilinguals (n=19)		
Mean age at testing	22 (range=18–27; SD=3.1)		
Place of Birth and Residence	Spain, Palma de Mallorca		
Language background			
	Primary Language: CAT: 55%; SPAN: 33%; BOTH: 11%		
	Home lang. as child: CAT: 50%; SPAN 22%; BOTH 27%		
	Most comfortable lang.: CAT: 44%; SPAN:22%; BOTH: 33%		
Language spoken at:			
Home:	CAT: 61%; SPAN: 27%; BOTH: 11%		
School:	CAT: 59%; SPAN: 12%; BOTH: 29%		
Social Situations:	CAT: 27%; SPAN: 39%; BOTH: 33%		
Self-proficiency (1=poor; 4=excellent)			
CAT:	Reading (3.7); Writing (3.7); Speaking (3.6); Comprehension (3/9)		
SPAN:	Reading (3.9); Writing (3.8); Speaking (3.7); Comprehension (3/9)		

where *estar* is required in Spanish but optional in Catalan, and event locatives where *ser* is required in both languages.[8] We expected the participants to show more use of *estar* with locatives and adjectives in Catalan but no difficulties with their use of *ser* with event locatives as both languages behave the same in this context (*ser* required).

To elicit the use of *ser* and *estar* in both languages, we implemented an elicited production task with the aid of PowerPoint and a laptop computer (Cuza 2016; Crain & Thornton 1998). The participants were presented with a preamble followed by a question. The response had to be consistent with the preamble and a photo provided. Examples (9)-(10) show a sample of the task in Spanish:

(9) *Locative adverb – animate (ESTAR required)*

> **Preamble:** *Bart quiere jugar con Dora y Diego pero no los encuentra y te pregunta.* "Bart wants to play with Dora and Diego but he can't find them and he asks you..."
>
> *(here a photo of Dora and Diego on top of a tree)*

---

8 Event locatives included the following: *La boda es en la iglesia* ("The wedding is at the church"), *La clase es en la biblioteca (The class is at the library), La fiesta es en casa de los Sympsons* ("The party is at the Simpsons"), *El festival es en la Plaza Mayor* ("The festival is at the Plaza Mayor"), *La competencia de barcos es en el puerto* ("The regatta is at the port").

Prompt: *Dile a Bart dónde.* "Tell Bart where..."
Expected response: *Dora y Diego* **están** *encima del árbol.* "Dora and Diego are on top of a tree."

(10) *Adjectival Predicate* (*ESTAR* required)

Preamble: *Lisa no tiene mucho tiempo para cenar pues ya tiene que salir con sus amigos. Ella quiere tomarse la sopa que su mamá le preparó rápidamente pero no puede.* "Lisa does not have too much time to have dinner because she is going out with her friends. She wants to eat the soup her mother prepared for her but she can't.

(here a photo of a steaming soup)

Prompt: *¿Por qué Lisa no puede tomarse la sopa rápido* "Why can't Lisa eat the soup quickly?
Expected response: *Porque está caliente.* "Because it is hot."

(11) *Event locatives* (*SER required*)

Preamble: *Hoy hay una carrera de barcos en Palma y Dora quiere ir pero no sabe dónde y te pregunta.* "Today there is a regatta in Palma and Dora wants to go but she does not know where it is, and she asks you..."

(here a photo of a regatta in Palma de Mallorca's port)

Prompt: *Dile a Dora dónde...* "Tell Dora where..."
Expected response: *La competencia de barcos es en el puerto.* "The regatta is at the port."

The same task was implemented in Catalan. The Spanish task was conducted first and the Catalan after in one sitting. For each task, there were a total of 25 test tokens plus 4 distractors and 2 practice items. The participants were interviewed at the participants' school or at a public place. The tasks were counterbalanced and randomized. Responses were audio-recorded for later analysis.

5 Results

In what follows we discuss our results. We present the group results by condition and then discuss the individual data to have a better of understanding of any existing variation within each language. Furthermore, we explore any potential correlations with external variables such as patterns of language exposure and use, and proficiency, among others.[9]

Locatives

Regarding locative constructions in Catalan, results showed much higher proportions of copular *estar* use vs. *ser* with both animate (*estar*=50%; *ser*=36%) and inanimate subjects (*estar*=44%; *ser*=35%). In Spanish, the participants used *estar* about 90% of the time, with no cases of copula *ser*. This is represented in Figure 1:

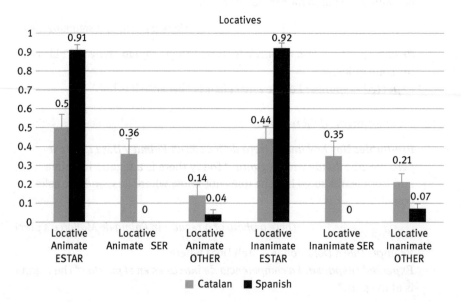

Figure 1: Proportion of copula verbs and other constructions used in locative constructions in Catalan and Spanish.

In addition to copulas *ser* and *estar*, the participants also showed some cases of 'other' responses, crucially with inanimate locatives in Catalan (21%). The category 'other' included other verbal forms expressing similar meanings. For example, some participants used the verb *es troba* in Catalan or *se encuntra* in Spanish ("it is located") instead of the copula *estar*. There were also a few cases

---

9 One of the participants did not complete the task in Spanish. Therefore, we ran the quantitative analysis on the basis of 18 participants for both languages.

of 'other' responses in Spanish with animate (4%) and inanimate subjects (7%), where some participants used the verbal form *se encuentra* ("it is located").

An overall repeated measures ANOVA on animate locatives with language (Spanish, Catalan) and condition (proportion of *ser* and *estar*) as the within-subject factors and group (bilinguals) as the between subject factor showed no significant effects by language ($F(1,48) = 1.74$, $p = 0.19$) but significant interaction by condition ($F(1,48) = 69.01$, $p<.001$). In order to find out where the differences lie, we conducted a series of post-hoc pairwise comparisons using the Bonferroni type I error rate adjustment procedure. Regarding Catalan, the results showed no significant differences in the distribution of *estar* and *ser* ($p = 0.22$). Although the participants used *estar* much more than *ser*, this difference was not significant. In regard to Spanish, the participants used *estar* almost categorically. There was not one single instance of *ser* use. Furthermore, the results showed that the participants distinguished between the two languages as far as copula use was concerned. They used *estar* significantly more in Spanish compared to Catalan ($F(1,48) = -4.35$, $p<.001$), and they used *ser* significantly more in Catalan compared to Spanish ($F(1, 48) = 3.60$, $p<.001$). A repeated measures ANOVA with inanimate locatives showed no significant effects by language ($F(1,32) = 1.97$, $p = 0.17$) but significant interaction by condition ($F(1,32) = 98.15$, $p<.001$), as in the case of animate locatives. Post-hoc comparisons showed no significant differences in the distribution of *estar* and *ser* in Catalan ($p = 0.20$). In regard to Spanish, the participants behaved target-like in the selection of copula *estar* vs. *ser*. In fact, they did not use *ser* ungrammatically. The proportion of *estar* use in Spanish was significantly higher than in Catalan ($p<.001$), and so was the proportion of copula *ser* use in Catalan ($p<.001$). This means that although both languages tended to use *estar* more than *ser* with locatives, the rates of *estar* and *ser* use between the two of them was not the same. Each language behaved quite differently from the other, which counters a previous proposal of the existence of "an attrited" non-standard Catalan-variety in contact with Spanish.

In order to observe if the group differences were supported at the individual level, we conducted an individual analysis on the use of locatives with animate and inanimate subjects in Catalan and Spanish. As represented in the group results, the majority of the participants preferred *estar* over *ser* with animate and inanimate subjects in Catalan and Spanish. This is represented in Table 2 below.

With animate locatives in Catalan, 10/18 participants were either in the high range (22%) or in the medium range (33%) of *estar* realization, with 3 to 4 *estar* items realized. This contrasts with the use of *ser*, where most of the participants were either in the low range (27%) or produced no instances of *ser* (39%). With inanimate contexts, the participants behaved much the same, with a marked preference towards *estar*. Furthermore, in both contexts, 39% of the participants showed no realization of *ser*. These results provide support for *estar* overextension

Table 2: Individual results: Ser and estar use with animate and inanimate locatives per language.

Language		# of items	Locatives Animate		Locatives Inanimate	
			estar	ser	estar	ser
Catalan	high use	4–5	**4/18 (22%)**	3/18 (17%)	**4/18 (22%)**	4/18 (22%)
	medium use	3	**6/18 (33%)**	3/18 (17%)	**3/18 (17%)**	2/18 (11%)
	low use	1–2	5/18 (27%)	**5/18 (27%)**	9/18 (50%)	5/18 (27%)
	zero use	0	3/18 (17%)	**7/18 (39%)**	2/18 (11%)	**7/18 (39%)**
Spanish	high use	4–5	**17/18 (94%)**	0/18 (0%)	17/18 (94%)	0/18 (0%)
	medium use	3	1/18 (5%)	0/18 (0%)	1/18 (5%)	0/18 (0%)
	low use	1–2	0/18 (0%)	0/18 (0%)	0/18 (0%)	0/18 (0%)
	zero use	0	0/18 (0%)	0/18 (0%)	0/18 (0%)	0/18 (0%)

in Catalan, even though the differences are not statistically different, and confirm previous research (Sanz & González, 1995). As far as *estar* overextension with locative constructions in Catalan, Hypothesis 1a is confirmed. However, in Spanish, the results were drastically different, with most participants (17/18) using *estar* across the board with locatives, confirming Hypothesis 3a. As discussed earlier, it is clear that copula alternation works differently in the two languages. Although the participants use *estar* more than *ser* in Catalan with locatives, they still use *ser* in some instances.

We found a small correlation between the use of *estar* in these contexts and patterns of language use in Catalan. For example, there were four participants who consistently used *estar* in animate and inanimate contexts, and showed almost no use of *ser*. Interestingly, these participants indicated that they spoke more Spanish than Catalan at home, at work and in social situations. They all had Spanish-speaking parents, 3/4 of them indicated that they felt more comfortable speaking Spanish, and 1/4 indicated to be equally comfortable in both languages. However, this correlation was less strong with the use of *ser* among participants who indicated that they spoke Catalan at home. In contrast to what one would expect if *ser* was the preferred option in standard Catalan, only 4/11 participants who claimed to speak Catalan at home showed a preference for *ser*. The rest, used both copulas interchangeably or preferred *estar*. This pattern of preference towards *estar* use suggests two possibilities: (1) that there is crosslinguistic influence from Spanish into Catalan that is independent of language dominance, or (2) that the Catalan acquired by these speakers is indeed different from other "standard" varieties of Catalan where *estar* is more restricted, and it has incorporated the use of both copulas as possible alternatives for locative constructions (Sanz & González, 1995). Although not completely clear, it seems as if the semantic scope initially reserved for copula *ser* with locatives has expanded to include *estar*.

Adjectives

Regarding stage-level predicates, results showed a preference for *estar* over *ser* in both Catalan and Spanish (79% vs. 96% respectively).[10] The participants selected *ser* in a few cases in Catalan (11%) but almost none did so in Spanish (1%). This is represented in Figure 2:

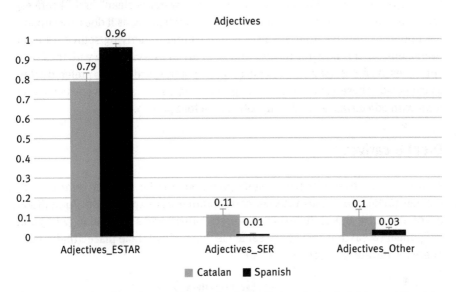

Figure 2: Proportion of copula use with stage-level adjectival predicates in Catalan and Spanish.

As is normally the case with elicited production tasks (Cuza, 2016; Crain & Thornton, 1998), the adults also showed a few instances of 'other' structures. A repeated measures ANOVA with condition (proportion of *ser* and *estar* in Catalan) as the within-subjects factor and group as the between-subjects factor showed significant effects by condition ($F(1,17)= 103.46$, $p<.001$). The participants used *estar* significantly more than *ser* in Catalan, even though either copula is acceptable. A subsequent repeated measures ANOVA with condition (proportion of *ser* and *estar* in Spanish) as the within-subjects factor and group as the between-subjects factor also showed significant effects by condition ($F(1,17)= 1742.82$, $p<.001$). As in the case of Catalan, participants used *estar* significantly more than *ser*, as is required in Spanish. Although the participants used *estar* significantly more than

---

10 Stage-level adjectives (*estar* required) included *caliente* (hot), *frío* (cold), *abiertas* (open), *cerradas* (closed), *encendidas* (turn on), *apagadas* (turned off), *limpia* (clean), and *sucia* (dirty).

ser in both languages, the rate of *estar* use in Catalan (79%) was significantly lower than in Spanish (96%) (*F*(1,17)= 12.80, *p*<.002).

A look at the individual data confirms the group results. Most of the participants (12/18) selected *estar* over *ser* in 70% of the cases or more in Catalan. Given the homogenous distribution of the data, there were no correlations with patterns of language use. A few participants selected *ser*, but this was limited, primarily, to two specific items: L'aigua és/està neta "The water is clean" and El cafè és/està fred "The coffee is cold". This item effect is interesting as it does not support the notion of transfer from Spanish as the leading underlying source for *estar* overextension. It is possible that *ser* and *estar* are in free variation with these two adjectives. As far as Spanish was concerned, all of the participants prefered *estar*, as expected. These results confirm hypothesis 1b for Catalan (overextension of *estar* with adjectives) as well as hypothesis 3a for Spanish.

Event locatives

With event locatives, the participants preferred copular *ser* over *estar* in both Catalan (61%) and Spanish (68%), corroborating our expectations. In addition to copula verbs, the participants also used "other" verbs in Catalan (28%) and in Spanish (24%) that convey the same meaning of 'will take place' (*tindrà lloc*). These results are represented in Figure 3:

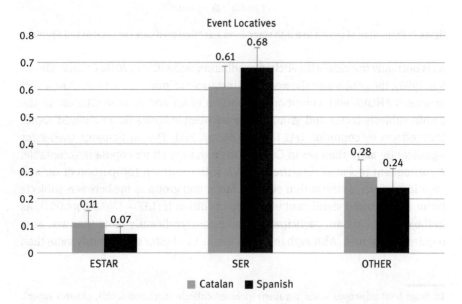

Figure 3: Proportion of copula use with event locatives in Catalan and Spanish.

To measure whether the proportions of *ser* and *estar* in each language were significantly different we conducted two separate repeated measures ANOVA with condition (proportion of *ser* and *estar*) as the within-subjects factor and group as the between-subjects factor showing significant effects by condition. In regard to Spanish, results showed significant differences in the proportion of *ser* vs. *estar* use ($F(1, 17)= 46.87$, $p<.001$). As predicted, the participants behaved target-like in their use of copular *ser*. In Catalan, the participants also behaved target-like in the use of copula *ser* compared to *estar* ($F(1, 17)= 20.23$, $p<.001$). The proportion of *ser* use in Catalan and Spanish was not significantly different ($p=.653$), nor was the proportion of *estar* use ($p=.496$). A look at the individual data confirms the group results (Table 3). The participants behaved target-like at the individual level using *ser* over *estar* almost categorically in Catalan and Spanish. Copula *estar* was not used much among the participants in either of the two languages. This confirms hypotheses 2 and 3:

Table 3: Individual results: *ser* and *estar* use with event locatives per language.

Language		# of items	Event Locatives		
			estar	ser	other
Catalan	*high use*	4–5	0/18 (0%)	8/18 (44%)	1/18 (5%)
	medium use	3	1/18 (5%)	3/18 (16%)	0/18 (0%)
	low use	1–2	4/18 (22%)	5/18 (28%)	12/18 (67%)
	zero use	0	13/18 (72%)	2/18 (11%)	5/18 (28%)
Spanish	*high use*	4–5	0/18 (0%)	11/18 (61%)	3/18 (16%)
	medium use	3	0/18 (0%)	1/18 (5%)	1/18 (5%)
	low use	1–2	5/18 (28%)	6/18 (33%)	5/18 (28%)
	zero use	0	13/18 (72%)	0/18 (0%)	9/18 (50%)

In contrast with adjectives and adverbial locatives, 3/18 participants used 'other' structures much more than copula *ser* in Spanish. In Catalan, 12/18 participants also used 'other' structures in one or two cases. This is because 'other' structures (i.e. *tendrá lugar* "it's going to take place") are in complementary distribution with copula *ser* in both languages. As mentioned earlier, other verbal forms compete with the copular *ser* to express the same meaning, which is the reason why the use of *ser* is not categorical in this particular context.

6 Discussion and conclusions

The goal of our study was to examine the status of copulas *ser* and *estar* in the grammars of Spanish and Catalan bilinguals. Regarding Catalan, we expected the participants to show a bias toward *estar* with locative adverbs and adjectives due to transfer from Spanish, where *estar* is obligatory. However, we did not predict difficulties with the use of *ser* with event locatives, as this is the required copula in both languages. Furthermore, we did not predict *estar* overextension with locatives and adjectives in Spanish or with the use of *ser* with event locatives. As discussed earlier, most residents of Palma have native-like competence in Spanish and the use of *estar* with locatives and stage-level adjectives is very salient in the input.[11] More variation, however, was expected with events due to the use of other verbs expressing the same meaning.

As far as locatives and adjectives in Catalan are concerned, our results suggest cross-linguistic influence effects from Spanish. In regard to locatives, specifically, the participants used *estar* more than *ser* in animate and inanimate contexts. Although the differences were not significant at the group level, individual results (Table 2) do show a much higher preference for the use of *estar* than *ser*. As discussed earlier, copula *ser* was not used by almost 40% of the participants (7/18). These results support previous work arguing a gradual substitution of *ser* by *estar* with locative constructions in Catalan (Sanz & González 1995; Solà 1985).

With regard to adjectives, the participants used *estar* almost 80% of the cases in Catalan. This was significant at the group level in comparison to the use of *ser*, and it was also corroborated by the individual analysis. The use of *ser* with adjectives was very restricted. As in the case of locatives, it seems as if *estar* was being substituted by *ser*. However, these results must be taken with caution; the rate of *estar* use in Catalan was significantly different from the rate of *estar* use in Spanish. This suggests that the participants were not using *estar* across the board in Catalan, as was the case in Spanish. Most Catalan-dominant speakers, preferred *estar* with adjectives in both Spanish and Catalan, but also used *ser* and *estar* in a statistically significant way with locatives in Catalan.

The question that arises then is why do the participants overextend *estar* with adjectives more than with locatives in Catalan. We argue that this might be related to the type of adjective that we tested. The adjectives we tested unanimously select *estar* in Spanish. Therefore, it is possible that this trend is also being introduced

---

11 A quick search for the adjective *caliente* "hot" in the Corpus of Spanish by Mark Davies resulted in 747 entries with *estar* vs. 330 with *ser*. Although the use of *ser* is possible in certain individual-level contexts in Spanish (e.g., El agua del Lago Ontario **es** muy fria para bañarse durante el verano "The water in Lake Ontario is too cold to swim in during the summer"), the stage-level contexts examined in the current study were clearly a circumstantial characterization where *estar* was required (*El café está frio* "The coffee is cold"). With locatives, *estar* is almost always required in Spanish, crucially with animate subjects (*Rosa está en la bodega* "Rosa is at the food store").

into Catalan, and that the distinction in this specific context is becoming much more neutralized than with locatives. Future research would benefit from examining adjectives that unanimously select for *estar* in Spanish as well as those where both *estar* and *ser* are possible depending on the context. This type of analysis would allow us to tease apart the extent to which *estar* has been extended into Catalan adjectival predicates due to crosslinguistic influence from Spanish.

From a theoretical perspective, the results suggest that copula selection with locatives and stage-level predicates in Catalan cannot be accounted for by the same theoretical approach. If, as argued by Zagona (2013), *ser* and *estar* alternation is regulated by an uninterpretable aspectual feature ([*u*P]) that determines the complements of copular *estar* but not those of *ser*, then this is not supported by Catalan locatives, as the participants did not categorically preferred *estar* over *ser*. As far as Catalan locatives are concerned, it does not seem that there must be aspectual agreement between the stative *u*P of copular *estar* and a stative preposition expressing a single location. However, an interpretable aspectual feature [+*u*P] does seem to determine the selection of *estar* with stage-level predicates, as this was the preferred choice among the participants.

Regarding event locatives, the results confirmed what we predicted. The participants behaved target-like in their use of *ser* in both Catalan (*ser*=61%; *estar*=11%) and Spanish (*ser*=68%; *estar*= 7%). However, our task was limited in the sense that the participants also had the option of using other structures with the same "eventive" meaning provided by the copula *ser* (e.g., to take place). This is the reason why none of the participants behaved at ceiling (Figure 3). There were only six instances of *estar* use in Spanish, crucially with the items *La boda está en la iglesia "The wedding is at the church" (x2) and *La clase está en la biblioteca "The class is in the library" (x2). In the case of the latter item, it is possible that the participants interpreted *la clase de dibujo* "the drawing class" as a physical location, and not as an event locative, in which case the use of *estar* is grammatical. This was also the case in Catalan, where three participants used *estar* with this item, and with the test token El festival está a la Plaça Major "The festival is at the Plaza Mayor". In both cases, the subject (*class, festival*) could have been interpreted as a physical entity, not necessarily as an event. Despite these minor instances of ungrammatical *estar* use explained above, the results do confirm Zagona's (2013) aspectual approach as most participants selected copular *ser*. The copula verb *estar* is ungrammatical in this case since the PP has an eventive aspectual meaning (+Theme), given by the subject DP, which clashes with the stative *u*P of *estar*.

Regarding locatives and adjectives in Spanish, the participants overwhelmingly used copula *estar*, as required. These results counter previous research arguing for structural influences from Catalan into Spanish, and morphosyntactic reinterpretation (Blass-Arroyo 2011; Perpiñán, 2015; Serrano, 1996). The restructuring found by Serrano (1996) with *ser* overextension with inanimate locatives in Spanish (El pan **es** a la mesa "The bread is on the table") is not supported by our data, confirming recent research (Perpiñán 2015). This does not mean, however, that a Catalan-dominant speaker with much less competence in Spanish could not make these errors; this is simply not a common occurrence among balanced Spanish/Catalan bilinguals in Palma. Furthermore, our data support Perpiñán's (2015) findings of target use of *ser* with event locatives in Spanish. From a theoretical perspective, the Spanish data support Zagona's (2013) aspectual approach to copula selection in the three contexts under analysis.

To summarize, the results of the current study support previous work in documenting *estar* overextension to stage-level adjectives and adverbial locatives in Catalan (Sanz & González 1995) but no difficulties with the use of copula *ser* with event locatives. The use of *ser* was particularly restricted with adjectives in Catalan, but not with adverbial locatives or event locatives. These results are relevant to current proposals on vulnerable domains and structural overlap as key constraints on cross-linguistic influence/transfer effects (Hulk & Müller 2000; Müller & Hulk 2001). The lack of transfer from Catalan into Spanish is not surprising. As discussed earlier, Spanish is the dominant language in Palma de Mallorca, especially for social interactions among the youth, and the use of *estar* or *ser* in the contexts examined is very categorical. Thus, it is not surprising that the participants showed target behavior in these contexts.

Future research would benefit by investigating more closely adjectival predicates where the use of one copula vs. the other depends on the preceding context in Spanish, as well as contexts where only *estar* is required. Furthermore, it would be interesting to triangulate the current production data with the participants' intuition and comprehension in order to have a better understanding of the extent to which these types of bilinguals are able to tease apart the relevant distinctions.

References

Argyri, E. & Sorace, A. 2007. Crosslinguistic influence and language dominance in older bilingual children. *Bilingualism: Language and Cognition* 10. 79–99.

Arnaus-Gil, L. & N. Müller. 2015. The acquisition of Spanish in a bilingual and a trilingual L1 setting. Combining Spanish with German, French and Catalan. In T. Judy and S. Perpiñán (eds.), *The acquisition of Spanish in understudied language pairings*, 135–168. Amsterdam: John Benjamins.

Baker, C. 1996. *Foundations of bilingual education and bilingualism*, 2nd edn. Clevedon: Multilingual Matters.

Blass-Arroyo, J. L. 2007. Spanish and Catalan in the Balearic Islands. *International Journal of the Sociology of Language* 184. 79–93.

Bourhis, R., H. Giles, & D. Rosenthal. 1981. Notes on the construction of a 'subjective vitality questionnaire' for ethnolinguistic groups. *Journal of Multilingual and Multicultural Development* 2(2). 145–155.

Brucart, J.M. 2012. Copular alternation in Spanish and Catalan attributive sentences. *Revista de Estudos Linguísticos da Universidade do Porto* 7. 9–43.

Bruhn de Garavito & E. Valenzuela. 2008. Eventive and stative passives in Spanish L2 acquisition: A matter of aspect. *Bilingualism: Language and Cognition* 11. 323–336.

Bruyèl-Olmedo, A. & M. Juan-Garau. 2010. English as a *lingua franca* in the linguistic landscape of the multilingual resort of S'Arenal in Mallorca 6(4). 386–411.

Bruyèl-Olmedo, A. & M. Juan-Garau. 2015. Minority languages in the linguistic landscape of tourism: the case of Catalan in Mallorca. *Journal of Multilingual and Multicultural Development* 36(6). 598–619.

Camacho, J. 2012. Ser and estar: The individual/stage-level distinction and aspectual predication. In José Ignacio Hualde and Antxón Olarrea (eds.), *The Blackwell handbook of Hispanic linguistics*. Oxford: Wiley-Blackwell.

Cuza, A. 2016. The status of interrogative subject-verb inversion in Spanish-English bilingual children. *Lingua* 180. 124–138.

Cuza, A., N. Reyes & E. Lustres. 2017. *The acquisition of copular choice in child heritage speakers of Spanish*. Oral presentation at the *2017 Hispanic Linguistics Symposium*. Texas Tech University. October 26–28, 2017.

Cuza, A., & P. Guijarro-Fuentes. 2017. Semantic rdistribution of copula ser/estar in Catalan/ Spanish bilingual children and adults. In *Proceedings for 41st Boston University Conference in Language Development (BUCLD)*. Somerville, MA: Cascadilla Press.

Cuza, A. & R. Pérez-Tattam. 2016. Grammatical gender selection and phrasal word order in child heritage Spanish: A feature reassembly approach. *Bilingualism: Language and Cognition* 19. 50–68.

Cuza, A. 2013. Cross-linguistic influence at the syntax proper: interrogative subject-verb inversion in heritage Spanish. *The International Journal of Bilingualism* 17(1). 71–96.

Crain, S. & R. Thornton. 1998. *Investigations in universal grammar. A guide to experiments on the acquisition of syntax and semantics*. Cambridge, MA: MIT Press.

Demonte, V. & P. Masullo. 1999. La predicación: los complementos predicativos. In Ignacio Bosque & Violeta Demonte (eds.), *Gramática descriptiva de la lengua española*, vol. 2, 2461–2523. Madrid: Espasa.

Diesing, M. 1992. *Indefinites*. Cambridge, MA: MIT Press.

Falk, J. 1979. Ser y estar con atributos adjetivales. Uppsala: Almqvist and Wiksell.

Fernández-Leborans, M. J. 1995. Las construcciones con el verbo estar: aspectos sintácticos y semánticos. *Verba* 22. 253–284.

Fernández-Leborans, M. J. 1999. La predicación: las oraciones copulativas. In I. Bosque & V. Demonte (eds.), *Gramática descriptiva de la lengua Española*, 2354–2460. Madrid: Espasa.

Geeslin, K. 2002. The second language acquisition of copula choice and its relationship to language change. *Studies in Second Language Acquisition* 24. 419–451.

Geeslin, K. 2003. A comparison of copula choice in advanced and native Spanish. *Language Learning* 53(4). 703–764.

Geeslin, K. & P. Guijarro-Fuentes. 2006. The second language acquisition of variable structures in Spanish by Portuguese speakers. *Language Learning* 56(1). 53–107. Geeslin, K. & P. Guijarro-Fuentes. 2007. Linguistic and social predictors of copula use in Galician Spanish. In Kim Potowski and Richard Cameron (eds.), *Spanish in contact: Policy, social and linguistic inquiries*, 253–273. Amsterdam: John Benjamins.

Geeslin, K. & P. Guijarro-Fuentes. 2008. Variation in contemporary Spanish: Linguistic predictors of estar in four cases of language contact. *Bilingualism: Language and Cognition* 11(3). 356–380.

Gutiérrez, M. 1992. The extension of estar: A linguistic change in progress in the Spanish of Morelia, México. *Hispanic Linguistics* 5. 109–141.

Holtheuer, C. 2011. The distribution of ser and estar with adjectives: A critical survey. *Revista Signos* 44. 33–57.

Hulk, A. & N. Müller. 2000. Bilingual first language acquisition at the interface between syntax and pragmatics. *Bilingualism: Language and Cognition* 3(3). 227–244.

Liceras, J., R. Fernández Fuertes & A. Alba de la Fuente. 2012. Subject and copula omission in the English grammar of English-Spanish bilinguals: on the issue of directionality of interlinguistic influence. *First Language* 32. 88–115.

Meisel, J. 2007. The weaker language in early child bilingualism: acquiring a first language as a second language. *Applied Psycholinguistics* 28. 495–514.

Melia, J. 1997. La llengua dels joves. Palma de Mallorca: Universitat de les Illes Balears.

Montrul, S. 2004. Subject and object expression in Spanish heritage speakers: A case of morphosyntactic convergence. *Bilingualism: Language and Cognition* 7(2). 125–142.

Montrul, S. 2008. *Incomplete acquisition in bilingualism*. Amsterdam: John Benjamins

Montrul, S. 2015. Dominance and proficiency in early and late bilingualism. In C. Silva-Corvalán & J. Treffers-Daller (eds.), *Language dominance in bilinguals: Issues of measurement and operationalization*. Cambridge: Cambridge University Press.

Montrul, S. & T. Ionin. 2012. Dominant language transfer in Spanish heritage speakers and L2 learners in the interpretation of definite articles. *The Modern Language Journal* 96(1). 70–94.

Montrul, S. & N. Sánchez-Walker. 2013. Differential object marking in child and adult Spanish heritage speakers. *Language Acquisition* 20. 109–132.

Müller, N., & A. Hulk. 2001. Cross-linguistic influence in bilingual language acquisition: Italian and French as recipient languages. *Bilingualism: Language and Cognition* 4. 1–21.

Paradis, J. & F. Genesee. 1996. Syntactic acquisition: autonomous or interdependent? *Studies in Second Language Acquisition* 18. 1–25.

Pérez-Leroux, A. T., Y. Álvarez & T. Battersby. 2010. Cuando era feliz, e indocumentado: An aspectual approach to copula choice in L2 Spanish. In C. Borgonovo, M. Español-Echevarría & P. Prévost (eds.), Selected proceedings of the 12th Hispanic Linguistics Symposium, 209–220. Somerville, MA: Cascadilla Press.

Pérez-Leroux, A.T., A. Cuza & D. Thomas. 2011. From parental attitudes to input condition Spanish-English bilingual development in Toronto. In Kim Potowski and Jason Rothman (eds.), *Bilingual youth: Spanish in English-speaking societies*, 49–176. Amsterdam: John Benjamins.

Perpiñán, S. 2015. The locative paradigm in the L2 Spanish of Catalan Speakers. In T. Judy & S. Perpiñán (eds.), *The acquisition of Spanish in understudied language pairings*, 105–132. Amsterdam: John Benjamins.

Pieras-Guasp, F. 2002. Direct versus indirect attitudes measurement and the planning of Catalan in Mallorca. *Language Problems and Language Planning* 26. 51–68.

Pirvulescu, Mihaela, Ana-Teresa Pérez-Leroux, Yves Roberge, Nelleke Strik & Danielle Thomas. 2014. Bilingual effects: Exploring object omission in pronominal languages. *Bilingualism: Language and Cognition* 17(3). 495–510.

Polinsky, M. 2011. Reanalysis in adult heritage language: A case for attrition. *Studies in Second Language Acquisition* 33. 305–328.

Putnam, M. & L. Sánchez. 2013. What's so incomplete about incomplete acquisition? A prolegomenon to modeling heritage language grammars. *Linguistic Approaches to Bilingualism* 3. 478–508.

Sanz, C. & M.J. González. 1995. Ser and estar in Tortosi Catalan: Language contact, language variation, and language change. *Sintagma* 7. 5–25.

Schmitt, C., C. Holtheuer, K. Miller. 2004. Acquisition of copulas ser and estar in Spanish: learning lexico-semantics, syntax, and discourse. *Proceedings of Boston University Conference on Language Development*. Cascadilla Press, Somerville, MA.

Schmitt, C. & K. Miller. 2007. Making discourse-dependent decisions: the case of the copulas "ser" and "estar" in Spanish. *Lingua*, 117, 1907–1929.

Sera, M.D. 1992. To be or not to be: use and acquisition of the Spanish copulas. *Journal of Memory and Language* 31. 408–427.

Sera, M.D. 2008. Commentary on "copular acquisition" – a response to Silva-Corvalán and Montanari. *Bilingualism: Language and Cognition* 11(3). 361–363.

Serrano, M. 1996. Interferencias léxicas y semánticas en una situación de contacto entre dos lenguas, catalán y castellano. *Diálogos Hispánicos* 18. 375–394.

Siguan, M. 1999. *Conocimiento y uso de las lenguas*. Madrid: Centro de Investigaciones Sociológicas.

Silva-Corvalán, C. 1986. Bilingualism and language change: The extension of *estar* in Los Angeles Spanish. *Language* 62. 587–608.

Silva-Corvalán, C. 1994. *Language contact and change: Spanish in Los Angeles*. Oxford: Clarendon Press.

Silva-Corvalán, C. & S. Montanari. 2008. The acquisition of ser, estar (and be) by a Spanish–English bilingual child: The early stages. *Bilingualism: Language and Cognition* 11. 341–360.

Solà, J. 1987. *Qüestions controvertides de sintaxi catalana*, 1st edn. Barcelona: Edicions 62.

Sorace, A. 2005. Selective optionality in language development. In L. Cornips & K. Corrigan (eds.), *Syntax and variation: Reconciling the biological and the social*, 46–111. Amsterdam: John Benjamins.

Unsworth, S. 2013. Assessing the role of current and cumulative exposure in simultaneous bilingual acquisition: The case of Dutch gender. *Bilingualism: Language and Cognition* 16. 86–110.

Unsworth, S. 2015. Amount of exposure as a proxy for dominance in bilingual language acquisition. In C. Silva-Corvalán & J. Treffers-Daller (eds.), *Language dominance in bilinguals: issues of measurement and operationalization,* 156–173. Cambridge University Press.

VanPatten, B. 1985. The acquisition of ser and estar by adult learners of Spanish: a preliminary investigation of transitional stages of competence. *Hispania* 68. 399–406.

Zagona, K. 2013. *Ser and estar: phrase structure and aspect. Cahiers Chronos* 25. 303–327.

Laia Arnaus Gil, Amelia Jiménez-Gaspar
and Natascha Müller

The acquisition of Spanish SER and ESTAR in bilingual and trilingual children: Delay and enhancement

Abstract: The use of the Spanish copula verbs SER and ESTAR has been argued to be subject to delay effects in bilingual children's language production. If compared with monolinguals, they exhibit difficulty with contexts which require SER: They omit SER and generalize ESTAR to SER-contexts. The present article focusses on the use of SER and ESTAR in adjectival contexts. The Spanish adult system comprises adjectives which can be used with only one copula verb or with both. 4 bilingual and trilingual children participated in the longitudinal study which analyzes the use of the two copulas in the children's spontaneous speech. SER contexts are much more difficult for all children, but the children who acquire Catalan, exhibiting a similar (but not identical) dual copula system as Spanish, are delayed with respect to bilingual and trilingual children who acquire languages with only one copula (French, Italian). Assuming that omission is a strategy on the part of the child to cope with linguistic complexity, delay is argued to be due to the fact that the Catalan syntactic derivations for the two copulas and those of Spanish interfere in language production. The observation that the delay effect is more visible in contexts requiring SER is assumed to be related to the fact that only Spanish ESTAR exhibits a less complex syntactic derivation. The cross-sectional study with 72 bilingual, trilingual and multilingual children elicited comprehension of permanent/temporary properties expressed by Spanish adjectives and assigned to animals in four stories. As expected, the SER-condition was much more difficult for all children than the ESTAR condition, irrespective of the level reached in the receptive (hearing) vocabulary test, language dominance and age. Only the trilinguals who acquire another language with a dual copula system like Spanish (Catalan, Portuguese), which make a difference between the encoding of permanent and temporary properties, showed an advantage in the SER condition. This possibility is reminiscent of the advantage multilingual children have in attentional control (Martin-Rhee & Bialystok 2008: 91). The advantage in the SER-condition as observed in the trilingual children who acquire Catalan/Portuguese together with German/French cannot be due to

Laia Arnaus Gil, Amelia Jiménez-Gaspar and Natascha Müller, Bergische Universität Wuppertal

https://doi.org/10.1515/9781501509988-005

cross-linguistic influence within the competence system since it was absent in the bilingual children who acquire Spanish with Catalan. It is therefore argued to be related to the mere fact of acquiring more than two languages.

1 Introduction

It is generally agreed upon that bilingual children who grow up with two languages from birth can separate their two languages (cf. Genesee 1989; Lleo 2002; Lleó & Kehoe 2002; Meisel 1989) but that the acquisition path is characterized by cross-linguistic influence. Cross-linguistic influence characterizes bilingual phonology (Lleó & Rakow 2006; Lleó 2016), morphology (Nicoladis 1999, 2003), and syntax (Gawlitzek-Maiwald & Tracy 1996; Döpke 1992, 1997, 1998; Hulk & Müller 2000; Müller & Hulk 2001). Paradis & Genesee (1996) argue that it has two effects: delay (in comparison with monolinguals) and acceleration (also in comparison with monolinguals). In contrast to delay effects, acceleration effects are understudied in early child bilingualism. They exist in bilingual German/English-Romance children (Kupisch 2006 for determiner realizations in German; Liceras et al. 2011 for copula realizations in English). Recently, Patuto, Repetto & Müller (2011) have asked the question of whether these two effects, as it has generally been assumed in the literature, are both routed in cross-linguistic influence. The following article will support the idea, as outlined in Patuto et al. (2011), that acceleration effects are rooted outside the linguistic systems and are thus not an instance of an influence of two linguistic systems.

Until today, early child trilingualism is understudied (but see the works of Arnaus Gil 2013 and Hager 2014). Cross-linguistic influence is also assumed to play a role when a child acquires three languages from birth, the effect being delay or acceleration in comparison with monolinguals and bilinguals (Arnaus Gil 2013 for copula use and Hager 2014 for gender marking on determiners). As with bilinguals, it is assumed that cross-linguistic influence is at play in early child trilingualism. Until today, rare are the studies on the acquisition of three languages from birth and this might be the reason of why "for the time being, most of us are still working within the theoretical framework of bilingualism" (Hoffman 1999: 16). Montanari (2013: 63) claims that the reason for the rarity of trilingual studies is the time-consuming and expensive methods which must be used to document language development in trilingual children. But the reason might also be related to the underlying assumption that trilingualism is only an extension of bilingualism as to how many languages are acquired and that the language acquisition theory developed on the basis of bilinguals will do for trilinguals as well (see Jeßner 1997; however, see also the criticism in Hoffmann 2000). Indeed, similarities exist between early child bilingualism and the acquisition of three languages from birth. But Hoffmann (2001) also reports differences (see also Quay 2011a,b) which should invite acquisitionists to consider the necessity of a theory of trilingual first language acquisition in its own. The differences between bilinguals and trilinguals are quantitative and qualitative in nature (Hoffmann 2001: 1). For example, trilinguals are assumed, in contrast to bilinguals, never to be balanced; there will always be one language which is dominant and the other two are "weaker". The quality of the input and the language-internal properties play a role in how well each language is mastered by the trilingual child (Montanari 2013: 63). Quay (2011a: 3) concludes that "trilingual children need to be considered as speakers in their own right."

The present paper will argue that both delay and acceleration play a role in early child trilingualism and that both have different sources, as has been argued for bilinguals. It is noteworthy that trilingual children do not always behave as their bilingual peers. Therefore, there is a need for a theory of early child trilingualism. Section 1 introduces the grammatical domain under investigation, namely the copula verbs in Spanish. Since Catalan plays an important role in the acquisition of the Spanish copula system in bilinguals and trilinguals, it will be presented together with the Spanish system. Section 2 contains a short overview of previous studies on the acquisition of SER and ESTAR. The longitudinal and the cross-sectional study are presented in section 3. 4 bilingual and trilingual children participated in the longitudinal study, while the cross-sectional study included 72 bilingual, trilingual and multilingual (> 3 languages) children. Section 4 presents the results for the longitudinal and the cross-sectional study separately. Section 5 discusses the results against the background of the source of delay and acceleration effects and a theory of trilingualism in its own. The article has an appendix which presents the statistical data.

2 The syntax of copula verbs in Spanish and Catalan

Spanish and Catalan belong to the languages (like many other languages of the world, Romance and Germanic languages among them) in which the functional category T must be associated with morphological content. A T without morphological content is only licit in expressive constructions like "oh you fool" which lie outside the scope of the present paper (cf. Potts & Roeper 2006). Both languages, Spanish and Catalan, exhibit two copula verbs SER/ÉSSER and ESTAR, in contrast to other Romance languages like French. SER and ÉSSER are used alike in some predicative contexts, as in (1) and (2). There are, however, also contexts for which the uses do not completely overlap, as in (3), (4) and (5).

(1) a. Sp   Silvia es/*está médico
    b. Cat La Sílvia és/*està metge
            Silvia is-SER/ÉSSER/*is-ESTAR (a) doctor

(2) a. Sp   Juan *es/está enfermo
    b. Cat El Joan *es/ està malalt
            John is-*SER/ÉSSER/ is-ESTAR sick

(3) a. Sp   Ana *es/está en casa
    b. Cat L'Ana és/està a casa
            Ana is-*SER/ÉSSER/is-ESTAR at home

(4) a. Sp   Las calles *eran/estaban desiertas
            The streets *were-SER/were-ESTAR empty
    b. Cat Els carrers eren deserts   (Ramos 2008:2012)
            The streets were-ÉSSER empty
    c. Cat Quan el jardí estava desert tornava al seu balcó
                                                        (Ramos 2008:2012)
            When the garden was-ESTAR empty (he) returned to his balcony

(5) a. Sp   Esta figura *es/está hecha a mano
    b. Cat Aquesta figura és/està feta a mà   (Arnaus Gil 2013:47)
            This figure is-*SER/ÉSSER/ESTAR done by hand

Generally speaking, the examples (3) and (4) show that Spanish is more restrictive with non-eventive locative PPs (3), with certain adjectives, such as *desierto* in (4) and with deverbal adjectives such as in (5) for which only ESTAR is allowed,[1] whereas Catalan makes use of both ÉSSER and ESTAR, the former being more frequently used than the latter.[2]

---

[1] A reviewer points out that the example (5a) is acceptable with SER in several Spanish varieties. These varieties thus resemble Catalan in this respect. Note that the variety of Spanish studied in the present article does not tolerate SER in example (5).

[2] Whether this variation depends on intra-linguistic (grammatical person, temporal reference, etc.) and extra-linguistic variables (socio-economic class, locality, sex, school year and arguably

The examples above on copula selection clearly show that Catalan allows both copulas in the same predicative context where Spanish actually allows ESTAR. From a historical perspective, Catalan only allowed the ÉSSER-examples in (4) and (5). However, ESTAR has been gaining importance so that the ESTAR-cases in (4) and (5) are also grammatical for Catalan native speakers. In addition, to our knowledge, there are no cases in which Catalan shows a more restrictive copula use than Spanish. Furthermore, the generalization which follows from the comparison of Catalan and Spanish, namely that ESTAR takes over SER and not vice versa, seems to hold also for Spanish varieties in America.

In this paper, we would like to focus on the uses of SER and ESTAR in adjectival contexts. These cases are particularly interesting, since, for some adjectives, only one copula verb is grammatical, as in (6), while for other adjectives, SER or ESTAR can be selected, as shown in (7). This distribution can be observed for these adjectives in Spanish as well as in Catalan.

(6) a. Sp Marta es/*está española
   a'. Cat La Marta és/*està espanyola
       Marta is-SER/ÉSSER/*ESTAR Spanish
   b. Sp Pablo *es/está cansado
   b'. Cat En Pau *és/està cansat
       Pablo is-*SER/*ÉSSER/ESTAR tired

(7) a. Sp Laura es/está fea
   a'. Cat La Laura és/està lletja
       Laura is-SER/ÉSSER/ESTAR ugly
   b. Sp El perro es/está nervioso
   b'. Cat El gos és/està nerviós
       The dog is-SER/ÉSSER/ESTAR nervous

For Gumiel-Molina, Moreno-Quibén & Pérez-Jiménez (2016) among many authors, the restrictive use of the copula in (6) has to do with the type of adjective: Whereas relational adjectives are only allowed to be accompanied by SER, perfective adjectives can only be selected by ESTAR. All the other gradable adjectives (ambivalent adjectives following Marín 2009) such as the ones in (7) are allowed with

---

language use restriction (the extent to which an individual uses Catalan in his/her daily life, unrestricted speakers using Catalan both in and outside of the home)) lies outside the scope of the present contribution. More research is necessary if it comes to social factors that condition variant use.

both SER and ESTAR. In the literature, it has been proposed that the difference in copula selection for the ambivalent adjectives in (7) has to do, for example, with the semantic features or with the syntactic derivation of these adjectives. For a first group of linguists, the semantic differences obtained by using SER or ESTAR with an adjective are aspectual in nature: When SER is selected, the adjectival property is attributed to the individual represented by the DP in subject position; we are dealing with an Individual Level Property (ILP, Carlson 1997, Lema 1995) which is applied to the person as a whole and which has no temporal boundaries (i.e. it is inherent and permanent). By contrast, ESTAR is selected in order to express a temporary property applied to the referent of the DP in subject position (Stage Level Predicate, SLP). This group of linguists assumes that there is a one-to-one relation between the choice of SER-ESTAR and the ILP-SLP interpretation of the adjective (cf. Schmitt 1992, Camacho 2012). The second group of linguists postulates different syntactic configurations for the Spanish copulas and the aspectual differences. The aspectual interpretation for ambivalent adjectives as in (7) is deduced from the syntactic derivation or the syntactic features that SER and ESTAR have. For Zagona (2009) and Camacho (2012), ESTAR is specified for more features than SER: it has an uninterpretable prepositional [uP]-feature and an interpretable aspectual inchoative [iAsp]-feature respectively, being responsible for the selection of those adjectives that only allow ESTAR as in (6b) or can be accompanied by this copula, as in (7). For SER, both authors claim that there is no particular feature characterizing this copula verb and so it fulfills an elsewhere-condition. In the same vein, Raposo & Uriagereka (1995), Arnaus Gil (2013), Arnaus Gil & Müller (2015), Camacho (2016), Romeu (2016) and Gallego & Uriagereka (2016) propose that the Spanish copula verbs are inserted in two different syntactic structures and that these different syntactic configurations give rise to the different readings in (7). For the adjectives in (6) as well as for relational (only allowed with SER) and perfective (only possible with ESTAR) adjectives, Arnaus Gil (2013) and Arnaus Gil & Müller (2015) claim that these belong to the semantic class of adjectives that are already marked in the lexicon with the corresponding property. Once they enter the syntactic derivation with their IL- or SL-property, syntax makes the corresponding syntactic derivation available (SER for IL, ESTAR for SL). Turning again to the ambivalent adjectives in (7), these authors proposed that Spanish SER is merged in v^0 in order to be able to assign the permanent property to an ambivalent adjective[3] (it is then moved to

---

[3] One reviewer points out that this syntactic proposal would not explain, for example, why the Spanish adjective *muerto* 'dead' only allows ESTAR, although it conveys a permanent property. Luján (1981) discusses this adjective, together with *temporario* 'temporary' which only selects

the functional category which host finiteness, T for example, for independent reasons, i.e. tense and agreement features). Evidence for this proposal comes from passive structures which are always built with SER,[4] as in (8), and causative and gerundive constructions as in (9) which are only grammatical with SER (s. Arnaus Gil & Müller 2015:138ff). All the preceding constructions which are licit with SER are completely ungrammatical with ESTAR. This differing grammaticality of SER and ESTAR is interpreted by Arnaus Gil & Müller (2015) as giving rise to a *v*P-layer for SER, the copula which is involved in constructions manipulating the subject argument, as in passive and causative constructions. In contrast to SER, Spanish ESTAR is merged directly in T, the *v*P-layer is not projected.

SER. She defends the view that these cases are not counterexamples for the permanent (SER) and change-of-state (ESTAR) proposal, since *muerto* 'dead', for example, conveys a change of state (from alive to dead) and therefore it can only be accompanied by ESTAR. Moreover, these two examples would belong to a predefined semantic class of adjectives (cf. Arnaus Gil 2013, Arnaus Gil & Müller 2015) and they behave as the examples in (6) above, namely, they are already marked with the corresponding property in the lexicon and therefore syntax is only responsible for making the corresponding syntactic derivation available.

4 There exists the so-called resultative or adjectival passives as in *El bizcocho está hecho* 'The cake is-ESTAR done', as noted by one reviewer. These are claimed to be built in the lexicon (cf. Wasow 1977, as cited in Bruhn de Garavito 2009) and express a change-of-state of the subject referent. But what is actually the category of the predicate? If we take into consideration that we are confronted with deverbal adjectives, these constructions do not differ from those in (i) where we have a non-deverbal adjective:

(i) a. El patio está sucio
       The courtyard is-ESTAR dirty
   b. Juan y Pedro están enfermos
      Juan and Pedro are-ESTAR ill

One piece of evidence in favor of this view comes from across-language comparisons: Deverbal adjectives in resultative or adjectival passives in Spanish may reflect non-deverbal adjectives in other languages. Compare the examples in (ii):

(ii) a. Sp   El bizcocho está hecho
            The cake is-ESTAR done
    b. Eng The cake is ready
    c. Ger Der Kuchen ist fertig

The different syntactic structures for Spanish SER and ESTAR are presented in (11) for the examples in (10)[5]:

(8) Sp   La canción ha sido/*estado escuchada por la banda
         The song has been heard by the band

(9) a. Sp El profesor hace ser/*estar más valiente al alumno
             The teacher makes be-SER/*ESTAR more courageous to the student
     b. Sp El vendedor está siendo/*estando muy pesado
             The salesman is-ESTAR being-SER/*being-ESTAR very annoying

(10) a. Sp Juan es guapo   b. Sp La profesora está guapa
             Juan is-SER handsome   The teacher is-ESTAR pretty

---

5 One reviewer points out that T selects for an AP in structure (11) with ESTAR. The analysis presumes that, within phase theory (Chomsky 2000), the sister of T is not a proposition (*v*P) or phase. In other words, T either selects for a phase, a relatively complete syntactic object from a semantic perspective, as in the case of SER, or for (just) a syntactic category like an AP. Possibly, this is a wrong generalization and we have to say, more cautiously, that SER is reminiscent of a complete phase (with an external argument which is manipulated to a certain degree), whereas ESTAR is associated with an incomplete, dependent syntactic object, both awaiting a formal definition within syntactic theory. It could be argued that one problem of our analysis is that it violates the *Uniform Theta-role Assignment Hypothesis* (UTAH) as formulated by Baker (1988, 1997) because in (11a) the external argument occupies Spec, *v*P, whereas in (10b) it is inserted directly in SpecTP. Since the need of mapping a d-structure onto an s-structure has disappeared in the minimalist framework, UTAH has become obsolete. Notice however that there are minimalist analyses which argue in favor of the maintenance of (a reformulated version of) UTAH (Wells 2015). Our analysis would be compatible with such view. Note that control verbs like *to promise* in 'John promised Mary PRO to be elected/to go to the party' are instances of UTAH violations. Furthermore, the discussion of ergative languages for which it has been assumed that Themes are linked to (VP-) external positions and Agents to (VP-) internal positions is reminiscent of a redefinition of the UTAH. Our analysis would be compatible with the view that the Agent is merged above the Theme. It nicely captures the intuition that the subject of SER is a "normal" subject in the sense that it can be manipulated as any other subject (passivized, "degraded" via causativization). We are aware of the fact that the validity of UTAH would be of help for the child in order to acquire language.

(11)

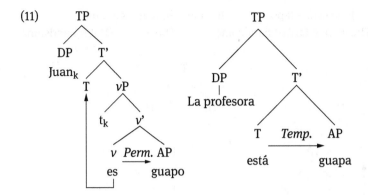

In contrast to Spanish, Catalan ESTAR is involved in passivization, as shown in (12), and the passive construction is grammatical with both, ÉSSER and ESTAR, as the example in (13) illustrates.

(12) Cat La cançó ha estat interpretada per la banda
           The song has been-ESTAR played by the band

(13) Cat La cançó és/està interpretada per la banda
           The song is-SER/ESTAR played by the band

In contrast to Spanish which does not allow causativization of verbs corresponding to deverbal adjectives like *enfadado* 'angry' that need ESTAR, Catalan can causativize *enfadar*, as in (14b):

(14) a. Sp   *Su hija ha hecho enfadar a María[6]
                His daugther has made to-annoy to-Mary
      b. Cat El seu fill ha fet enfadar la Maria

These examples are evidence in favor of an active *v*P-layer in Catalan constructions where Spanish only allows SER. In other words, Catalan ESTAR, as it was the case for Spanish SER, has to be in principle higher in the derivation than Catalan ÉSSER. Together with the earlier observation as exemplified in (3), (4) and (5), illustrating that Spanish ESTAR contexts are often translated by either ÉSSER or ESTAR in Catalan, Arnaus Gil & Müller (2015: 141) suggest the structures in (16) for ÉSSER and ESTAR in the Catalan adjectival contexts in (15):

---

6 For some native speakers of Spanish this sentence seems to be grammatical.

(15) a. Cat   En Joan està guapo   b. Cat   En Joan és guapo
         The Joan is-ESTAR handsome   The Joan is-ÉSSER handsome

(16)

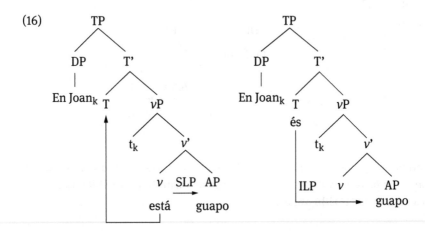

Although both structures contain the same functional layers, as opposed to the Spanish copula verbs SER and ESTAR, the structure with ÉSSER is derivationally less complex than the one with ESTAR since it requires less movement steps. Whereas ESTAR is assumed to be inserted in $v°$ and later moved higher up in the structure, ÉSSER is directly merged in T°. In this position, as it was the case for Spanish SER, the copula will assign its corresponding property (SLP or ILP) to the AP, illustrated in both structures in (16) with an arrow heading to the right side.

In a nutshell, following this syntactic proposal for Spanish and Catalan copula verbs, we could conclude that both languages convey the permanent and temporary interpretations of adjectival predicative contexts by introducing the respective copulas in different syntactic positions. In terms of syntactic complexity, Spanish SER and Catalan ESTAR would be more complex than Spanish ESTAR and Catalan ÉSSER, since they are merged in v to convey their correspondent meaning and require more movement steps (i.e. movement to T°) than the respective other copula. Notice further that both Catalan ÉSSER and ESTAR instantiate a vP which makes both copulas more complex than Spanish ESTAR. The focus of the present paper is the acquisition of copula verbs in Spanish. If the two systems are viewed together, we can conclude that Spanish ESTAR requires the least complex derivation since the copula is directly inserted into T (hence, no movement of the finite copula is needed) and the construction does not involve a vP. All other structures, Spanish SER and Catalan ÉSSER and ESTAR involve a vP-layer and/or movement of the copula to T.

3 Previous studies on the acquisition of the Spanish copula verbs

A complete overview of the literature on the acquisition of the Spanish copulas SER and ESTAR by monolingual and bilingual children can be found in Arnaus Gil (2013: 162–175). Arnaus Gil & Müller (2015: 143–146) confine the overview to two main observations with respect to errors of omissions and commission.

Especially with adjectives which allow both copula verbs, SER and ESTAR, monolingual Spanish children, if they use the copulas in a target-deviant way, tend to omit the copula (mainly SER) or overgeneralize ESTAR which is the first copula verb to appear. Both errors of omission and commission, however, are rare (target-deviant uses do not exceed the 4% limit, cf. Arnaus Gil 2013: 436). As for bilingual children, most studies have looked at the language pair English-Spanish. The simultaneous acquisition of these two languages seems to delay the Spanish system as compared with monolinguals (Silva-Corvalán & Montanari 2008, among others), while the distinction between SER and ESTAR in Spanish is argued to enhance copula use in English (Liceras, Fernández Fuertes & Alba de la Fuente 2011, among others). The German-Spanish and French-Spanish children analyzed by Arnaus Gil (2013) pattern with the Spanish-English children in Spanish, namely they mostly omit SER and overgeneralize ESTAR, but more so than monolingual Spanish children. Thus, the errors found in bilinguals are similar to those found in monolinguals, they involve SER contexts, but the German/French system which does not exhibit two copulas, delays the acquisition of the dual copula system in Spanish. Arnaus Gil (2013) bases her results on a longitudinal and a cross-sectional study. To date, no results exist for the acquisition of Spanish together with a language like Catalan which exhibits a similar (but not identical) copula system as Spanish.

As for trilinguals, the only study available is the one by Arnaus Gil (2013). She argues that trilingual children are sensitive to the dual copula system in Spanish. Their target-deviant copula use can be compared qualitatively with that of bilingual children with the difference that trilinguals tend to overgeneralize ESTAR, while bilinguals tend to omit SER. Overall, the trilingual children who acquire Catalan and German together with Spanish, and who are compared with bilingual children who acquire Spanish and German/French, exhibit less difficulty with the Spanish copula system than the bilingual children. It is noteworthy that Arnaus Gil did not have access to Spanish-Catalan bilingual data. Her study is based on longitudinal data. A cross-sectional study with a specific test for the Spanish copula verbs comparing bilinguals and trilinguals on their performance of SER and ESTAR is lacking.

4 The data

Longitudinal data

Participants

We analyzed one bilingual and three trilingual children longitudinally.[7] The children were born and live in France or Spain. Table 1 contains information about the language combination, the country of residence, the age span of the recordings and the number of recordings available for each child and language. The data of the bilingual German-Spanish children are presented and discussed in Arnaus Gil (2013).

Table 1: The children of the longitudinal study.

Child	Language combination	Country of residence	Age	Number of recordings
Syca-Inés	Sp-Fr	France	2;2 – 3;8	35[a] / 35
Frank	Sp-Cat-Ger	Spain	1;11 – 4;9	74 / – / 74
Milena	Sp-Cat-Ger	Spain	1;6 – 2;3	13 / – / 14
Diego	Sp-Fr-It	France	2;8 – 4;9	41[b] / 38 / 41

Notes:
[a] We analyzed 29 recordings in Spanish. In Arnaus Gil (2013), 8 recordings have been investigated.
[b] We analyzed 23 recordings in Spanish.

---

7 The data were collected and transcribed in four research projects which have been financed by the DFG (*Deutsche Forschungsgemeinschaft*) since 1999: 1) Frühkindliche Zweisprachigkeit: Italienisch-Deutsch und Französisch-Deutsch im Vergleich (Hamburg, 1999–2005, under the direction of Natascha Müller); 2) Die Architektur der frühkindlichen bilingualen Sprachfähigkeit: Italienisch-Deutsch und Französisch-Deutsch in Italien, Deutschland und Frankreich im Vergleich (Wuppertal, 2005-2008, under the direction of Natascha Müller); 3) Code-Switching bei bilingual aufwachsenden Kindern in Deutschland, Italien, Frankreich und Spanien: Italienisch-Deutsch, Französisch-Deutsch, Spanisch-Deutsch, Italienisch-Französisch, Italienisch-Spanisch, Französisch-Spanisch (Wuppertal, 2009–2013, under the direction of Natascha Müller), 4) Frühkindlicher Trilinguismus: Deutsch – Französisch – Spanisch in Deutschland (Wuppertal, 2014-2017, under the direction of Laia Arnaus Gil and Natascha Müller). For details about the projects cf. Cantone, Kupisch, Müller & Schmitz (2008), Hauser-Grüdl, Arencibia Guerra, Witzmann, Leray & Müller (2010), Müller, Arnaus Gil, Eichler, Geveler, Hager, Jansen, Patuto, Repetto & Schmeißer (2015), Müller, Cantone, Kupisch & Schmitz (2002) and Müller, Kupisch, Schmitz & Cantone (2011). The quantitative analysis of the child corpora has been provided by Laia Arnaus Gil.

Methodology

The children have been videotaped every fortnight in the interaction with a mono-lingual adult (a parent) who is a native of the respective language. The interactions are spontaneous and were transcribed by native speakers.

Cross-sectional data

Participants

Table 2 illustrates the participants of a cross-sectional study of bilingual, trilingual and multilingual children who reside in Germany or Spain. The multilingual children speak more than three languages. 72 children who have acquired Spanish as one of their native languages participated in the study. The vast majority of children is younger than 6;6, i.e. more or less comparable with the children of the longitudinal study.

Methodology

We measured language proficiency with the PPVT (Peabody Picture Vocabulary Test, Dunn et al. 1986) from which the size of the receptive vocabulary can be inferred. The PPVT is a standardized test designed for children who speak the respective language as a native language and live in a country where it is spoken. It is used in clinical assessment in order to detect language impairments and to analyze language development. The test offers a comparison with the children of the norming sample (control groups) in several age groups. In the present case, it was used to measure the linguistic competence in the different L1s of children who acquire more than one language from birth.

Based on their proficiency in the PPVT, the children were ranked into low, average and high on the basis of a comparison with the norming sample of each language. The norming sample consisted of 1219 children from Mexico and 1488 children from Puerto Rico, both countries where Spanish is the national language, together with a great number of common languages, indigenous languages and English among them. The punctuation system and its interpretation in the Spanish PPVT is shown in Figure 1.

The test which elicited the two copulas is based on Schmitt & Miller (2007) and was composed of four stories with four different animals. The permanent properties of the animals were affected by actions which gave rise to temporary

Table 2: The children of the cross-sectional study.

	Language combination	2;6–3;5	3;6–4;5	4;6–5;5	5;6–6;5	6;6–7;5	7;6–8;5	8;6–9;5	9;6–10;5	TOTAL
Bilingual (n=32)	Sp-Ger	5	5	6	4	1	1	1		23
	Sp-Fr		2	2						4
	Sp-Cat	2		1	1				1	5
Trilingual (n=31)	Sp-Cat-Ger		1		1					2
	Sp-Cat-Fr			3	6		1			10
	Sp-Ger-Fr		1		1	1				3
	Sp-Fr-X[a]			2	2					4
	Sp-Ger-X	3	4	4	1					12
Multilingual (n=9)	2 Romance languages (Sp+X) + 2 other languages	1	2	2						5
	3 Romance languages (Sp-Cat-Fr) + 1 other language	1	1		1	1				4
TOTAL		12	16	20	17	3	2	1	1	72

Note: [a] We have analysed trilingual and multilingual children who have languages which have not been studied in this study, such as Russian, Italian, among others. We have indicated with a cross the presence of a non-studied language.

properties. Before the test started, practice items were used in order to guarantee that the child understood the game. Distractors were used to avoid that the child gets used to one response. Figure 2 illustrates the story in which the permanent vs. temporary property of a bear were asked.

The experimenter used the sentences in (17). (17a) represents the SER-condition and (17b) the ESTAR-condition. Put differently, in the SER-condition we expected the child to use the adjective which expresses the permanent property (here: brown), whereas in the ESTAR-condition the child had to produce the adjective that expresses the temporal/accidental property, namely blue.

(17) a. *El oso es* _____
       The bear is-SER_____
    b. *El oso está* _____
       The bear is-ESTAR_____

The order of SER- and ESTAR-test sentences was changed for each story in order to avoid routine processes.

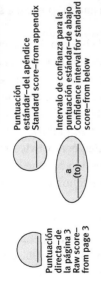

PUNTUACIONES DEL TEST E INTERPRETACION DE LA PUNTUACION–Véase la Parte 3 del manual
TEST SCORES AND THEIR INTERPRETATION–See Part 3 of the manual

Puntuación
directa–de
la página 3
Raw score–
from page 3

Puntuación
estándar–del apéndice
Standard score–from appendix

Intervalo de confianza para la
puntuación estándar–de abajo
Confidence interval for standard
score–from below

a
(to)

Rango percentil–del
apéndice o de abajo
Percentile rank–from
appendix or below

Intervalo de confianza para el
rango percentil–de abajo
Confidence interval for percentile
rank–from below

a
(to)

Edad equivalente–del
apéndice
Age equivalent–from appendix

Intervalo de confianza
para la edad equivalente–
del apéndice
Confidence interval for age
equivalent–from appendix

a
(to)

RECOMENDACION: Use sólo los intervalos de confianza cuando informe los resultados del TVIP.   RECOMMENDATION: Use only confidence intervals in reporting TVIP results.

INTERVALOS DE CONFIANZA PARA LA PUNTUACION ESTANDAR Y EL RANGO PERCENTIL
CONFIDENCE INTERVALS FOR STANDARD SCORE AND PERCENTILE RANK

En la escala de arriba marque la puntuación estándar obtenida. Trace una línea vertical que cruce la escala de abajo para marcar el rango percentil obtenido. También en la escala de arriba, sombree una franja a ambos lados de la línea vertical, utilizando los datos de la tabla de la derecha para determinar el ancho de la franja. Anote, en los espacios indicados, ei rango percentil obtenido, y los dos intervalos de confianza, uno para la puntuación estándar (la escala de arriba) y otro para el rango percentil (la escala de abajo). Vea los ejemplos en la Figura 3.2 del manual.

On the top scale, mark the obtained standard score. Draw a vertical line through it and across the second scale to mark the obtained percentile rank. Also on the top scale, shade a band on both sides of the vertical line, using the data in the table to the left to determine the band width. Record, in the spaces provided above, the obtained percentile rank and the two confidence intervals, one for standard scores (top scale) and one for percentile ranks (second scale). See Figure 3.2 in the manual for examples.

Puntuación estándar obtenida (Obtained standard score)	Área para sombrear (Area to shade)	
	A la izquierda de la línea (Left of line)	A la derecha de la línea (Right of line)
55–69	2	6
70–84	3	5
85–114	4	4
115–130	5	3
131–145	6	2

Puntuaciones estándar Standard scores																			
55	60	65	70	75	80	85	90	95	100	105	110	115	120	125	130	135	140	145

Rangos percentiles
Percentile ranks

1   5   10   15   20 25 30 35 40 45 50 55 60 65 70 75 80   85   90   95   99

Categorías descriptivas
Descriptive categories

Puntuación extremadamente baja
Extremely low score

Puntuación moderadamente baja
Moderately low score

Baja
Low

Puntuación promedio
Average score

Alta
High

Puntuación moderadamente alta
Moderately high score

Puntuación extremadamente alta
Extremely high score

Figure 1: Punctuation and interpretation: Spanish PPVT.

Figure 2: Spanish copula test.

5 The results

The longitudinal data

In what follows, we will present the use of SER and ESTAR in the trilingual and bilingual children of the longitudinal study. All children except for Diego have been analyzed in Arnaus Gil (2013) and Arnaus Gil & Müller (2015). From the work by Arnaus Gil (2013), we can anticipate that we will have to pay attention particularly to errors of omission and overgeneralization (i.e. commission) of one copula. For reasons of space, we collapsed the results from all analyzed recordings into one bar, although the analyzed time spans differ immensely.[8] This was also done because the use of the two copulas differs from child to child and for comparable age spans with sometimes very low absolute numbers. Since the present article focusses on adjectival contexts, the following figures (3) and (4) present a subset of all SER and ESTAR instances.

If presented in one bar, figures 3 and 4 show that all children, irrespective of whether they were bilingual or trilingual, had more problems in contexts which require SER than in ESTAR-contexts. Notwithstanding, there was a difference among the children: The trilingual children who acquire Spanish together with Catalan omitted both copulas more frequently than the bilingual child Syca-Inès and the trilingual child Diego, more so in SER-contexts than in ESTAR-contexts. If we compare the two contexts, the copula is being omitted nearly twice as often in SER contexts than in ESTAR contexts. An error of omission has the inconvenience that it is unclear what the underlying syntactic derivation of the structure

---

8 A reviewer identifies correctly that by collapsing all results from all recordings we might hide potential differences in the acquisition process. For reasons of space and focus of this article, we want to compare both the longitudinal and the cross-sectional data.

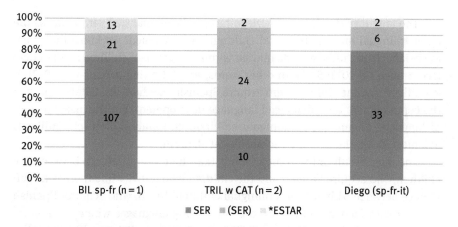

Figure 3: SER-adjectival contexts in the data from three trilingual children and one bilingual child: Spanish realizations, omissions of a possible SER, overgeneralizations of ESTAR.

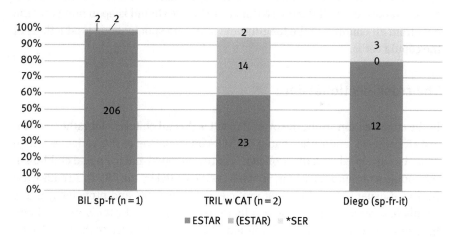

Figure 4: ESTAR-adjectival contexts in the data from three trilingual children and one bilingual child: Spanish realizations, omissions of a possible ESTAR, overgeneralizations of SER.

with an omitted copula verb was. It could be, as alluded to by the figures 3 and 4, the target-like structure, 51 cases in an underlying SER structure and 16 cases in an underlying ESTAR structure. However, the data can also be seen from a different angle. One could also say that 67 omissions of an undefined underlying syntactic structure face 415 realizations of either SER or ESTAR. Since the trilingual children with Catalan rarely overgeneralize the copula verbs, we believe that the view that SER is more often omitted than ESTAR is tenable.

The language dominance of Diego has not been analyzed yet. As far as the other trilingual and the bilingual children are concerned, we know that there are balanced and unbalanced children within the group of children studied here (see Arnaus Gil 2013: 5.1.3). In other words, and following Arnaus Gil (2013), it is unlikely that the children who acquire Spanish together with Catalan omitted the copula due to an unbalanced language development. For the measurement of language dominance in bilingual children, cf. Cantone, Kupisch, Müller & Schmitz (2008), Hager (2014), Schmeißer et al. (2016).

The main result of the comparison is that there is a difference between the children who acquire Catalan and the children who don't, while there is no difference between trilingual and bilingual children. Diego, who acquires Spanish together with French and Italian, the latter being languages where a comparable distinction between SER and ESTAR does not exist, behaves like the bilingual child who acquires Spanish together with French, a language which exhibits only one copula verb (*être* 'be'). He differs from the children who acquire Spanish together with Catalan: These trilingual children omit the copula to a considerable extent, SER more so than ESTAR. One should keep in mind that the data from all children in the longitudinal study are spontaneous productions of the copula verbs.

The cross-sectional data

In the cross-section study, the overall result is that all children did rather well for ESTAR-contexts, and rather badly for SER-contexts. One of the variables which could be correlated with the proficiency of the bilingual and trilingual children in the copula test is proficiency in Spanish (as measured by the PPVT). Arnaus Gil & Jiménez-Gaspar (2016) show that proficiency in the PPVT and proficiency in the copula test cannot explain the results in the copula test. Figure 5 nicely shows that the bilingual and trilingual children performed rather well in the ESTAR condition and rather badly in the SER condition. The result of the Chi-squared test shows that there is no statistical difference between the different PPVT groups in each condition (SER/ESTAR), but all differences within the same PPVT group (for example low ESTAR vs. low SER: 0.012, p<0.05) are highly statistically significant (for a comprehensive presentation of the statistical data, cf. the appendix below).[9]

---

9 The statistical analysis has been done by Amelia Jiménez-Gaspar.

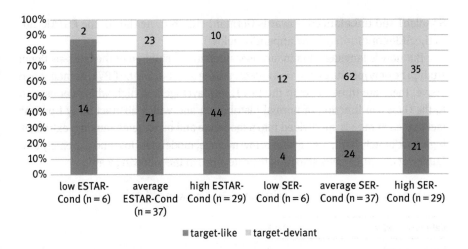

Figure 5: Proficiency in the copula test according to the proficiency level in the PPVT (Arnaus Gil & Jiménez-Gaspar 2016).

A similar result is obtained, if we look at the language dominance of the bilingual and trilingual children. Figure 6 shows that unbalanced as well as balanced children master the ESTAR condition in a much more target-like way than the SER condition. Balanced as well as unbalanced children perform worse in the SER condition. There is no statistical significance between unbalanced (towards

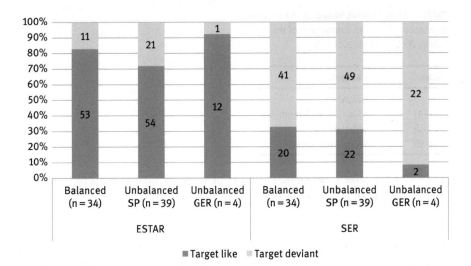

Figure 6: Proficiency in the copula test according to language balance (Arnaus Gil & Jimenéz-Gaspar 2016).

Spanish) and unbalanced (towards German) children, neither in the ESTAR- nor in the SER-condition (cf. the appendix below).

But how is language dominance measured in the children of the cross-sectional study? The only measure which is available are the results from the PPVT. As mentioned above, there are three ranks in the PPVT: low, average and high which correspond to the Gaussian function of normal distribution and which abstract away from the fact that each rank is subdivided into a moderate and an extreme ranking: extremely high, moderately high, high average, low average, moderately low and extremely low. Kubina et al. (2016) suggest to rank the categories in the following way[10]:

Table 3: Ranks of proficiency in the PPVT (Kubina et al. 2016: 5)

Category in PPVTs	Rank
Extremely Low	0
Moderate Low	1
Average	2
Moderate High	3
Extremely High	4

In order to calculate language (un)balancy, the rank value obtained in language A is subtracted from the rank value as obtained in language B. The resulting value stands for one out of four dominance labels (cf. Hager 2014).

Table 4: Balance types based on the difference as obtained from the subtraction of the PPVT-values (Kubina et al. 2016: 6).

Value	Category
0	balanced
(-1/+1)	balanced with tendency
(-2/+2)	unbalanced
(-3/+3)	more unbalanced

The following table gives some examples of such calculation for some bilingual children in the cross-sectional study.

---

10 The PPVT also divides the average level into two different subcategories (low average and high average); however, in order to avoid the establishment of too many categories and due to the fact that average is considered the "normal" group of the norming sample, we decided to collapse the two average levels into one in table (3).

Table 5: Calculation of language dominance of bilingual children in the cross-section study: some examples. (Adapted from Kubina et al. 2016: 6)

language combination	Child	PPVT-value L_A	PPVT-value L_B	value L_A	value L_B	value of PPVT-difference	category
ger-sp	Rosa	Average	Average	2	2	0	balanced
ger-sp	Tino	Mod. High	Average	3	2	1	balanced tendency (ger)
ger-fr	Fleur	Extr. Low	Average	0	2	-2	unbalanced
ger-fr	Balthasar	Average	Mod. High	2	3	-1	balanced tendency (fr)
fr-sp	Etienne	Mod. High	Mod. Low	3	1	2	unbalanced

If we apply the above calculation to trilingual children, we obtain balanced children when they have the same category in their different L1s, that is, if one child has achieved an average level in Spanish, French and German, this child is considered "balanced". Besides, it is possible to categorize children as balanced, but with a tendency towards a particular language. It occurs when the difference between the different L1s is small (1/-1). Nevertheless, there are children who obtained different values in their different L1s, therefore, in those cases, we specify in which language the child has higher scores. In this case, children obtain 2 or -2 points in the calculation of their different L1s.

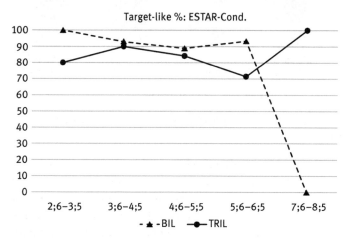

Figure 7: Proficiency in the copula test (ESTAR-condition) according to age (Arnaus Gil & Jimenéz-Gaspar 2016).

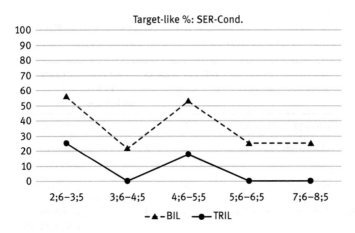

Figure 8: Proficiency in the copula test (SER-condition) according to age (Arnaus Gil & Jimenéz-Gaspar 2016).

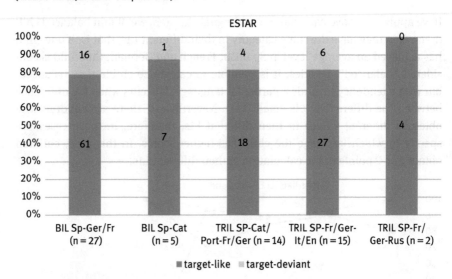

Figure 9: Proficiency in the copula test according to language combination (Arnaus Gil & Jimenéz-Gaspar 2016): ESTAR-condition.

Another variable which could have influenced the children's proficiency in the copula test is age. In order to study this variable, we grouped the children into 5 age periods. The differences between the bilingual and trilingual children for both conditions along the age periods are statistically not significant (cf. the appendix below). The last age span (7;6–8;5) could not be taken into account for the ESTAR-condition because the number of children in this group was 0. Figure 7 shows the results for ESTAR, figure 8 for SER.

Since we have observed an effect of the language combination in the production of SER and ESTAR in the longitudinal study, the next variable to be studied in the cross-sectional study is the language combination. Let us start with the ESTAR-condition. The languages which, in addition to Spanish, exhibit two copulas are Catalan and Portuguese. Figure 9 shows that the children with Catalan (bilingual or trilingual) performed similarly in the ESTAR-condition to the children who do not acquire a language with two copulas together with Spanish. At least 80% of all items with ESTAR were handled in a target-like way by the children, i.e. they correctly produced the adjective with the temporary property.

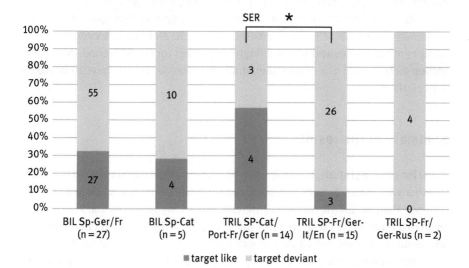

Figure 10: Proficiency in the copula test according to language combination (Arnaus Gil & Jimenéz-Gaspar 2016): SER-condition.
Note: In addition to the Chi-Squared test, we analysed the data with the SPSS program to achieve a more sophisticated testing. We correlated the relation between the language combination and the children's answers in the different conditions (SER or ESTAR). We found a significant result (see Table 2 in the appendix). As we observed that in the test of homogeneity of variances (see table below) the language combination was an important variable, we decided to analyse the data across the difference between bilinguals, trilinguals and multilinguals, taking into account whether the child had Catalan or Portuguese as their L1s or not (that is, six different groups of children), because we had observed in the first analysis (chi-square) significant differences among the trilingual children who acquire Catalan or Portuguese as one of their first languages and trilingual children with different language combinations.

Levene's statistics	df1	df2	Sign.
5.23	5	310	.000

Test of homogeneity of variances: the SER and ESTAR condition across the language combinations

Let us turn to the SER-condition. Figure 10 reveals that there is no statistical difference between the bilingual groups, even though one group acquires Catalan together with Spanish. The trilingual group with Catalan/Portuguese performs better than the trilingual/multilingual groups with only one dual copula system (Spanish). The difference is statistically significant (0.012, p<0.05). The difference between the bilingual group with Spanish and Catalan and the trilingual group with two languages with two copula systems is not statistically significant. The higher percentage that we observe for the trilinguals cannot be due to the third L1 since this is either French or German, languages that have unitary copula systems. In other words, only if the child is trilingual with a second language which exhibits a dual copula system like Spanish will the performance in the SER-condition be enhanced. Notice, however, that the number of target-like and target-deviant responses for the SER-condition in the enhanced trilingual group is rather small and thus our results have to be taken with caution.

Summary of the results

In the longitudinal study, the children who acquire a dual copula system (Catalan) together with Spanish were characterized by errors of omission, more so in SER contexts than in ESTAR contexts. Interestingly, trilingualism as such is unlikely as an explanation for these errors of omission, since the trilingual child with two additional languages which do not exhibit a dual copula system as in Spanish patterned with the bilingual French-Spanish child. The longitudinal data are production data.

In the cross-sectional study, the SER-condition was much more difficult for all children than the ESTAR-condition, irrespective of the level reached in the PPVT, language dominance and age. Only the trilinguals who acquire another language with a dual copula system like Spanish (Catalan, Portuguese) showed an advantage in the SER condition. Although the correct adjective had to be produced by the child, the test tested comprehension of permanent/temporary properties assigned to the animals in the stories.

6 Discussion

Derivationally, Spanish SER is more complex than ESTAR, the former being merged in *v* and moved to T for independent reasons. The different derivational complexity can nicely explain why the longitudinal data exhibit more omissions in SER-contexts than in ESTAR-contexts.[11] However, if only the syntactic derivation of the Spanish system counted, we would expect the bilingual child Syca-Inès and the trilingual child Diego to omit the two copulas in a similar way and to a similar degree which is not the case. Therefore, the respective other language(s) seem(s) to play an important role. But how can this role be defined?

A trilingual child who acquires Spanish and Catalan has to handle another language with a dual copula system, in the case of Catalan a language in which both copulas instantiate a vP and ÉSSER is directly merged in T and ESTAR in v and moved for independent reasons to T. Principally speaking and taking into account that multilingualism is characterized by cross-linguistic influence (cf. Hulk & Müller 2000, Müller & Hulk 2001), a multilingual child who produces Spanish SER or ESTAR could err on the underlying syntactic representation and use the Spanish verb in an otherwise Catalan syntactic derivation.

Spanish SER   merged in v (according to Spanish adult system) vP present
Spanish SER   merged in T (according to Catalan adult system) vP present
Spanish ESTAR merged in T (according to Spanish adult system) vP absent
Spanish ESTAR merged in v (according to Catalan adult system) vP present

If we compare the four cases, it is only Spanish ESTAR which is less complex and which exhibits a unique syntactic derivation. All derivations which involve SER exhibit a kind of complexity which could lead the child into omitting this copula more often than ESTAR, the latter exhibiting the least complex derivation in adult Spanish. That we are dealing with cross-linguistic influence from Catalan to Spanish is likely if we consider the developmental path of the children who acquire Spanish together with a language which does not exhibit a dual copula system, either bilingual or trilingual: Syca-Inès and Diego do not have problems with the selection of ESTAR and its spell-out in Spanish if we consider 90% as a quantitative acquisition criterion (cf. Brown 1973) and the fact that for Diego only 15 ESTAR-contexts were available. In a nutshell, we would like to suggest that the SER-omissions

---

11 One reviewer suggests that omission could be seen as a default strategy in child grammar. This view is interesting and would be able to account for the observation that there are omissions with SER and with ESTAR. Arguably, a default is used when the child has to cope with structures which overcharge the child's linguistic or cognitive capacities. In other words, we would need the notion of complexity even if we assume default strategies to be in place. Another reviewer points out that our analysis makes the prediction that SER-contexts are more difficult to produce than ESTAR-contexts across the board, i.e. in contexts other than those which contain an adjective. This prediction concerning the production of the two copula verbs is corroborated by the data analyzed in Arnaus Gil (2013).

in the Spanish of the trilingual children who acquire Catalan instantiate a Spanish or a Catalan underlying structure, while (the less frequent) ESTAR-omissions are always omissions in an otherwise Catalan underlying structure.[12]

Let us turn to the results of the cross-sectional task. This test, in contrast to the production of the copula in the longitudinal study, tested the children's sensitivity for the SER- and the ESTAR-condition. Remember that the children had to provide the correct adjective according to the permanent/temporary property of the animal in the story. Here, the result was that the SER-condition was much more difficult than the ESTAR-condition. The SER-condition represented the permanent property of the animal, the background information at the time when this property had been overridden by the changing, temporary property of the animal in the foreground. It goes without saying that at the time when this temporary property was introduced, the background information is more difficult to access (encoded by SER). This was true for all children tested, irrespective of their proficiency in the PPVT, their language balance and their age. Only the children who were trilingual with Catalan or Portuguese, another dual copula system comparable to Spanish, performed better in the SER-condition, i.e. they had less difficulty to access the background information than the other children. Why is this so? If only the respective other language which is acquired together with Spanish played a role, then we would also expect this advantage in the SER-condition with bilingual Spanish-Catalan children, where it was absent. What is the difference between a bilingual Spanish-Catalan child and a trilingual child who acquires Spanish and Catalan together with a language like French or German, both having only one copula verb?

The difference may rely in decision-taking. Upon speaking Spanish, the trilingual child decides (subconsciously) whether the system is like Catalan or like French/German, perhaps due to efficient computation, i.e. in order to avoid the use of representations which are unknown and therefore costly to instantiate/acquire. In the case of the trilingual child who acquires Spanish together with Catalan or Portuguese, there is another language which makes use of the same background-foreground or permanent/temporary distinction

---

12 Another way of looking at the longitudinal data has been proposed to us by a reviewer. If we take a look at the target-deviant productions of the multilingual children we observe approximately 20% of overgeneralizations and the rest are omissions. S/he points out that this great amount of omissions could be seen as a default form. Usage of a default (omission) is likely in Catalan-Spanish trilinguals because they have competing copula systems (remember that the distribution of the copulas differs in the two languages). Notwithstanding, omissions are much more frequent in SER-contexts which our approach based on complexity would predict. In other words, we believe that the production data can best be predicted on the basis of a syntactic analysis which assigns a less complex derivation to Spanish ESTAR.

as Spanish. The linguistic expression of this distinction is enhanced for the more demanding situation, the background property or the property which was relevant before the change of state. The observation that bilingual children do not show the same enhancement as trilinguals might indicate that decision-taking or choice is important in order to unfold the enhancing characteristics of the Catalan/Portuguese system in situations when the child has to speak Spanish.

As such, the results of the longitudinal study and of the cross-sectional study seem to contradict one another. In the longitudinal study, it was the production of SER which was most problematic in the trilinguals who acquire Catalan together with Spanish. The errors of omission were less frequent in the case of the bilingual French-Spanish child and the trilingual Spanish-Italian-French child. Taking into account that cross-linguistic influence occurs in multilingualism, the least complex syntactic derivation is required by Spanish ESTAR. All other derivations, coupled from adult Spanish and Catalan, are derivationally complex and thus invite the child to omit the copula as a strategy to avoid this kind of complexity. In a nutshell, the Catalan syntactic derivations for the two copulas and those of Spanish interfere in language production. In the cross-sectional study, another skill was tested, namely whether the children could "go back" to the permanent property, a property which was relevant early in the story. This possibility is reminiscent of the advantage multilingual children have in attentional control (Martin-Rhee & Bialystok 2008: 91). The advantage in the SER-condition as observed in the trilingual children who acquire Catalan/Portuguese together with German/French is unlikely to be due to any linguistic property since it was absent in the bilingual children. It is most probably related to decision-making which trilinguals must do, presumably for reasons of efficient processing. In this case, it might be helpful for the child to know a similar language to Spanish, that is Catalan, that encodes permanent and temporary properties in the same way: Whereas permanent properties are related predominantly to background information, temporary properties rely mainly on foreground information. This was true for the four stories that were developed specifically for the elititation task.[13]

---

13 One reviewer alludes to the possibility that the results are due to a comprehension/production-asymmetry, in the present case, comprehension would (as observed with many grammatical domains) outrank production. We admit that more research has to be done on language comprehension in multilingual children. However, if a comprehension/production-asymmetry was at heart of the explanation of our results, we would expect the bilinguals to show an advantage in comprehension of the SER-condition as well, which is not the case. Therefore, we believe that the explanation is likely to come from the number of languages to be handled by the

Sekerina & Spradlin (2016) are the editors of a special issue on bilingualism and its effects on executive function. Indeed, their introduction makes clear that the Bilingual Advantage Hypothesis, as originally defended by Ellen Bialystok (1999) and her colleagues, could not be verified by a number of scientists. In other words, bilinguals do not always yield better performance than monolinguals. The authors ask the relevant question of whether "inhibition [is] the underlying mechanism moderating the ability to efficiently negotiate having two or more languages, and [whether] [...] it transfer[s] to non-linguistic tasks" (Sekerina & Spradlin 2016: 508). Remember that the general result of our production study is that children who acquire more than one language have problems to select the correct derivation especially for Spanish SER and therefore use the less complex derivation from the respective other language(s). In other words, multilingual children find it difficult to produce a derivationally complex linguistic analysis if there is a less complex one (remember that the children who acquire Spanish together with Catalan had more problems with SER contexts than children who acquired Spanish together with languages which exhibit only one copula verb). Sekerina & Spradlin point out that the evidence for inhibition is insufficient to explain some benefits of bilingualism. This seems to be the case in our study as well. If the ability of inhibition was the source for the advantage of the trilinguals who acquire Spanish together with Catalan or Portuguese in the SER-condition of our comprehension task in Spanish, and if there is permeability of the ability of inhibition in linguistic and non-linguistic tasks, then we would expect better results as we had in the production of Spanish SER. Sekerina & Spradlin (2016: 508) ask further whether monitoring is the key facility, "since bilinguals must monitor which language is appropriate". Both, inhibition and monitoring, are probably relevant but in specific areas. Arguably, inhibition is the source for the monolingual language mode which bilinguals can entertain. Monitoring is the source for the bilingual language mode which the bilingual considers for example if her/his interlocutor speaks more than one language as well. Carried over to the present study of children who acquire more than one language, inhibition of the non-requested language is costly and even more so if two or more languages have to be inhibited (as in the case of trilinguals and multilinguals). On the other hand, the ability of monitoring might benefit from the number of languages, explaining our result that the trilinguals had better performances than the bilinguals in the comprehension of the SER-condition because they have more experience with monitoring than their

---

child and the different processes involved in language production and comprehension. Note that the number of individuals we tested is small. Indeed, the ideas developed here should be studied in future research on the basis of a larger number of children, both bilingual and trilingual.

bilingual peers. Our results indicate that methodological issues should be given more attention in the future and that the field should address the question of exact replications: Although we obtained statistically significant results, the number of individuals who participated in the test was really small.

If we are on the right track, then "erroneous" linguistic behavior and enhancement have different sources: the one is rooted in cross-linguistic influence, the other in skills which have to do with more general cognitive skills, like decision-making. The different behaviour of the bilinguals and the trilinguals in the cross-sectional study who acquire, besides Spanish, a language with a dual copula system indicates that language acquisition research lacks a theory of early child tri-/multilingualism and that theories of bilingual language use cannot be carried over to trilingual and multilingual children. Future studies should combine different types of tasks in order to advance language acquisition theory. They should also stress the challenge of the task in order to weigh the importance of linguistic and cognitive influencing variables.

References

Arnaus Gil, L. 2013. *La selección copulativa y auxiliar: las lenguas romances (español – italiano – catalán – francés) y el alemán en contacto. Su adquisición en niños bilingües y trilingües.* Tübingen: Narr.

Arnaus Gil, L. & A. Jimenéz-Gaspar. 2016. *SER and ESTAR in coding permanent vs. temporal properties: Early bilingual and trilingual acquisition.* UIC Bilingualism Forum, October 20th – 21rd Chicago.

Arnaus Gil, L. & N. Müller. 2015. The acquisition of Spanish in a bilingual and in a trilingual setting: Combining Spanish with German, French and Catalan. In T. Judy & S. Perpiñán (eds.), *The acquisition of Spanish in understudied language pairings*, 135–168. Amsterdam: John Benjamins.

Baker, M. 1985. *Incorporation: A theory of grammatical function changing.* Cambridge, MA: MIT PhD thesis.

Baker, M. 1997. Thematic roles and syntactic structure. In L. Haegeman (ed.), *Elements of grammar*, 73–137. Dordrecht: Kluwer.

Bialystok, E. 1999. Cognitive complexity and attentional control in the bilingual mind. *Child Development* 70(3). 636–644.

Brown, R. 1973. *A first language: The early stages.* London: George Allen & Unwin.

Bruhn de Garavito, J. 2009. Eventive and stative passives: The role of transfer in the acquisition of *ser* and *estar* by German and English L1 Speakers. In J. Collentine, M. García, B. Lafford & F. Marcos Marín (eds.), *Selected Proceedings of the 11th Hispanic Linguistics Symposium*, 27–38. Somerville, MA: Cascadilla Press.

Camacho, J. 2012. *Ser* and *estar*: The individual/stage level distinction and aspectual predication. In J. I. Hualde, A. Olarrea & E. O'Rourke (eds.), *The handbook of Spanish linguistics*, 453–476. Oxford: Blackwell.

Camacho, J. 2016. What do Spanish copulas have in common with Tibetan evidentials? In S. Gumiel Molina (ed.), *New perspectives on the study of ser and estar*, 173–202. Amsterdam: John Benjamins.

Cantone, K. F., T. Kupisch, N. Müller & K. Schmitz. 2008. Rethinking language dominance in bilingual children. *Linguistische Berichte* 215. 307–343.

Carlson, G. 1977. *Reference to kinds in English.* University of Massachusetts, Amherst, PhD thesis.

Chomsky, N. 2000. Minimalist inquiries. In: R. E. A. Martin (ed.), *Step by step. Essays on minimalist syntax in Honor of Howard Lasnik*, 89–155. Cambridge: MIT Press.

Döpke, S. 1992. *One parent, one language: An interactional approach.* Amsterdam/ Philadelphia: John Benjamins.

Döpke, S. 1997. Is simultaneous acquisition of two languages in early childhood equal to acquiring each of the two languages individually? In: E. Clark (ed.), *Proceedings of the 28th Annual Child Research Forum*, 95–112. Stanford: CSLI Publications.

Döpke, S. 1998. Competing language structures: The acquisition of verb placement by bilingual German-English children. *Journal of Child Language* 25. 555–584.

Dunn, L. M., D. M. Dunn, A. Lenhard, W. Lenhard, R. Segerer & S. Suggate. 1986. *Peabody (Peabody Picture Vocabulary Test).* Diablo: Pearson.

Gallego, A. J. & J. Uriagereka. 2016. ESTAR = SER+ X. *Borealis: An International Journal of Hispanic Linguistics* 5. 123–156.

Hager, M. 2014. *Der Genuserwerb bei mehrsprachig aufwachsenden Kindern – Eine longitudinale Untersuchung bilingualer und trilingualer Kinder der Sprachenkombi- nationen deutsch-französisch/italienisch/spanisch, französisch-italienisch/spanisch und deutsch-spanisch-katalanisch.* Bergische Universität Wuppertal, http://elpub.bib. uni-wuppertal.de/edocs/dokumente/fba/romanistik/ diss2014/hager/da1401.pdf.

Gawlitzek-Maiwald, I. & R. Tracy. 1996. Bilingual bootstrapping. *Linguistics* 34. 901–926.

Genesee, F. 1989. Early bilingual development: One language or two? *Journal of Child Language* 16. 161–179.

Gumiel Molina, S., N. Moreno Quibén & M. I. Pérez Jiménez. 2016. The inference of temporal persistence and the individual/stage level distinction: the case of ser and estar in Spanish. In S. Gumiel Molina (ed.), *New perspectives on the study of ser and estar*, 119–146. Amsterdam: John Benjamins.

Hauser-Grüdl, N., L.A. Guerra, F. Witzmann, E. Leray & N. Müller. 2010. Cross-linguistic influence in bilingual children: can input frequency account for it? *Lingua* 120(11). 2638–2650.

Hoffmann, C. 1999. Trilingual competence: linguistic and cognitive issues. *Applied Linguistic Studies in Central Europe* 3. 16–26.

Hoffmann, C. 2000. Bilingual and trilingual competence: Problems of description and differen- tiation. *Estudios de Sociolingüística* 1(1). 83–92.

Hoffmann, C. 2001. Towards a description of trilingual competence. *International Journal of Bilingualism* 5(1). 1–17.

Hulk, A. & N. Müller. 2000. Crosslinguistic influence at the interface between syntax and pragmatics. *Bilingualism: Language and Cognition* 3(3). 227–244.

Jeßner, U. 1997. Towards a dynamic view of multilingualism. In: M. Pütz (ed.), *Language choices: conditions, constraints and consequences*, 17–30. Amsterdam: John Benjamin.

Kubina, C., A. Jiménez-Gaspar & Laia Arnaus Gil. 2016. *Measuring linguistic competence in early bilingualism and trilingualism: Applying the PPVT in a cross-sectional study with children acquiring Spanish and French in different language combinations.* VIIIth

International Conference of Language Acquisition, September 7–9, Palma de Mallorca, Spain.

Kupisch, T. 2006. *The acquisition of determiners in bilingual German-Italian and German-French children*. München: Lincom Europa.

Lema, J. 1995. Distinguishing copular and aspectual auxiliaries: Spanish ser and estar. In J. Amastae, G. Goodall, M. Montalbetti & M. Phinney (eds.), *Contemporary research in Romance linguistics: Papers from the XXII Linguistic Symposium on Romance Languages*, 257–274. El Paso/Juárez, Febrero 22–24, 1992Amsterdam: John Benjamins.

Liceras. J., R. Fernández Fuertes & A. Alba de la Fuente. 2011. Overt subjects and copula omission in the Spanish and the English grammar of English-Spanish bilinguals. On the locus and directionality of interlinguistic influence. *First Language* 32 (1–2). 88–115.

Lleó, C. 2002. The role of markedness in the acquisition of complex prosodic structures by German-Spanish bilinguals. *International Journal of Bilingualism* 6(3). 291–313.

Lleó, C. & M. Kehoe (eds.). 2002. Special issue on the interaction of phonological systems in child bilingual acquisition. *International Journal of Bilingualism* 6(3). 233–237.

Lleó, C. 2016. Acquiring multilingual phonologies (2L1, L2 and L3): Are the difficulties in the interfaces? In S. Fischer & C. Gabriel, *Manual of Grammatical Interfaces in Romance*. Berlin: Walter de Gruyter.

Lleó, C. & M. Rakow 2006. The prosody of early two-word utterances by German and Spanish monolingual and bilingual children. In C. Lleó (ed.), *Interfaces in multilingualism*, 1–26. Amsterdam/Philadelphia: John Benjamins.

Luján, M. 1981. The Spanish copulas as aspectual indicators. *Lingua* 54. 165–210.

Marín, R. 2009. *Spanish individual-level and stage-level adjectives revisited*. http:// semanticsarchive.net/Archive/mY5NjQzZ/Spanish_IL_SL_adjectives.pdf.

Martin-Rhee, M. & E. Bialystok. 2008. The development of two types of inhibitory control in monolingual and bilingual children. *Bilingualism: Language and Cognition* 11(1). 81–93.

Meisel, J. 1989. Early differentiation of languages in bilingual children. In K. Hyltenstam & L. Obler (eds), *Bilingualism across the lifespan: aspects of acquisition, maturity, and loss*, 13–40. Cambridge: Cambridge University Press.

Montanari, S. 2013. Productive trilingualism in infancy: What makes it possible? *World Journal of English Language* 3(1). 62–77.

Müller, N., L. Arnaus Gil, N. Eichler, J. Geveler, M. Hager, V. Jansen, M. Patuto, V. Repetto & A. Schmeißer. 2015. *Code-switching: Spanisch, Italienisch, Französisch. Eine Einführung*. Tübingen: Narr.

Müller, N., K. F. Cantone, T. Kupisch & K. Schmitz. 2002. Zum Spracheneinfluss im bilingualen Erstspracherwerb: Italienisch–Deutsch. *Linguistische Berichte* 190. 157–206.

Müller N. & A. Hulk. 2001. Crosslinguistic influence in bilingual language acquisition: Italian and French as recipient languages. *Bilingualism: Language and Cognition* 4(1). 1–21.

Müller, N., T. Kupisch, K. Schmitz, & K. F. Cantone. 2011. *Einführung in die Mehrsprachigkeitsforschung: Französisch, Italienisch*. Tübingen: Narr.

Nicoladis, E. 1999. Where is my brush-teeth? Acquisition of compound nouns in a French-English bilingual child. *Bilingualism: Language and Cognition* 2(3). 245–256.

Nicoladis, E. 2003. Cross-linguistic transfer in deverbal compounds of preschool bilingual children. *Bilingualism: Language and Cognition* 6(1). 17–31.

Paradis, J. & F. Genesee. 1996. Syntactic acquisition in bilingual children: Autonomous or interdependent? *Studies in Second Language Acquisition 18*. 1–25.

Patuto, M., V. Repetto & N. Müller. 2011. Delay and acceleration in bilingual first language acquisition: the same or different? In: E. Rinke & T. Kupisch (eds.), *The development of grammar: Language acquisition and diachronic change. Volume in honor of Jürgen M. Meisel*, 231–261. Amsterdam, Philadelphia: John Benjamins.

Potts, Ch. & T. Roeper. 2006. The narrowing acquisition path. From expressive small clauses to declaratives. In L. Progovac, K. Paesani, E. Casielles & E. Barton (eds.), *The syntax of nonsententials: multidisciplinary perspectives*, 183–201. Amsterdam/Philadelphia: John Benjamins.

Quay, S. 2011a. Introduction: Data-driven insights from trilingual children in the making. *International Journal of Multilingualism* 8(1). 1–4.

Quay, S. 2011b. Trilingual toddlers at daycare centers: the role of caregivers and peers in language development. *International Journal of Multilingualism* 8(1). 22–41.

Ramos Alfarín, J. R. 2008. Sintaxi. L'atribució. In J. Solà, M.-R. Lloret, J. Mascaró & M. Pérez Saldanya (eds.), *Gramàtica del català contemporani*, vol. 2. Barcelona: Editorial Empúries.

Raposo, E. & J. Uriagereka. 1995. Two types of small clauses (Toward a syntax of theme/rheme relations). In A. Cardinaletti & M. T. Guasti (eds.), *Small clauses*, 179–206. New York: Academic Press.

Romeu, J. 2016. Ser, estar and two different modifiers. In S. Gumiel Molina (ed.), *New perspectives on the study of ser and estar*, 51–83. Amsterdam: Benjamins.

Schmeißer, A., M. Hager, Arnaus Gil, V. Jansen, J. Geveler, N. Eichler, M. Patuto & N. Müller 2016. Related but different: the two concepts of language dominance and language proficiency. In C. Silva-Corvalán & J. Treffers-Daller (eds.), *Language dominance in bilinguals: issues of operationalization and measurement*, 36–65. Cambridge: Cambridge University Press.

Schmitt, C. 1992. *Ser* and *estar*. A matter of aspect. *Proceedings of the Northeastern Linguistic Society (NELS) 22*, 411–426. Amherst, MA: GLSA.

Schmitt, C. & K. Miller. 2007. Making discourse dependent decisions: The case of the copulas ser and estar in Spanish. *Lingua* 117 (11). 1907–1929.

Silva-Corvalán, C. & S. Montanari. 2008. The acquisition of ser, estar (and be) by a Spanish-English bilingual child: The early stages. *Bilingualism: Language and Cognition* 11. 341–360.

Sekerina, I. & L. Spradlin (eds.). 2016. Bilingualism and executive functions: An interdisciplinary approach. *Special Issue of Linguistic Approaches to Bilingualism* 6(5).

Wells, S. 2015. A minimalist movement account of ditransitives. University of York, http://etheses.whiterose.ac.uk/12587/1/A%20Minimalist%20Movement%20Account%20of%20Ditransitives%20-%20Wells%20(2015).pdf (accessed 3.3.2017)

Zagona, K. 2009. Ser and Estar: Phrase structure and aspect. *Cahiers Chronos*. 1–25.

Appendix

In the following table, we can observe the statistical data depending on the correlations across the children's proficiency in SER/ESTAR target-like uses, and (i) the proficiency in PPVT, (ii) the language balancy determined by bilinguals, trilinguals or the children in the norming sample, (iii) the different age stages and

Table 1: Correlations across the children's proficiency in SER/ESTAR target-like uses.

(i) Proficiency in PPVT and copula test				
low ESTAR	low SER	0.012	p < 0.05	significant
average ESTAR	average SER	0.166	p > 0.05	
high ESTAR	high SER	0.000	p < 0.05	highly significant
low ESTAR	average ESTAR	0.455	p > 0.05	
low ESTAR	high ESTAR	0.691	p > 0.05	
average ESTAR	high ESTAR	0.554	p > 0.05	
low SER	average SER	0.866	p > 0.05	
low SER	high SER	0.512	p > 0.05	
average SER	high SER	0.396	p > 0.05	
(ii) Language balance and proficiency copula test				
multi ESTAR	multi SER	0.419	p > 0.05	
tril ESTAR	tril SER	0.000	p < 0.05	highly significant
bil SER	bil ESTAR	0.002	p < 0.05	highly significant
multi ESTAR	tril ESTAR	0.267	p > 0.05	
multi ESTAR	bil ESTAR	0.604	p > 0.05	
tril ESTAR	bil ESTAR	0.372	p > 0.05	
bil SER	tril SER	0.204	p > 0.05	
bil SER	multi SER	0.704	p > 0.05	
multi SER	tril SER	0.154	p > 0.05	
(iii) Age and proficiency in copula test				
bil (2;6–3;5) ESTAR	bil (2;6–3;5) SER	0.150	p > 0.05	
tril (2;6–3;5) ESTAR	tril (2;6–3;5) SER	0.243	p > 0.05	
multi (2;6–3;5) ESTAR	multi (2;6–3;5) SER	0.470	p > 0.05	
bil (3;6–4;5) ESTAR	bil (3;6–4;5) SER	0.007	p < 0.05	highly significant
tril (3;6–4;5) ESTAR	tril (3;6–4;5) SER	0.004	p < 0.05	highly significant
multi (3;6–4;5) ESTAR	multi (3;6–4;5) SER	0.605	p > 0.05	
bil (4;6–5;5) ESTAR	bil (4;6–5;5) SER	0.126	p > 0.05	
tril (4;6–5;5) ESTAR	tril (4;6–5;5) SER	0.005	p < 0.05	highly significant
multi (4;6–5;5) ESTAR	multi (4;6–5;5) SER	0.655	p > 0.05	
bil (5;6–6;5) ESTAR	bil (5;6–6;5) SER	0.004	p < 0.05	highly significant
tril (5;6–6;5) ESTAR	tril (5;6–6;5) SER	0.024	p < 0.05	significant
multi (5;6–6;5) ESTAR	Multi (5;6–6;5) SER	0.450	p > 0.05	
(iv) Language combination and proficiency in copula test				
bil with Cat/Port. SER	bil without Cat/Port. SER	0.820	p > 0.05	
tril with Cat/Port. SER	tril without Cat/Port. SER	0.023	p < 0.05	significant

multi= multilingual children, bil= bilingual children, tril= trilingual children finally (iv) the language combination, that is, if the children are bi-trilingual with or without Catalan/Portuguese, since these two languages have, like Spanish, two copula verbs (SER and ESTAR). We have calculated the p-value to know whether these correlations are statistically significant.

We found statistically significant results with the ANOVA analysis regarding the language combination (bi-trilinguals/multilinguals with(out) Catalan or Portuguese) and the conditions (SER, ESTAR):

Table 2: Anova analysis regarding the language combination and the conditions of the copula verbs, SER and ESTAR.

	Sum of squares	df	Mean square	F	Sig.
Intra groups	8.67	5	1.73	2.28	.047
Inter groups	235.88	310	.76		
Total	244.54	315			

Pilar Barbosa, Cristina Flores and Cátia Pereira

On subject realization in infinitival complements of causative and perceptual verbs in European Portuguese: Evidence from monolingual and bilingual speakers

Abstract: This study aims to investigate knowledge of a heritage language (HL), i.e. the language of origin of bilingual speakers who grow up in the context of migration with exposure to the HL and the dominant language of the host country. We focus on European Portuguese (EP), and concentrate on bi-clausal infinitival complements of causative and perception verbs. These may have different forms depending on whether the infinitival complement is inflected or uninflected. In particular, the subject may be Nominative or Accusative. Two experimental tasks were applied, a Completion Task and an Acceptability Judgment Task, to a total of 60 adult informants: 30 native speakers raised in a monolingual context, and 30 heritage speakers (HSs), raised in a bilingual context with EP as home language and German as environmental language. Overall both groups demonstrate an evident preference for Accusative over Nominative Case marked subjects, regardless of the presence of inflection on the infinitive. Concerning the monolingual group, the most striking result regards the residual rates of Nominative Case marked subjects in the presence of an inflected infinitive in both tasks. This result is unexpected under standard assumptions concerning clause structure in EP. We offer an alternative analysis based on the idea that pre-verbal Nominative Case marked subjects in EP are (typically) left-dislocated topics (Alexiadou & Anagnostopoulou 1998; Barbosa 1995). Left-dislocated topics in EP are assigned Nominative Case by default. On this view, preference for avoiding a Nominative subject in the presence of an inflected infinitive reduces to preference for the operation of raising to object over the last resort operation of default (Nominative) Case assignment. This preference can be viewed as an instance of the Paninian principle Blocking, whereby a general, default form is blocked by the existence of a more specific rival form. In this case, the default Case option is blocked by the more specific operation of raising to object. The most significant difference between monolinguals and bilinguals concerns a higher rate of acceptance of Nominative pronouns by HSs, including in uninflected infinitives. This means that, on a par with the predominant raising to object option, the HSs allow

Pilar Barbosa, Cristina Flores and Cátia Pereira, Universidade do Minho

https://doi.org/10.1515/9781501509988-006

for the default Case strategy; i.e., they fail to apply blocking. This strategy has also been attested in early stages of the acquisition of these constructions by EP monolingual children (Santos et al. 2016), a fact that reinforces the view that the process of acquisition of the HL is native-like in the sense that it goes through the same stages as the process of monolingual acquisition. However, by retaining an option that is no longer available in mature grammars, the HSs reveal protracted development.

1 Introduction

Research into infinitival complements, either of control verbs or of causative and perception verbs has a long tradition, not only from a theoretical perspective (e.g., Rosenbaum 1967), but also in the field of language acquisition (see overview in Santos, Gonçalves & Hyams 2016). European Portuguese (EP) is a particularly attention-grabbing case of interest in this domain, because infinitives may be uninflected or inflected. In the latter case, a Nominative case marked subject is licensed in virtue of the presence of agreement inflection (Raposo 1987). Infinitival complements of perception and causative verbs are especially interesting since, in addition to the inflected infinitival option, uninflected infinitives show up with Accusative Case marked subjects. In addition, perception verbs allow yet another type of infinitival complement, namely the prepositional infinitival construction (PIC), in which the subject surfaces in the Accusative form regardless of the presence of agreement inflection. This means that infinitival complements of perception and causative verbs are a highly complex domain of variability raising interesting learnability issues, particularly in a context of language contact.

Taking the co-existence of these different structures as a starting point, the present study aims to determine, on the basis of experimental data, which structures are preferred by native speakers and how the presence/absence of agreement in the infinitival form is correlated with the Case of the complement's subject. The distribution of these constructions in native EP will be assessed not only by looking at the performance of native speakers raised in a monolingual context, but also of bilingual speakers, who acquired Portuguese as heritage language (HL) in a migration context, so-called heritage speakers (HSs). This allows us to evaluate if the context of native language acquisition, i.e. as primary language in a predominant monolingual context or as primary language in co-existence with another, more dominant environmental language, constrains the speakers' knowledge of the target structures.

The role of the context (and the resulting particular input conditions) in native language acquisition has been standing in the middle of theoretical debates for some time. Numerous authors argue that mature heritage grammars diverge qualitatively from mature monolingually acquired grammars because the process of HL acquisition is constrained by limited input and by the dominant presence of the majority language (see Benmamoun, Montrul & Polinsky 2013). According to the *incomplete acquisition hypothesis*, proposed by Montrul (2008), the development of a HL under reduced input conditions may result in incomplete grammars, which often resemble late acquired L2 knowledge (see also Montrul 2016). As influential as this proposal might be, it is also very challenging for formal perspectives on language acquisition, since it assumes that individuals exposed to a language since birth and growing up with uninterrupted naturalistic, even though reduced, exposure to this language may still not develop native knowledge. The construct of *incomplete acquisition* has been criticized in recent years (Guijarro-Fuentes & Schmitz 2015; Meisel 2013; Pascual y Cabo & Rothman 2012; Pires & Rothman 2009; Putnam & Sánchez 2013) and there has been an attempt to replace the label of incompleteness by less evaluative terms (see references in Kupisch & Rothman 2016). One major point of discussion, which we want to take up in the present work, is the debate on the nativeness of HSs' language competence (Rothman & Treffers-Daller 2014). Studies on HL development have consistently shown that HSs tend to differ from monolinguals in various domains of linguistic knowledge, from phonetics (Rao & Ronquest 2015) to morpho-syntax (Flores 2015). A closer look at these studies, particularly those focusing on morpho-syntactic properties, reveals, however, that HS groups usually amplify a linguistic behavior also observed in monolingual groups (Rinke & Flores 2014). An important (though not the only one) causal factor that explains differential and variable outcomes in HSs' test performances is general inaccessibility to different language registers (particularly more formal registers), to different language modes (written sources) and to formal instruction (Kupisch & Rothman 2016) in the HL.

Previous work on EP as HL has shown that second generation speakers from Portuguese communities in Germany tend to develop very stable knowledge of their HL, which is explained by their continuous, daily contact with the HL (Flores 2015). However, it has also been shown that some properties are acquired with delay when compared with monolingual peers, in particular late linguistic properties like clitic placement (Flores & Barbosa 2014) or the subjunctive (Flores, Santos, Jesus & Marques 2017). What is important to highlight in these cases is that the observed delay displays the developmental patterns described for L1 native acquisition, i.e. adolescent or adult HSs may show features of linguistic behavior consistent with an earlier developmental stage of L1 acquisition.

In this paper, we intend to evaluate the 'nativeness' of EP HSs' knowledge of the different types of infinitival complements of perception and causative verbs. In particular, we will show that heritage bilinguals develop native knowledge of these structures but retain features that are characteristic of early stages of the process of acquisition of EP by monolingual children, which seem not to be totally overcome. In this sense, we reject the idea of a non-native development of heritage grammars.

2 Infinitival complements of causative and perception verbs in European Portuguese

In EP, causative and perception verbs may select at least three different types of clausal complements: a finite clause (cf. (1)), an inflected infinitival clause (cf. (2)) and an uninflected infinitival complement (cf.(3)):

(1) a. O   pai   {mandou/deixou} que os   filhos   saíssem   do
      the father ordered/allowed that the kids   leave.SUBJ of.the
      quarto.
      room
      'The father {ordered/allowed} the kids to leave the room.'
    b. Eu {vi/senti/ouvi} que as   crianças saíam   do   quarto.
      I   saw/felt/heard   that the kids   left.IMP   of.the room
      'I {saw/felt/heard} the kids were leaving the room.'

(2) a. O   pai   {mandou/deixou} as   crianças falarem
      the father ordered/allowed the kids   to.talk.INF.3PL
      com a   professora.
      with the teacher
      'The father {ordered/allowed} the kids to talk to the teacher.'
    b. Eu {vi/senti/ouvi} as   crianças falarem   com a
      I   saw/felt/heard   the kids   to.talk.INF.3PL with the
      professora.
      teacher
      'I {saw/felt/heard} the kids talk to the teacher.'

(3) a. O   pai   {mandou/deixou} as   crianças falar   com a
      the father ordered/allowed the kids   talk.INF   with the
      professora.
      teacher
      'The father ordered/allowed the kids to talk to the teacher'

b. Ele   {viu/sentiu/ouviu}   as   crianças falar   com   a
   he   saw/felt/heard   the kids   talk.INF   with the
   professora.
   teacher
   'The father {saw/felt/heard} the kids talk to the teacher'

In this paper, we focus on constructions that take infinitival complements (as illustrated in (2) and (3)). These differ from each other with respect to verbal inflection: while (2a,b) contain agreement morphology on the infinitive, (3a,b) feature non-agreeing infinitives. The presence *versus* absence of agreement morphology on the infinitive has potential consequences for the syntax of these complements, particularly regarding the Case of the notional subject of the infinitival clause. According to Raposo (1987) and Gonçalves (1999), there is a one way relation between inflection and Case: an inflected infinitival complement takes a Nominative subject (cf. (4a)) and an uninflected infinitive takes an Accusative subject (cf. (4b)).

(4) a. O   pai   {mandou/deixou} [**elas** falarem   com   a
       the father   ordered/allowed   [they   speak.INF.3Pl   with   the
       professora].
       teacher]
       'The father {ordered-them/allowed-them} talking to the teacher.'
   b. Eu {vi/senti/ouvi}   [**elas** falarem   com   a   professora].
       I   saw/felt/heard   they   to.talk.INF.3PL   with the   teacher
       'I {saw-them/felt-them/heard-them} talk to the teacher.'

(5) a. O pai   {mandou-**os**/deixou-**as**}   falar   com   a
       the father   ordered-them/allowed-them   speak.INF   with the
       professora.
       teacher
       'The father {ordered-them/allowed-them} to speak with the teacher.'
   b. Ele {viu-**as**/sentiu-**as**/ouviu-**as**}   falar   com   a   professora.
       he   saw-them/felt-them/heard-them   talk.INF   with the   teacher
       'He saw/felt/heard them talk to the teacher.'

Raposo (1987) and Gonçalves (1999) propose that, when agreement inflection is present, Nominative case is available for the subject clause internally. Assuming that Nominative Case is connected to phi-agreement (rather than Finiteness), the subject of the infinitive is assigned Case by [-FIN] AGR (Raposo 1987). When agreement inflection is absent, the subject surfaces in the Accusative form (cf. (5)). Since Accusative pronouns are clitics in EP, the Accusative pronoun appears attached to the matrix verb. Sentences (5a,b) are analysed as instances of Exceptional Case Marking or, more recently, raising to object (Barbosa & Raposo 2013): given that the subject of the embedded infinitive cannot be assigned Case within the embedded clause, it raises to the matrix where it gets Case from the matrix verb.

This account works pretty well for the paradigm above, but fails when an additional observation is brought into the picture, namely that it is not uncommon to find examples with an inflected infinitive and an Accusative Case marked subject:

(6) Ela viu-os correrem.
     she saw-them run.INF.3Pl
     'She saw them run.'

Sentence (6) is not ungrammatical in EP, a fact that is unexpected under Case theory: since agreement inflection is present, Nominative Case is available, so raising to object should be a superfluous step in the derivation. Sentence (6) should be out in violation of Economy (Chomsky 1995), contrary to fact. Since, to date, these data have not been checked against a reasonable number of native speaker intuitions, our experimental tasks are designed so as to determine the preference patterns found not only in bilingual subjects, but also in monolinguals. The monolingual data will constitute the baseline for assessing the behavior of HSs.

One intriguing fact regarding such examples is that not all persons of the paradigm behave alike. Thus, (7a,b) below, with a first person plural subject and a second person singular subject appear to be more degraded than (6):

(7) a. ??Ela viu-nos corrermos.
          she saw-us   run.INFL.1PL
     b. ??Ela viu-te   correres.
          She saw-you   run.INFL.2SG

Hornstein, Martins and Nunes (2008) offer a formal account of these facts, but, to our knowledge, these data have never been the focus of empirical enquiry. In this study, our experimental tasks are designed so as to elicit data belonging to the different persons of the paradigm, and thus shed light on this puzzling asymmetry. Moreover, our experimental study is intended to clarify the status of examples such as (6–7).

The sentences discussed above containing an uninflected complement and an Accusative subject should be distinguished from superficially similar constructions involving complex predicate formation. Consider example (8):

(8) a. Eu {mandei/deixei} ler   o livro   às crianças.
         I   ordered/allowed read.INF the book   to.the children
         'I {ordered/allowed} the children to read the book.'
     b. Eu mandei-**lhes**   ler   o   livro. [*lhes = as crianças*]
         I   ordered-3PL.Dat read.INF   the   book
         'I ordered them to read the book.'

In (8), the subject surfaces in the Dative form, an NP introduced by the preposition *a* in (8a), or a Dative pronoun in (8b). As extensively argued in Gonçalves (1999), (8) is best analysed as a single clause headed by a complex predicate formed by the finite verb *mandei* ('ordered') and the infinitival form *ler* ('read'). Jointly the complex predicate assigns Dative case to the agent of *ler* 'read'.

One important point to make regarding this kind of clause union is that Dative case is assigned to the causee only when the embedded verb is transitive. If the embedded verb is intransitive, the Case assigned is Accusative:

(9) a. Eu [mandei sair]   as crianças.   *Clause Union*
         I   ordered leave.INF   the kids
     b. Eu [mandei-as sair].
         I   ordered-them leave.INF

(9b) is the pronominal counterpart to (9a). Note that, when the embedded verb is intransitive and the causee is a pronoun, the outcome of clause union is indistinguishable from the output of raising to object. (10a) below contains the representation of a raising to object construction with an intransitive verb. (10b) contains the pronominal counterpart to (10a), which is homophonouns with (9b):

(10) a. Eu mandei [as crianças]$_i$ [t_i sair].   *Raising to Object*
          I   ordered the kids   leave.INF
      b. Eu mandei-as$_i$ [t_i sair].
          I   ordered-them   leave.INF

What distinguishes the representations in (10) from those in (9) is their biclausal character: whereas (10a,b) are biclausal, (9a,b) are monoclausal constructions. Here we will not discuss the monoclausal construction any further, since all experimental items of our tasks are biclausal.

Perception verbs allow yet another type of infinitival construction, known as the Prepositional Infinitive Construction (PIC):

(11) a. Eu vi as crianças a falarem com a professora.
      I saw the kids at talk.INF.3PL with the teacher
   b. Eu vi as crianças a falar com a professora.
      I saw the kids at talk.INF with the teacher
      'I saw the kids talking to the teacher.'

In (11) the embedded infinitive is introduced by the preposition *a*. The infinitive may be inflected (11a) or uninflected (11b). Two key aspects characterize the PIC and distinguish it from bare infinitival complements. The first aspect concerns the aspectual properties of the PIC as opposed to the bare infinitive. The infinitival complement in (11) has a progressive interpretation that is very similar to that of the English gerund (as attested in the glosses). In order to better understand the difference in meaning between the PIC and bare infinitival complements, let us consider the following minimal pair:

(12) a. O Carlos viu o pássaro a morrer, mas conseguiu
      the Carlos saw the bird at die.INF, but managed.3SG
      salvá-lo.
      save.INF-it
      'Carlos saw the bird dying, but managed to save him.'
   b. # O Carlos viu o pássaro morrer, mas conseguiu
      the Carlos saw the bird die.INF, but managed.3SG
      salvá-lo.
      save.INF-it
      'Carlos saw the bird die, but managed to save it.'

While (12b) sounds contradictory, (12a) doesn't. Assuming that the bare infinitival form does not alter the lexical aspect of the verb (cf. Silvano & Cunha 2016), (12b) is expected to be contradictory, since the verb 'die' is an achievement and, as such, it denotes a culmination. Therefore, the clause is incompatible with a continuation that denies that culmination. When the infinitive combines with *a*, however, the aspectual properties of the base are altered so that the situation is viewed as a process in progress, namely the process that precedes the culmination of the event. It is this phase of the process that is taken to be the object of perception in (12a) and this is why the sentence is not perceived as a contradiction.

    The second aspect that distinguishes the PIC from the bare infinitival construction concerns the Case of the subject: the subject of the PIC is invariably assigned Accusative Case regardless of whether agreement inflection is present or not:

(13) a. O   Carlos viu as   crianças a falarem   com a
        the   Carlos saw the   kids   at talk. INF.3PL with the
        professora.
        teacher
        'Carlos saw the kids talking to the teacher.'
     b. O   Carlos viu-as   a   falarem   com a   professora.
        the   Carlos saw-them   at   talk.INF.3PL with the   teacher
        'Carlos saw them talking to the teacher.'
     c. *O   Carlos viu elas a   falarem   com a   professora.
        the   Carlos saw they at talk.INF.3PL with the   teacher

(14) a. O   Carlos viu as   crianças a falar   com a   professora.
        the   Carlos saw the   kids   at talk.INF   with the   teacher
        'Carlos saw the kids talking to the teacher.'
     b. O   Carlos viu-as   a   falar   com a   professora.
        the   Carlos saw-them   at   talk.INF   with the   teacher
        'Carlos saw them talking to the teacher.'
     c. *O   Carlos viu elas   a falar   com a   professora.
        the   Carlos saw they   at talk.INF   with the   teacher

(13c) shows that the DP *as crianças* ('the children') or its pronominal counterpart is not assigned Nominative Case in spite of the presence of agreement inflection on the embedded infinitive. This contrasts with the bare infinitival construction, where Nominative Case is reported to be available in the sources cited as long as the infinitive bears agreement inflection In order to better understand this contrast between the PIC and bare infinitival complements, we turn to an examination of the internal syntax of the PIC, as originally proposed in Raposo (1989).

Raposo (1989) suggested that the PIC has the internal syntax of a small clause that is projected by the preposition. He starts by observing that the sequence [NP *a* V_{INF} ...] behaves as a constituent and then goes on to offer two arguments in favor of the small clause analysis. In the first place, the PIC has a different distribution from that of other inflected infinitival complements. In particular, the PIC may occur in contexts in which a bare inflected infinitival clause is not allowed:

(15) a. Eu quero [os   meninos a   trabalhar(em)   já].
        I   want   the   kids   at   work. INF(3PL)   now
        'I want the kids working now.'

b. *Eu quero [os meninos trabalhar(em) já].
    I want the kids work.INF(3PL) now

On the other hand, the PIC has a distribution that is very similar to that of canonical small clauses headed by an adjective or a PP. The parallelism between the PIC and canonical small clauses can be seen in the context of perception verbs or *querer* 'want'.

(16) a. Eu vi [os meninos nus].
        I saw the kids naked
        'I saw the kids naked.'
    b. Eu vi [os meninos no quarto].
        I saw the kids in.the room
        'I saw the kids in the room.'
    c. Eu vi [os meninos a nadar(em)].
        I saw the kids at swim.INF(3PL)
        'I saw the kids swimming.'   (Raposo 1989: 284)

(17) a. Eu quero [a encomenda entregue ainda hoje].
        I want the parcel delivered still today
        'I want the parcel delivered today.'
    b. Eu quero [o livro na estante].
        I want the book in.the shelf.
    c. Eu quero [os meninos a trabalhar(em) já].
        I want the kids at work.INF.(3PL) now
        'I want the kids at work now.'   (Raposo 1989: 284)

Furthermore, the PIC is not possible in the contexts in which a small clause headed by a preposition is not allowed. This is shown by the predicates *considerar* ('consider') and *supor* ('suppose'). While the former precludes a prepositional small clause, the latter doesn't. The PIC patterns with the small clause headed by a preposition.

(18) a. Eu considero [os meninos inteligentes].
        I consider the kids intelligent
    b. *Eu considero [os meninos com febre].
        I consider the kids with fever
    c. *Eu considero [os meninos a trabalhar(em)].
        I consider the kids at work.INF.(3PL)   (Raposo 1989: 285)

(19)　a.　Eu　supunha [os　meninos　com febre].
　　　　　I　　supposed the　kids　　　with fever
　　　　　'I supposed that the kids were with a fever.'
　　　b.　Eu　supunha [os　meninos　a　trabalhar(em)].
　　　　　I　　supposed the　kids　　　at　work.INF.(3PL)
　　　　　'I supposed the kids were working.'　　　　　(Raposo 1989: 285)

According to Raposo (1989), these distributional facts argue in favor of the idea that the PIC is a small clause headed by a preposition. In addition, Raposo observes that there is a parallelism between the PIC and control structures such as (20).

(20)　Eu　obriguei　[os meninos]　[a　[*pro/PRO* ler(em)　　　esse livro]].
　　　I　　forced　　the kids　　　to　*pro/PRO* read.INF.(3PL) that book
　　　'I forced the kids to read this book.'　　　　　(Raposo 1989: 286)

Even though the embedded clause bears inflection in (20), the (null) embedded subject cannot have independent reference and must be controlled by the object of *obrigar* ('force'). The author proposes that the relation established between the notional subject of the PIC (NP in the structure NP *a* V_{INF}) and the infinitival complement is similar to the relation established between the matrix object and the infinitival complement in control structures. The infinitival complement of the PIC is a clause with a null subject which is controlled by the lexical subject of the small clause headed by the preposition. Assuming this theory, Raposo (1989) proposes the following structure for the PIC containing agreement inflection:

(21)　DP [$_{PP}$ *a* [$_{IP}$ *pro* Infl$_{[+AGR]}$ VP]]

In (21) the controlled null subject is *pro*, which is assigned Case by Infl$_{[+AGR]}$. When the infinitive is not inflected, the controlled null subject is PRO (Raposo assumes that, in this case, the complement of P is CP).

(22)　DP [$_{SP}$ *a* [$_{CP}$[$_{IP}$ *PRO* Infl$_{[-AGR]}$ VP]]]　　　(Raposo 1989 *apud* Cochofel 2003)

The parallelism between the PIC and small clauses can be extended to the domain of Case. Whenever a small clause occurs as complement of V, its subject is assigned Accusative Case from V:

(23)　Eu vi-os　　nús　／　com fome.
　　　I　saw-them naked　／　with hunger

Sentence (23) is analysed as in (24), a raising to object configuration:

(24) Eu vi-os$_i$ [t_i nús] / [t_i com fome].

In a similar fashion, the subject of the PIC is assigned Case by the matrix verb whenever the PIC occupies the object position, as is the case with perception verbs. Thus, (25a) is analysed as in (25b) and (26a) is analysed as in (26b):

(25) a. Eu vi-os   a trabalhar.
         I saw-them   at work.INF
         'I saw them working.'
      b. Eu vi-os$_i$ [t_i [$_{PP}$ a [$_{CP}$ PRO trabalhar]]].   (Raposo 1989: 287)

      Accusative

(26) a. Eu vi-os   a trabalharem.
         I saw-them   at work.INF.(3PL)
         'I saw them working.'
      b. Eu vi-os$_i$ [t_i [$_{PP}$ a [$_{CP}$ *pro* trabalharem]]].   (Raposo 1989: 287)

      Accusative   Nominative

Since the subject of the small clause is outside the embedded IP projection and the PP projection stands in the way between it and embedded Infl, it invariably gets its Case from a source that is external to IP, namely matrix V. Under this analysis, when the infinitive is inflected, *pro* is the element that gets Nominative Case from Infl. Thus, whenever the PIC is the complement of a perception verb, the Case of the lexical DP will be Accusative regardless of whether infinitival T is inflected or not.

When the PIC is not selected, the subject is assigned default Case, which is Nominative in EP. Example (26a) shows a small clause in absolute position, where Nominative Case is assigned by *default*. (26b) indicates that the PIC patterns in a similar way, i.e. the subject also surfaces as Nominative:

(26) a. Eles nús?   Nem pensar!
         they naked?   not   think.INF
         'Them naked? No way!'
      b. Eles a fumar(em)?   Nem pensar!
         they at smoke.INF.(3PL)? not think.INF
         'Them smoking? No way!'

Raposo's analysis of the PIC offers an elegant way of accounting for the Case patterns in the PIC and was further corroborated by data discussed in Barbosa and Cochofel (2005), so we will adopt it here (see Duarte 1992 for a different analysis). To conclude, the PIC is a small clause headed by P, which selects a clausal infinitival complement. It is a proleptic structure in the sense that the subject of the small clause controls a null subject (*PRO* or *pro*, depending on the presence of agreement inflection) contained in the clausal projection that is selected by P.

According to Raposo (1989), the difference regarding Case assignment between the PIC and bare infinitival complements of perception verbs is that, in the latter case, inflected and non-inflected infinitives are predicted to pattern differently. When nonfinite Infl bears agreement inflection, Nominative Case should be automatically available for the subject clause internally (the subject is in Spec-IP, wherefrom it is governed by Infl $_{[Agr]}$),

(27) $V_{CAUS/PER}$ [$_{IP}$ DP Infl$_{[+AGR]}$ VP]
                   Noninative

For this reason, the subject is predicted to surface in the Nominative Case in agreeing infinitives (economy considerations should bar the superfluous operation of raising to object). In the absence of agreement inflection, the only source for Case is matrix V, so raising to object must apply and the subject is predicted to surface in the Accusative Case.

(28) $V_{CAUS/PER}$ DP$_i$ [$_{IP}$ t_i Infl$_{[-AGR]}$ VP]
                  Accusative

In the PIC, by contrast, the source of Case is invariably matrix V, as outlined above.

Table 1 summarizes the different patterns predicted to occur under Raposo's (1989) analysis.

As mentioned above, there is one other pattern that is not predicted by Raposo's analysis and yet is attested in naturally occurring data, namely the (apparently uneconomical) derivation in which an Accusative Case-marked subject combines with a bare infinitive bearing agreement morphology (cf. (6)). Recall that the degree of acceptability of such examples appears to depend on the feature Person on the agreeing infinitive: 3rd person appears to yield better results than 1st or 2nd.

Table 1: Overview of the structures predicted under Raposo (1989).

Structure	Inflection	Expected Case
Infinitival complements of causative/perception verbs	+AGR	NOMINATIVE
	-AGR	ACCUSATIVE
PIC (only with perception verbs)	+AGR	ACCUSATIVE
	-AGR	ACCUSATIVE

3 The present study

Research questions

Based on the above description of infinitival complements, our research questions are two-fold. Our first question concerns the preferences of EP monolingual speakers regarding the acceptance and the production of different types of infinitival complements of perception and causative verbs. Although these structures have been thoroughly discussed from a formal perspective, as shown in the previous section, empirical evidence of EP native speakers' preferences is still lacking. We are interested in knowing which option – inflected infinitival complement *versus* uninflected infinitival complement – is more productive in native EP and how each option correlates with Case morphology on the subject of the infinitive (Nominative or Accusative).

From the perspective of standard Case theory, a very clear prediction is made concerning bare infinitival complements, namely that an Accusative Case marked subject should show up just in case agreement inflection is absent. In the presence of agreement, the expected form is Nominative, all other things being equal. The experimental tasks are designed so as to evaluate whether speakers in fact show the preferences predicted.

Our second question concerns the HSs of EP living in Germany. First, these speakers have had much less exposure to EP than monolingual speakers raised in Portugal and, second, they have had very limited formal instruction in EP and almost no contact with written sources and formal registers. Our goal is, therefore, to determine whether these speakers develop a knowledge of the target structures that is similar to that of monolinguals, despite unequal input conditions and coexistence with the dominant German language.

Similarly to EP, German perception and causative verbs take infinitival complements (see (29)). However, German differs from EP in several ways: (i) standard

German does not have clitic pronouns; (ii) it does not have inflected infinitives and, importantly, (iii) the subject pronoun always bears Accusative case, a structure traditionally known as 'accusative cum infinitivo' (ACI) (Felser 2000).

(29) a. Ich sah den Mann   / ihn   ins   Haus   hineingehen.
          I   saw the man.ACC/ him.ACC into.the   house   go.INF
          'I saw the man / him entering the house.'
      b. Der Vater ließ   seine Kinder   / sie   einen   Hamburger
          the father allowed his   kids.ACC / them.ACC   a   hamburger
          essen.
          eat.INF
          'The father allowed his kids/them to eat a hamburger.'

Consequently, if HSs of EP develop a divergent non-native grammar, for reasons of reduced input and cross-linguistic influence, they will not show the same preferences as the monolingual speakers.

Participants

A total of 60 adult informants participated in the present study: 30 native speakers of EP raised in a monolingual context, and 30 HSs of EP, raised in a bilingual context with EP as home language and German as dominant environmental language.

The monolingual group includes 30 university students in the age span of 18 to 36 years (mean age = 20.0; SD = 3.8). No informant of this group was raised bilingually or lived abroad for an extended period of time.

The HSs of EP are second generation immigrants in the age span of 14 and 47 years (mean age = 26.3; DP = 10.6), who live in Germany since birth or early childhood. They completed a detailed questionnaire, focused on sociolinguistic and biographical information such as age of migration, place of birth, amount of formal instruction in Portuguese, language habits, amount and type of contact with EP, knowledge of other languages, the parents' migration background. The age span of the experimental group is larger than that of the monolinguals, but all speakers share the fact that they were exposed to Portuguese since birth and speak that language frequently in their daily routines.

Twenty one speakers were born in Germany, the other participants were born in Portugal and immigrated to Germany with their families until the age of five years. All speakers have frequent contact with their heritage language; however, exposure to Portuguese is mainly restricted to oral input – no informant reports reading literature or newspapers in Portuguese. The only contact the bilingual HSs have or had with the written register occurred in the special program of instruction for child HSs, where Lusophone children become literate in Portuguese and are also taught some Portuguese History and Geography. Only one participant never attended these classes; nine are still enrolled. The others have attended a HL program for two to ten years but were no longer in school age at the time of data collection. In the self-assessment test, all participants rated their proficiency in German higher than in Portuguese, particularly the writing skills. This is in line with their statement to be German-dominant and to feel much more comfortable in speaking German than their HL.

Method

Data collection

Data collection consisted of a written biographic questionnaire, followed by the experimental tasks: a written Completion Task (CT) and an Acceptability Judgment Task (AJT). The monolingual controls' data were collected in a classroom at the University of Minho. The bilingual HSs were tested in different places in their area of residence in Germany: at their homes, in the headquarters of a cultural association or in a school. The untimed tasks were conducted as paper and pencil tests and took approximately 30 minutes to complete.

Experimental tasks

Two experimental tasks were applied, a CT and an AJT. The test conditions of both tasks result from the combination of the following variables:

i.   3 linguistic structures: sentences with the inflected infinitive, sentences with the simple infinitive (without agreement) and PIC structures (with and without verbal agreement features);
ii. Nominative *versus* Accusative Case marked pronouns as subjects of the infinitive;
iii. Grammatical person: 2P Sgl, 1P Pl, 3P Pl;
iv. Verbs: 3 perception verbs (*ver* 'to see', *ouvir* 'to hear', *sentir* 'to feel'); 2 causative verbs (*mandar* 'to order', *deixar* 'to let'), 3 control verbs (*convencer* 'to persuade', *aconselhar* 'to advise', *obrigar* 'to order').

Completion task

The CT task consists of four short narratives with 28 gaps: the 23 experimental items distributed according to the conditions shown in Table 2 (conditions I to VIII) and five additional distractor items (corresponding to missing articles). The test was preceded by a training exercise. An example of one short story is given in the appendix.

Table 2: Test conditions for the completion task with one example per condition.

Condition	Verbs	N° of items
I Perception verb without agreement	*ver, ouvir, sentir*	3
O pai viu eles / -os brincar àquela hora. the father saw they / them play.INF at.that hour		
II Perception verb with agreement	*ver, ouvir, sentir*	3
Eu vi tu / -te brincares ontem. I saw you.NOM / you.ACC play.INF.2SG yesterday		
III Causative verb without agreement	*mandar, deixar*	3
O professor deixou nós/-nos voltar ao ensaio. the teacher let we / us return.INF to.the rehearsal		
IV Causative verb with agreement	*mandar, deixar*	3
O patrão mandou nós / -nos irmos ao seu gabinete. the boss ordered we / us go.INF.1PL to.the his office		
V PIC without agreement	*ver, ouvir, sentir*	3
A professora viu tu / -te a conversar também. the teacher saw 2.SG.NOM./ 2.SG.ACC at talk.INF too		
VI PIC with agreement	*ver, ouvir, sentir*	3
A professora ouviu nós / -nos falarmos muito hoje. the teacher heard we / -us talk.INF.1PL a.lot today		
VII Control verb without agreement	*aconselhar, obrigar*	3
Eu aconselho tu / -te a treinar muito, a ti e a mim, para sermos tão bons como eles. I advise 2.SG.NOM./ -2.SG.ACC to train.INF a lot, you and me, to be as good as they		
VIII Control verb with agreement	*Convencer*	2
Um colega chamou por eles e convenceu eles / -os a voltarem ao a colleague called for them and persuaded they / -them to return.INF.3PL to.the ensaio. rehearsal		

Acceptability judgment task

The AJT consisted of 39 sentences, 36 sentences distributed between the conditions 1 to 8, listed in Table 3 below (6 sentences per condition 1 to 4; 3 sentences per condition 5 to 8). Conditions 8 and 9, with control verbs, were included as control items. All sentences included in this test were taken from the previous CT. Participants were asked to make a binary choice, judging the sentences either as 'sounding bad' or 'sounding fine'. An additional correction of all sentences judged as 'bad' was required.

Table 3: Test conditions for the AJT with one example per condition.

Condition	N° of items
1 Accusative pronoun without agreement	6
O pai viu-os brincar àquela hora. the father saw-them play.INF at.that hour	
2 Accusative pronoun with agreement	6
Eu vi-te brincares ontem. I saw-2SG.ACC play.INF.2SG yesterday '	
3 Nominative pronoun without agreement	6
O pai viu eles brincar àquela hora. the father saw they play.INF at.that hour	
4 Nominative pronoun with agreement	6
Eu vi tu brincares ontem. I saw 2SG.NOM play.INF.2SG yesterday	
5 PIC + Accusative pronoun without agreement	3
A professora viu-te a conversar. the teacher saw-2SG.ACC at talk.INF	
6 PIC + Nominative pronoun without agreement	3
A professora viu tu a conversar. the teacher saw 2SG.NOM at talk.INF	
7 PIC + Accusative pronoun with agreement	3
A professora viu-te a conversares. the teacher saw 2SG.ACC at talk.INF.2SG	

(continued)

Table 3: (continued)

Condition	N° of items
8 PIC + Nominative pronoun with agreement	3

A professora viu tu   a   conversares.
the teacher saw 2SG.NOM at   talk.INF.2SG

Condition	N° of items
9 Control verb without agreement	2

O   pai   obrigou tu   / -te   a dar-me   um abraço
the father forced   2SG.NOM / 2SG.ACC to give.INF-me a   hug

Condition	N° of items
10 Control verb with agreement	1

O   pai   obrigou tu   / -te   a dares-me   um abraço
the father forced   2SG.NOM / 2SG.ACC to give.INF.2SG-me a   hug

For codification, only the sentences judged as 'bad' with a correction targeting the tested structure were effectively counted as 'bad'. When the correction focused on other properties or on the content of the sentence, the answer was coded as 'sounds good'.

4 Results

In the following sections we will present the comparative results for each task. Statistics was performed in SPSS, version 21.0. Since the data are not normally distributed, non-parametric tests for inter-group comparisons were applied.

Completion task

As described above, in the CT the participants were instructed to always fill the blanks, so that null subjects were not an option. Since the rate of unfilled blankets was marginal, they were not considered for quantification. For reasons of simplification, we will present the results by indicating always the rate of **Accusative** selection (as opposed to Nominative). Figure 1 shows the mean rate of Accusative pronouns per condition for both groups, monolingual and bilingual speakers.

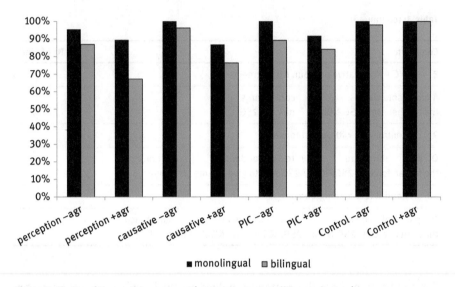

Figure 1: Choice of Accusative pronouns (mean rate per condition and group).

As shown in Figure 1, overall both groups demonstrate an evident preference for the use of the Accusative clitic instead of a Nominative pronoun in all conditions, but this preference is stronger in the monolingual group. Looking at the conditions in detail, the results show that in the sub-conditions with perception and causative verbs without agreement, i.e. in uninflected infinitival complements (conditions I and III) the values of both groups are very similar. In condition I (perceptual verb without agreement) the monolinguals select an Accusative pronoun in 95.5% (SD = 7.9) and the bilinguals in 86.9% (SD = 13.5) of all contexts. In condition III (causative verb without agreement) the rate is even higher with 100% Accusative Case in the monolingual group and 96.2% (SD = 0.2) in the bilingual group. Two Mann-Whitney tests indicate that inter-group differences are not statistically significant neither in condition I ($U = 334.500$; $p = .051$) nor in condition III ($U = 420.500$; $p = .154$). This means that, as expected, raising-to-object constructions are clearly favoured by EP speakers, both monolinguals and bilinguals, in these contexts.

In the constructions with perception and causative verbs with agreement, i.e. with inflected infinitives (conditions II and IV), the values of the two groups are more apart. Interestingly, the monolingual speakers still have a preference for the Accusative subject pronoun in 89.4% of all sentences (SD = 4.7) with perception verbs, while the bilingual group presents only a mean rate of 67.2% (SD = 8.5). A Mann-Whitney test confirms that this difference is statistically significant (U = 244.000; p = .003). This means that in the presence of agreement features the bilingual HSs select the Nominative case more often than their monolingual counterparts. With causative verbs the between-group difference is less evident (monolinguals: 86.8%, SD = 3.5; bilinguals: 76.4%, SD = 9.3). A Mann-Whitney test confirms that this difference is not statistically significant (U = 351.000; p = .172). What is interesting to bear in mind is that, overall (and rather unexpectedly), also in infinitival complements with inflected infinitives the speakers of EP show a preference for raising-to-object structures.

Concerning the PIC conditions (V and VI), also in this case both groups use high rates of Accusative pronouns. Again, however, this rate is lower in the bilingual group than in the monolingual group. In condition V (PIC without agreement) the monolinguals always selected the Accusative clitic (100%), while the bilingual HSs use Accusative clitics in 89.2% (SD = 3.4) of the contexts. In condition VI (PIC with agreement), clitic pronouns are selected in 91.7% (SD = 5.6) of all contexts by monolingual EP speakers and in 84.1% (SD = 7.2) of the contexts by heritage bilinguals. In both conditions, this difference is statistically significant (V: U = 345.00, p = .017; VI: U = 321.00, p = .04).

The conditions with control verbs (VII and VIII) function as control items, since in this case it is only possible to use Accusative pronouns. Indeed, as expected, the monolingual controls use exclusively Accusative pronouns in both conditions with control verbs (with and without agreement). Also the bilingual group selects almost exclusively Accusative clitics, with 100% in condition VIII and 98.0% (SD = 3.4) in conditions VII. A Mann-Whitney test shows that the slight difference in conditions VII is not significant (U = 390.000, p = .292).

Along with inter-group comparisons, also intra-group analyses were run in order to assess the statistical differences between the different conditions within the two groups. For this purpose, the conditions with and without inflection were pair-wise compared using Wilcoxon Z tests. The results show that, in the monolingual group, only the difference between the use of Accusative subjects in complements of causative verbs without (condition III) and with inflection (condition IV) was significant (Z = -2.232; p = .026). In all other conditions the rate of Accusative subjects does not differ significantly from each other. There are also no statistical differences between the verbs (causative vs. perception verbs).

As for the bilingual group, the difference between the use of Accusative subjects in complements with and without inflection is significant not also in the conditions with causative verbs (III vs. IV: Z = -2.507; p = .012), as in the monolingual group, but also in the conditions with perception verbs (I vs. II: Z = -2.139; p = .032). There are, similarly to the monolingual group, no statistical differences between perception and causative verbs.

In sum, the results of the completion task show that the performance of bilingual HSs is very similar to that of monolingual speakers concerning Case assignment to the subject pronoun in infinitival complements of perception and causative verbs. As their monolingual counterparts, they prefer Accusative clitics over Nominative pronouns, even in constructions with inflected infinitives. There are, however, differences between the groups. The most evident differences are found in inflected complements of perception verbs and in the PIC construction, particularly with inflected infinitives. In both cases, the heritage bilinguals select the Nominative case more often than their monolingual peers.

Acceptability judgment test

In the AJT, participants were asked to judge sentences from the previous task by giving a binary response ('sounds good' *versus* 'sounds bad') and by correcting the unaccepted sentences. Figure 2 shows the mean rate of accepted items per sub-condition and per group.

The results given in Figure 2 indicate that, overall, both groups show similar tendencies when judging the given sentences. Starting with condition 1, i.e. simple infinitives as complements of perception and causative verbs with an Accusative clitic as subject (raising-to-object constructions), results reveal that, in fact, this

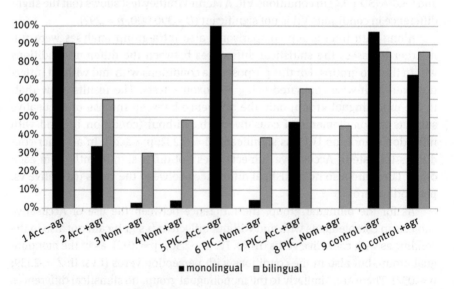

Figure 2: Mean rate of acceptance (per condition and per group).

construction is the preferred option for both speaker groups, with 88.8% acceptance in the monolingual group and 90.4% in the bilingual one. A Mann-Whitney test confirms that there are no statistically significant differences between the groups ($U = 367.500$; $p = .352$). Conversely, in condition 2 (inflected infinitive with Accusative), the rate of acceptance lowers considerably, to 33.9% in the monolingual and to 59.5% in the bilingual group. A Mann-Whitney test shows that this difference is statistically significant ($U = 239.500$, p = .004).

As for the structures with Nominative pronouns (i.e. conditions 3 and 4 with and without agreement), the results show evident differences between the groups. The monolingual speakers clearly disfavor the selection of strong Nominative pronouns in infinitival complements, with simple infinitives (2.8% of acceptance) as well as with inflected infinitives (4.1% of acceptance). In this case, all corrections consisted in using either an Accusative pronoun with a simple infinitival complement or a PIC structure with a simple infinitive. This shows, again, that these structures are clearly the most favored by EP speakers. In the bilingual group the acceptance of Nominative pronouns in these constructions is also lower than with Accusatives, but clearly higher than in the monolingual group. The bilinguals accept Nominative pronouns with simple infinitives in 30.1% of all cases (against 2.8% in the monolingual group) and in 48.3% with inflected infinitives (against 4.1% in the monolingual group).

Also conditions 6 and 8 test the speakers' intuitions with Nominative subject pronouns, in this case in PIC structures, where the use of Nominative pronouns is not grammatical in EP. Here we see the same differences between monolingual and bilingual speakers as in conditions 3 and 4. The monolinguals clearly reject Nominative case in PIC structures (4.4% and 0% of acceptance, respectively). In the correction exercise they consistently substitute the Nominative by the Accusative case. In the bilingual group the rate of acceptance is 38.7% in PIC structures with simple infinitives and 45.2% with inflected infinitives. Mann-Whitneys confirm that the inter-group differences are very significant in both conditions (5.2: $U = 168.000$, $p = .000$; 6.2: U = 150.000, $p = .000$).

The condition that, in general, is most favoured by both groups is the PIC construction with the simple infinitive and an Accusative Case marked subject (conditions 5), with 100% acceptance in the monolingual group and 84.5% of accepted sentences in the bilingual group. Still, this difference is statistically significant ($U = 315.000$, $p = .004$). Also the sentences with control verbs, with and without agreement (conditions 9 and 10), present high rates of acceptance in both groups (condition 9: 96.7% for monolinguals and 85.7% for bilinguals; condition 10: 73.3% for monolinguals and 85.7% for bilinguals). The differences between the groups are not statistically significant (7.1: $U = 356.000$, $p = .096$; $U = 368.000$, $p = .249$). Despite the high rates of acceptance in both conditions, the monolingual speakers still prefer the structures without agreement. This is a consistent observation in all conditions when the structure without agreement (simple infinitive) is compared with the structure with agreement (inflected infinitive).

Additionally, Table 4 indicates the distribution of the structures chosen in order to correct an item that was rejected. The results show very clearly that the most favoured structures in both groups are the simple infinitival complements with an Accusative subject (MON: 37.4; BIL: 46.8) and the PIC without agreement marking and an Accusative subject (MON: 46.8; BIL: 26.3), thus corroborating the results of the completion task. The corrections proposed by the speakers consisted mainly in maintaining the Accusative pronoun and removing agreement morphology or changing Case assignment from Nominative to Accusative. With perception verbs, many monolingual and bilingual participants who deleted the agreement markers also added the preposition *a*, turning the structure into a PIC construction.

Table 4: AJT Correction task: Distribution of the structures chosen for correction.

	Monolingual group	Bilingual group
Acc −agr	37.4	42.9
Acc +agr	8.1	14.1
Nom −agr	0	1.4
Nom +agr	0	5.6
PIC Acc −agr	46.8	26.3
PIC Nom −agr	0	1.1
PIC Acc +agr	7.7	7.3
PIC Nom +agr	0	1.1

Finally, we intend to take a closer look at the rejection rate of the constructions with Accusative Case-marked subjects in the presence of agreement morphology, organized by grammatical person. Table 5 presents rejection rates per grammatical person in the cases in which the participants deleted agreement morphology in the correction task. The results reveal differences related with grammatical person. In bare infinitival complements 1st person plural is the most rejected structure (monolinguals: 88%; bilinguals: 34.5%), followed by 2nd person singular (monolinguals: 62.5%; bilinguals: 31.3%). 3rd person plural is the least rejected structure (monolinguals: 45.5%; bilinguals: 24.4%). The results concerning the PIC condition show the same tendency in both groups. Monolinguals reject the combination of 1st person plural with agreement morphology in 93.3% of the cases, 2nd person singular is rejected in 44.8% of the

Table 5: Rejection rates for ACC-subject + Inflected infinitive per grammatical person.

	Monolingual group			Bilingual group		
	2nd Sg	1st Pl	3rd Pl	2nd Sg	1st Pl	3rd Pl
Acc +agr	62.5%	88.0%	45.5%	31.3%	34.5%	24.4%
PIC Acc +agr	44.8%	93.3%	20.0%	16.0%	42.3%	8.0%

cases and 3rd person plural in only 20%. In the bilingual group the rejection rate is 42.3% for 1st person plural, 16% for the 2nd person singular and only 8% for 3rd person plural.

In sum, the results of the AJT with the correction task are in line with the data obtained in the completion task. In general both speaker groups show a marked preference for structures with Accusative clitics instead of Nominative pronouns. Unaccepted sentences tend to be corrected by deleting the agreement markers and by substituting Nominative for Accusative Case. However, there are significant differences between monolingual e bilingual EP speakers regarding the structures with Nominative pronouns, either in the bare infinitive construction or in the PIC. While monolingual speakers clearly dislike the use of Nominative pronouns, with and without agreement, HSs are more prone to using Nominative pronouns, with simple infinitival complements, with inflected infinitives and even in PIC structures, which do not allow for Nominative pronouns in the target grammar. A further interesting finding is that the rates of acceptance of the combination of an ACC-subject with an inflected infinitive vary according to grammatical person. In both groups the 1st person plural is the least accepted and the 3rd person plural the most accepted structure.

5 Discussion and conclusion

We start by examining the results of the monolingual group in order to answer the first research question; then we move on to the bilinguals and to the second question.

Concerning the monolingual group, the most striking result regards the residual rates of Nominative Case marked subjects in the presence of an inflected infinitive in both tasks. This result is unexpected since, under standard assumptions, the presence of inflection should automatically entail Nominative Case assignment (Raposo 1987). Moreover, in the completion task, the monolingual speakers of EP show a preference for raising-to-object in infinitival complements with inflected infinitives. In the AJT, the rates of acceptance of an Accusative subject in the presence of agreement inflection are lower. This may be an effect of the task: AJTs are more permeable to the influence of prescriptive grammar than production tasks. Quite generally, EP prescriptive grammars tend to advise against the use of the inflected infinitive in contexts in which the presence of agreement morphology leads to redundancy. Since the structures with an inflected infinitive are perceived as more redundant than their counterparts with an uninflected infinitive, it is not surprising that they should get lower rates in the judgement task. Setting this effect aside, what defies explanation is that the choice of a Nominative subject with an inflected infinitive is indeed residual in both tasks. In principle, an inflected infinitive should automatically entail a Nominative Case marked subject. Moreover, this derivation should be less costly than a derivation with raising to object, contrary to fact.

Even though this result is unexpected under standard assumptions concerning clause structure in EP, it actually comes as no surprise when other alternatives are considered. In effect, since the mid-nineties there has been a growing body of work (Alexiadou & Anagnostopoulou 1998; Barbosa 1995; Kato 1999; Manzini & Savoia 2002; Ordoñez & Treviño 1998; Platzack 2004; Pollock 1997, among others) making the claim that, in consistent Null Subject Languages (NSLs), the head bearing subject agreement is interpretable. This insight is not just meant to capture the old intuition that rich agreement in these languages is, in some sense, "pronominal", or "affix-like" (Rizzi 1982); it was also meant to capture a number of contrasts in the distribution and interpretation of overt subjects in the consistent NSLs as opposed to the non-NSLs. The particular implementations of this proposal vary, but all of them have one key feature in common: the functional head bearing subject agreement has a nominal specification ([+D]; valued phi-features; probably also Case) to the effect that it has the status of a pronominal affix/clitic on V raised to T. As a consequence of this, there is no EPP related movement to Spec-TP, the thematic subject stays inside the post-verbal field and pre-verbal subject constructions are not derived by A-movement. Since, in the particular case of the Romance NSLs, there is v/V raising to Infl/T, when the subject is a fully specified nominal, this yields a postverbal subject construction (so-called "free inversion"). Thus, example (30a) is analysed as in (30b):

(30) a. Telefonou   a   Maria
          called   the Maria
      b. [[T telefonou] [vP a Maria ~~telefonou~~]]

When the subject is silent, there are in theory two possibilities: either pronominal Agr is the theta-role bearer, in which case *pro* can be dispensed with (Kato 1999;

Ordoñez & Treviño 1999; Platzack 2004), or there is a *pro* in Spec,*v*P/VP (Alexiadou & Anagnostopoulou 1998; Barbosa 2009). In (31b) we adopt the latter hypothesis:

(31) a. Telefonaram.
        called
        'They called.'
     b. [[$_T$ telefonar**am**] [$_{vP}$ *pro*]]

In a configuration such as (31b), the semantic content for the pronominal argument is supplied by the situational context, or it can be supplied linguistically, by a topic. Example (32a), with an apparent pre-verbal subject, is analysed as an instance of subject left dislocation (cf. (32b)).

(32) a. A   Maria telefonou.
        the Maria called
        'Maria called.'
     b. [[A Maria] [$_{TP}$ telefonou [*pro*]]

We assume that clitic left dislocated topics are *base-generated* in a position of adjunction to the clausal projection that is predicated of them and are licensed by rules of predication (Chomsky 1977). Alternatively, the configuration above can be recast in terms of a TopicP projection. Here we do not wish to dwell on this aspect of the analysis, the important point being that the DP *a Maria* is base-generated in place and licensed by predication: *pro* supplies the open position required to establish a predication relation with the topic. The reader is referred to Demirdache (1992) and Anagnostopoulou (1997) for arguments in favor of a base-generation analysis of clitic left dislocated topics. Within this framework of assumptions, *pro* gets Nominative Case from T and the Nominative Case that shows up on the left-dislocated topic is assigned by *default* (recall that Nominative is the *default* Case in EP; cf. the discussion surrounding example (26) above).

  With this analysis in mind, we now return to infinitival complements of perception and causative verbs. Under the theory just sketched, the fact that monolingual speakers avoid using a Nominative Case-marked pre-verbal subject reduces to avoiding a left-dislocation configuration[1] in which default Case is

---

1 That there are restrictions on the distribution of preverbal subject constructions in inflected infinitives can be shown also with other types of verbs, such as epistemics (Barbosa 2000; Raposo 1987).

assigned to the left dislocated DP. From this perspective, the most econominal derivation is indeed the derivation with an uninflected infinitive and raising to object. This is the option that is preferred by monolingual speakers in the AJT.

Even though monolingual speakers disprefer sentences with an inflected infinitive and an Accusative subject in the AJT task, in the production task, they do produce such sentences. Under the framework of assumptions adopted in the preceding paragraphs, a sentence with an inflected infinitive and an Accusative Case marked subject is analysed as a left dislocation construction in the sense that the DP that is raised to object is base generated in a position external to the clause (33) and is licensed by rules of predication (mediated by *pro*).

(33)   Eles viram-**nos**ᵢ [[*t*ᵢ] [TP correrem [*pro*]]
                              └──────────┘
                              Predication

Curiously (33) has a structure that is very similar to that of the PIC under Raposo's analysis (recall that the PIC also contains a null subject that is obligatorily controlled by the Accusative marked subject). And in effect there are some striking parallelisms between the two. In particular, both constructions are sensitive to grammatical person. As mentioned, all the participants show a preference for rejecting inflected infinitives with 1st person plural, followed by 2nd person singular, while 3rd person plural is the least rejected structure. This applies both in the case of the PIC and in the case of the bare infinitival construction and can actually be seen as an argument in favor of the idea that the phi-feature set on T is interpretable. Consider the following examples:

(34) a. Ela viu-os   fazerem   isso.
          she saw-them.3S do.INF.3PL that
          'She saw them doing it.'
      b. ??Ela viu-nos fazermos isso.
          she saw-us.1PL do.INF.1PL that
      c. ??Ela viu-te   fazeres isso.
          she saw-you.2S do.INF.2S that

(35) a. Ela viu-os   a fazerem isso.
          she saw-them.3S at do.INF.3PL that
      b. ??Ela viu-nos   a fazermos isso.
          she saw-us.1PL at do.INF.1PL that
      c. ??Ela viu-te   a fazeres isso.
          she saw-you.2S at do.INF.2S that

To our ear, (34a-c) and (35a-c) are comparable in status. In evaluating these examples, one gets a sense of redundancy, which is sharper in the case of first and second persons. We assume that first and second person pronouns are specified for a [+Part(icipant)] feature and a Number feature ([±Pl(ural)] whereas third person pronouns are specified as [-Part; ±Pl]. When the infinitive is inflected, a similar feature specification is assigned to the interpretable [+D] set of phi-features in T (<+D i:phi>). Since both the pronoun and <+D i:phi> are interpretable, the structure is perceived as redundant (in comparison with its counterpart with an uninflected infinitive) particularly when the set of phi-features on T has the same feature specification as the set of phi-features on the pronoun. This is the case of first and second person. In the case of third person, however, the two feature sets are not the same: the pronoun has a gender feature that is absent from verbal inflection. For this reason, the sense of redundancy is less sharp.

In sum, since, on our view, preverbal subject constructions are not instances of EPP related movement to Spec-TP, the observed preference for avoiding a Nominative subject in the presence of an inflected infinitive is no longer problematic. It reduces to preference for the operation of raising to object over the last resort operation of *default* (Nominative) Case assignment. This preference can be viewed as an instance of the Paninian principle *Blocking,* whereby a general, default form is blocked by the existence of a more specific rival form. In this case, the default (Nominative) Case option is blocked by the more specific operation of raising to object.

Now we turn to the bilingual group. The first aspect to note is that inflected infinitives are without doubt part of EP heritage grammars. This has already been shown by Pires and Rothman (2009), who identified significant differences between HSs of EP and Brazilian Portuguese (BP) regarding knowledge of this structures. This discrepancy is explained by the fact that, in contrast to BP, inflected infinitives are very frequent in colloquial EP. The same observation holds also for the particular case of inflected infinitives in complements of perception or causative verbs and in the PIC, the structures under investigation.

A second important observation is that the HS group also displays a clear preference for Accusative Case marked subjects, so the HSs do not differ from monolinguals in this regard. This is robust indication of shared native knowledge in this domain, a fact that supports the claim that early, continuous exposure to EP, even under reduced input conditions, ensures the development of a native grammar that bears properties in common with the system acquired in a monolingual context. *A priori*, this contradicts the idea of incomplete HL acquisition.

However, the results also show differences between monolingual and bilingual speakers. A first difference is related with an overall higher rate of acceptance of agreement inflection by the bilingual group, particularly in infinitival

complements with Accusative subjects. As discussed above, the low rates of acceptance of inflected infinitives by the monolingual speakers can be explained with the
activation of prescriptive knowledge in acceptability judgment tasks, especially in
educated speakers as the ones we tested. Heritage speakers, in contrast, do not
possess the same knowledge of prescriptive grammar as their monolingual counterparts due to reduced contact with formal language registers and with formal
instruction. The absence of prolonged formal schooling is a strong predictor of performance differences between monolingual and bilingual groups in test situations
(Kupisch & Rothman 2016), which we believe may explain part of our results.

The most significant and most striking difference between monolinguals and
bilinguals concerns a higher rate of acceptance of Nominative pronouns by HSs,
with simple infinitives, with inflected infinitives and even in PIC constructions. In
our perspective, this means that HSs are more prone to using a configuration in
which *default* Case is assigned (recall that Nominative is the default Case in EP).

Interestingly, there is evidence that the *default* (Nominative) Case strategy is
an option at early stages of the acquisition of these constructions by monolingual
children. Santos, Gonçalves and Hyams (2016), who study the acquisition of sentential complementation under causative, perception, and object control verbs in
EP, report a tendency of their child groups to use Nominative subjects (36b) in PIC
structures instead of the Accusative form (36a).

(36) a. (A zebra) viu-os a dançar. (4;08,09)
          the zebra saw them.ACC ASP dance.INF
          'The zebra saw them dancing.'
      b. (A zebra) viu eles a dançar. (4;05,12)
          the zebra saw they ASP dance.INF
          'The zebra saw them dancing.' (Santos, Gonçalves & Hyams 2016: 220)

The authors relate the use of the Nominative form in (36b) to the occurrence,
in the target grammar, of Nominative subjects when the PIC is used in root
environments:

(37) (Olha!) Os meninos / Eles a nadar(em)
      (look!) the children they ASP swim.INF(.3PL)
      '(Look!) The children are swimming.' (Santos, Gonçalves & Hyams 2016: 210)

In (37), there is no external source for Case and the subject of the PIC is assigned
Nominative by *default*. The authors suggest that the same strategy applies in the
case of (36b): the reason why children allow a Nominative Case marked subject
in the PIC is that they allow for *default* Case assignment in this context. In the

target grammar, in the PIC, Nominative is available just in case an external Case assigner is not present, namely in root environments. When an external Case assigner is present, as in the contexts in which the PIC is selected by a perception verb, raising to object obtains and the *default* Case option is blocked. Thus, knowing the conditions under which the *default* Case option is blocked is part of the process of acquiring the PIC in EP.

Returning to the HSs, we observe that they moderately accept Nominative pronouns in infinitival complements of perception and causative verbs (regardless of the presence of inflection). In our perspective, this means that, on a par with the predominant raising to object option, these speakers allow for the *default* Case strategy. In other words, occasionally they fail to apply blocking, just like monolingual children. Hence, even though the mental grammar of HSs is not very distinct from that of monolinguals in this domain, it crucially retains features that are characteristic of a particular stage in the acquisition of the PIC in EP. This reinforces the view that the process of acquisition of the HL is native-like in the sense that it goes through the same stages as the process of monolingual acquisition; however, HSs seem to maintain an option that is no longer available in mature grammars,[2] revealing protracted development.

In our view, this outcome cannot be described as incomplete, non-native competence, but as native competence that has not stabilized knowledge of the conditions under which the *default* Case option is blocked. In this sense, we support claims in favor of nativeness of HL grammars such as those defended by Rothman and Treffers-Daller (2014). Variation observed in HSs is, by hypothesis, due to reduced exposure to the target language. Note in this context that the divergent behavior of the HSs cannot be attributed to cross-linguistic influence from the environmental language, since German does not allow for Nominative Case marked subjects in these complements (it rather has raising-to-object). Instead, an intra-linguistic explanation should be favoured.

Acknowledgments: We thank Daniela Neves for help in data collection, as well as the Portuguese community in Frankfurt area. This work was developed within the project Portuguese as Heritage Language and language change (Grant EXPL/MHC-LIN/0763/2013), funded by Fundação para a Ciência e Tecnologia.

---

2 At least in the monolingual speakers tested in the present study, this stage is overcome. However, it cannot be ruled out that also monolinguals sometimes use Nominative subjects in PIC structures, particularly less educated speakers. We will pursue this question in further work.

References

Alexiadou, A. & Anagnostopoulou, E. 1998. Parametrizing AGR: Word order, V-movement, and EPP-checking. *Natural Language and Linguistic Theory* 16. 491–540.

Anagnostopoulou, E. 1997. Clitic left dislocation and contrastive left dislocation. In E. Anagnostopoulou, H. Van Riemsdujk and F. Zwarts (eds.), *Materials on Left Dislocation*, 151–192. Amsterdam: John Benjamins.

Barbosa, P. 1995. *Null Subjects*. Cambridge, MA: MIT PhD dissertation.

Barbosa, P. 2000. Clitics: a window into the null subject property. In J. Costa (ed.), *Portuguese syntax: comparative studies*, 31–93. New York: Oxford University Press.

Barbosa, P. & Cochofel, F. 2005. A Construção de Infinitivo Preposicionado em PE. *Actas do XX Encontro Nacional da APL*, 387–400. Lisboa: APL.

Barbosa, P. & E. P. Raposo. 2013. Subordinação argumental infinitiva. In E. Paiva Raposo et al. (eds.), *Gramática do Português*, vol. 2, 1899–1977. Lisbon: Fundação Calouste Gulbenkian.

Benmamoun E., S. Montrul & M. Polinsky. 2013. Heritage languages and their speakers: Opportunities and challenges for linguistics. *Theoretical Linguistics* 39. 129–181.

Chomsky, N. 1977. On wh-movement. In P. Culicover, T. Wasos & A. Akmajian (eds.), *Formal syntax*, 71–132. New-York: Academic Press.

Chomsky, N. 1995. *The minimalist program*. Cambridge, MA: MIT Press.

Cochofel, F. 2003. *O infinitivo preposicionado em português europeu*. Universidade do Minho, Portugal, Master's dissertation.

Dermidache, H. 1992. *Resumptive chains in restrictive relative chains, appositives and dislocation structures*. Cambridge, MA: MIT, MA. PhD dissertation.

Duarte, I. 1992. Complementos infinitivos preposicionados e outras construções temporalmente defectivas em português europeu. In *Actas do VIII Encontro da Associação Portuguesa de Linguística*, 145–158. Lisboa: APL.

Felser, C. 2000. Aspectual complement clauses and the (un-)availability of verb raising. In H. Janßen (ed.), *Verbal projections*, 163–193. Tübingen: Niemeyer.

Flores, C. 2015. Understanding heritage language acquisition. Some contributions from the research on heritage speakers of European Portuguese. *Lingua* 164. 251—265.

Flores, C. & P. Barbosa. 2014. When reduced input leads to delayed acquisition: a study on the acquisition of clitic placement by Portuguese heritage speakers. *International Journal of Bilingualism* 18(3). 304–325.

Flores, C., A.L. Santos, A. Jesus & R. Marques. 2017. Age and input effects in the acquisition of mood in Heritage Portuguese. *Journal of Child Language* 44(4). 795–828.

Gonçalves, A. 1999. *Predicados complexos verbais em contextos de infinitivo não preposicionado em Português Europeu*. Universidade de Lisboa PhD thesis.

Hornstein, M., A.M. Martins & , J. Nunes. 2008.. Perception and causative structures in English and European Portuguese: phi-feature agreement and the distribution of bare and prepositional infinitives. *Syntax*, 11(2). 198–222.

Kato, M. A. 1999. Strong pronouns and weak pronominals in the null subject parameter. *Probus* 11(1). 1–37.

Kupisch, T. & Rothman, J. 2016. Terminology matters! Why difference is not incompleteness and how early child bilinguals are heritage speakers. *International Journal of Bilingualism*. OnlineFirst.

Manzini, M-R. L. & Savoia. 2002. Parameters of subject inflection in Italian dialects. In P. Svenonius (ed.), *Subjects, expletives and the EPP*, 157–200. New York: Oxford Press.

Meisel, J. M. 2013. Heritage language learners: Unprecedented opportunities for the study of grammars and their development? *Theoretical Linguistics* 39(3–4). 225–236.

Montrul, S. 2016. *The acquisition of heritage languages*. Cambridge: Cambridge University Press.

Montrul, S. 2008. *Incomplete acquisition in bilingualism: Re-examining the age factor.* Amsterdam: John Benjamins.

Ordoñez, F. & E. Treviño. 1999. Left dislocated subjects and the pro-drop parameter: a case study of Spanish. *Lingua* 107. 39–68.

Pascual y Cabo, D. & J. Rothman. 2012. The (il)logical problem of heritage speaker bilingualism and incomplete acquisition. *Applied Linguistics* 33(4). 450 - 455.

Pires, A. & J. Rothman. 2009. Disentangling sources of incomplete acquisition: An explanation for competence divergence across heritage grammars. *International Journal of Bilingualism* 13(2). 211–238.

Platzack, C. 2004. Agreement and the person phrase hypothesis. *Working Papers in Scandinavian Syntax* 73. 83–112.

Pollock, J.-Y. 1997. *Langage et cognition: introduction au programme minimaliste de la grammaire générative.* Paris: Presses Universitaires de France.

Putnam, M. & L. Sánchez. 2013. What's so incomplete about incomplete acquisition? A prolegomenon to modeling heritage language grammars. *Linguistic Approaches to Bilingualism* 3(4). 476–506.

Rao, R. & R. Ronquest. 2015. The heritage Spanish phonetic/phonological system: Looking back and moving forward. *Studies in Hispanic and Lusophone Linguistics* 8(2). 403–414.

Raposo, E. l987. Case theory and infl-to-comp: The inflected infinitive in European Portuguese. *LI.* 18.85–109.

Raposo, E. 1989. Prepositional infinitival constructions in European Portuguese. In O. Jaeggli & K. J. Safir (eds.), *The null subject parameter,* 277–305. Dordrecht: Kluwer.

Rinke, E. & C. Flores. 2014. Heritage Portuguese bilinguals' morphosyntactic knowledge of clitics. *Bilingualism. Language and Cognition* 17(4). 681–699.

Rizzi, L. 1982. *Issues in Italian syntax.* Dordrecht: Foris.

Rosenbaum, P. 1967. *The grammar of English predicate complement constructions*. Cambridge, MA: The MIT Press.

Rothman, J. & J. Treffers-Daller. 2014. A prolegomenon to the construct of the native speaker: heritage speaker bilinguals are natives too! *Applied Linguistics* 35(1). 93–98.

Santos, A. L., A. Gonçalves & N. Hyams. 2016. Aspects of the acquisition of object control and ECM-type verbs in European Portuguese. *Language Acquisition* 23(3). 199–233.

Silvano, P. & L. Cunha. 2016. Sobre a Caracterização temporal de frases complexas com orações finais com *para* em Português Europeu. *Revista da Associação Portuguesa de Linguística*, 2. 381–402.

Appendix

Example of a short narrative:

A Família Fonseca

O João e a Maria estavam a conversar no quarto quando o pai entra. O pai fica chateado com os dois irmãos, pois viu [1] _____ brincar àquela hora.

A mãe da Maria ouviu o alarido e foi ter com os seus filhos ao quarto, acon-
selhando [2] _____ a ir dormir. No dia seguinte, a Maria dirigiu-se ao
irmão e disse-lhe:
– Eu vi [3] _____ brincares ontem, não respeitaste o que a mãe nos disse.
O irmão indignado ralhou-lhe:
– Tu também querias ir e, além do mais, se estivéssemos os dois a brincar, a
mãe ia ouvir [4] _____ a fazer barulho.

The Fonseca family
João and Maria were talking in their room when their father came in. Father
was angry with the sibling, because he saw [1] ____ *play.INF* at this late
hour. Marias mother heard the noises and joined their children in the room,
advising [2] _____ *at go.INF* sleep The next day, Maria turned to her
brother and said:
"I saw [3] _____ play.INF.2S yesterday, you did not follow mum's orders."
Furious, her brother scolded her:
"You also wanted to go and, besides, if we both were playing, mum would
hear [4] _____ *at make.INF* noise.

Raquel Fernández Fuertes and Juana M. Liceras
Bilingualism as a first language: language dominance and crosslinguistic influence

Abstract: Even though research on bilingual first language acquisition (2L1) could be conceptualized as monolingual acquisition (L1) of two individual languages, the fact that in 2L1 acquisition there is exposure to input from two languages has consequences in terms of how the two language systems interact in the mind of the bilingual. This century has seen two important developments in this respect. First, a consensus seems to have been reached on the idea that the two systems are differentiated from the early stages (e.g. Genesee 1989; De Houwer 1990; Genesee, Nicoladis & Paradis 1995; Köppe & Meisel 1995; Genesee 2003). The second development is related to how the 2L1 language faculty compares to the L1 language faculty and the consideration that the grammatical processes and operations in both bilingual and monolingual speech must be accounted for in the same terms (MacSwan 2000; Liceras, Spradlin & Fernández Fuertes 2005; Liceras et al. 2008, among others). However, while it is unquestionable that L1 and 2L1 acquisition share similar mechanisms and processes, there are core issues such as language dominance, crosslinguistic influence and code-mixing that are specific to simultaneous bilingual acquisition.

In this chapter, we address these three language contact phenomena by analyzing spontaneous and experimental data from the simultaneous bilingual acquisition of English and Spanish by two identical twins in Spain (FerFuLice corpus in CHILDES) as it compares to data from other 2L1 and L2 children and adults. We conceptualize language dominance in terms of the computational value of grammatical features in a given language. And so, the dominant language is the one that provides the functional category whenever that category is highly grammaticized. Crosslinguistic influence between the two languages of a bilingual is analyzed in the case of sentential subjects and copula predicates and we propose that the occurrence as well as the directionality of influence is linked to lexical specialization. Therefore, the presence of two sets of subjects (i.e. overt and null) and two sets of copulas (i.e. *ser* and *estar*) in Spanish leads to a lack of negative influence from English into Spanish. However, a facilitation effect appears in bilingual English as seen in bilinguals' lower copula omission rates and lower null subject rate. In terms of code-mixing patterns between

Raquel Fernández Fuertes, Universidad de Valladolid
Juana M. Liceras, University of Ottawa and Universidad Nebrija

https://doi.org/10.1515/9781501509988-007

Determiners and Nouns, child and adult spontaneous production data differ from experimental data in that while the former show a preference for the Spanish Determiner (the category which is more grammaticized), the latter prefer the English Determiner.

We propose constructs such as the Grammatical Features Spell-Out Hypothesis or the Analogical Criterion to account for these patterns. The analysis of these language contact phenomena provides an insight on how language properties shape bilingual production.

1 Introduction

While the mechanisms and processes that shape bilingual first language acquisition (2L1) should, in principle, resemble those of monolingual acquisition (L1) in the case of each of the languages involved, the fact that in 2L1 acquisition there is exposure to input from two languages forces us to confront two fundamental research questions: whether and how the two language systems interact in the mind of the bilingual and what the outcomes of this interaction may be. Consequently, the main objective of this chapter is to discuss specific ways in which these research questions have been approached in the acquisition literature.

The very title of the chapter makes it clear that we will be dealing with simultaneous bilingual acquisition, namely with children who are exposed to the two languages from birth, rather than so-called sequential (or consecutive) bilingual acquisition which deals with children who are exposed to the second language after being exposed to the first language for at least two or three years (Baker 2011; De Houwer 2009; Silva-Corvalán 2014, among others). When the acquisition of a second language occurs past three years of age, it is usually referred to as child second language acquisition (cL2) rather than sequential bilingual acquisition (Meisel 2008).

Some of the most salient outcomes of 2L1 acquisition are language dominance, crosslinguistic influence, and language mixing. Language dominance has been defined in terms of relative proficiency (Grosjean 1982, among others) or relative speed of development (Wapole 2000) and it has been measured in relation to language production and to language processing. While there is not a unified definition of language dominance in young bilinguals, an inventory of linguistic diagnostics, along with other types of diagnostics, has been proposed to identify the dominant language. A first objective of this chapter is to propose a definition of language dominance that is not necessarily equated to proficiency but to the grammaticalization of features in the various languages.

As for crosslinguistic influence (i.e. Döpke 2000; Genesee, Nicoladis & Paradis 1995; Liceras, Fernández Fuertes & Alba de la Fuente 2012; Müller 1998; Nicoladis 2002; Yip & Matthews 2000), it is important to point out that, within the view of the bilingual mind that we maintain, and even if the two language systems share a single computational component, the realization of universal principles is to be mediated by the existence of two lexicons and two phonological components. This implies that the combinations of features present in the functional categories (i.e. pronouns, determiners, auxiliaries, complementizers ...) and the lexical or substantive categories (i.e. nouns, lexical verbs, adjectives ...) in the two languages may differ and, therefore, may result in crosslinguistic influence. It may also be the case that a feature or a set of features be realized as one lexical item in one language but as two lexical items in the other language. A case in point is the values of copula *be* in English that are realized as two different lexical items – *ser* and *estar* – in Spanish. The obligatory use of overt subjects in English but not in Spanish and the systematic availability of null subjects in Spanish but not in English have also been discussed as relevant *loci* for crosslinguistic influence. Thus, a second objective of this chapter is not only to discuss some potential *loci* for crosslinguistic influence in 2L1 acquisition but also to show that, while crosslinguistic influence can cause interference, it can also have a facilitating effect.

Finally, code-mixing or code-switching has also been investigated as an outcome of 2L1 acquisition, both as a diagnostic for language dominance as well as a reflection of how the properties of the two language systems may interact. We will use code-mixing and code-switching interchangeably even though the first term has been used to refer to mixing that occurs before children have incorporated the functional categories of the two languages (Köppe & Meisel 1995).

In order to discuss the above-mentioned outcomes, we will use data from the simultaneous bilingual acquisition of English and Spanish in Spain. We will specifically discuss 2L1 data from the bilingual twins in the FerFuLice corpus in CHILDES (MacWhinney 2000; Fernández Fuertes & Liceras 2010) in relation to L1 monolingual acquisition of both Spanish and English and paying special attention to copula omission and null and overt subject production, two constructions that have received a great deal of attention in the 2L1 acquisition literature (i.e. Paradis & Navarro 2003; Silva-Corvalán 2014). This will contribute to the understanding of individual bilingualism which can then be used as a point of comparison with societal bilingualism (Bathia & Ritchie 2012).[1] In our specific case, we will be discussing a case of individual rather than societal bilingualism

---

1 The type of contact that has been mainly studied is the one in which the language that may eventually become non-dominant, and here we are using the term as the equivalent of proficiency

and a situation where Spanish is the majority language while English is the minority language. Nonetheless, we want to address language dominance, crosslinguistic influence and code-mixing as outcomes of bilingualism that can be investigated across the board, as determined by the mere contact between two different language systems and, in principle, abstracting from the specific setting as such or the specific amount of input.

2 The characterization of bilingual first language acquisition

As Baker (2011), referring to Grosjean (1995, 2008) and Jesnner (2008), points out, two contrasting views of individual bilinguals have been argued for in the literature: the view of the bilingual as "two monolinguals in one person" (the "fractional" view) and the view of the bilingual as having a unique linguistic profile which is not the sum of two monolinguals (the "holistic" view). While the conceptualization of the problem is different because it pertains only to the initial stages of acquisition, the availability of two language systems is also at the core of the debate between those who argue that the mind of the young bilingual child contains a single language system (Lindholm & Padilla 1978; Redlinger & Park 1980; Vihman 1985; Volterra & Taeschner 1978) and those who defend that the two language systems are differentiated from the early stages (De Houwer 1990; Genesee 1989, 2003; Genesee et al. 1995; Köppe & Meisel 1995). This debate seems to have been won by the latter. However, we would like to frame the fractional/holistic debate as well as the single/two different language system view within the Minimalist framework, as argued by MacSwan (2000, 2014), where the grammatical processes and operations in both bilingual and monolingual speech must be accounted for by the same universal mechanisms. This is so because the bilingual language faculty is made up of two lexicons and two phonological components but a single language-specific computational system: the only one available for human language.[2] That is, under Minimalist premises, this view of the bilingual

---

(e.g. Spanish as minority / heritage language in the US), may have a facilitating effect in the acquisition of the dominant language (e.g. English as majority language in the US).

2 Even though the two lexicons proposal is intrinsic to MacSwan's model, a distributed morphology account can dispense with the two lexicons requirement, as was timidly suggested in Liceras, Fernández Fuertes, Perales, Pérez-Tattam, and Spradlin (2008, footnote 8) and recently argued for by Burkholder (2018).

language faculty offers a universal framework within which feature activation will proceed depending on the specific language, as well as feature valuation and the outcomes of the operations MOVE, MERGE, and AGREE. Therefore, this view provides us with the framework needed to discuss the outcomes that are specific to 2L1 acquisition but are, at the same time, shaped by the mechanisms and processes that pertain to L1 acquisition. It also implies that Universal Grammar is a central component of the Language Acquisition Device (LAD) and that linguistic structures reflect mentally represented knowledge (Meisel 2011, among others).

Even though in terms of ability, the field of bilingualism differentiates between active and passive bilinguals, we will only be discussing the acquisition of two languages that leads to active (comprehension and production) bilingualism. It is a fact that ability is a dimension of a continuum (Valdés Kroff et al. 2011) and that in the course of development the bilinguals whose data we will be discussing might become passive bilinguals in one of the two languages, but discussing this potential developing outcome is out of the scope of this chapter.

Active bilingualism may not necessarily imply that the receptive and productive competence in the two languages is "balanced" and this is why language dominance has been systematically discussed in the bilingual literature in general and in the 2L1 acquisition literature in particular.

Petersen (1988) lists prevalence of overall functional words from one of the two languages as a diagnostic internal to the linguistic system and parents' perception and amount of exposure as diagnostics external to the linguistic system. Nicoladis and Secco (1998) define language dominance in terms of relative vocabulary size in each of the two languages while for Genesee et al. (1995) or for Yip and Matthews (2006) the dominant language is the one for which the child has a higher Mean Length of Utterance (MLU).

We agree with Baker (2011) that balance and dominance tests are dependent upon language proficiency and performance and can only partially access the bilingual's language capacity and language ability. Also, dominance need not coincide with balance and, as Baker (2011) puts it, "it is possible to be approximately equally proficient in two languages, yet one may be dominant" and so, for instance, "speed of processing may provide evidence about balance but not about dominance in actual language use" (p. 35). In fact, language dominance can change overtime and it may be easier to identify at the lexical and phonological levels than at the morphosyntactic level, a difference that has been systematically pointed out in the case of language transfer.

As for transfer, while it may not be possible to differentiate transfer from crosslinguistic influence, some researchers (i.e. Silva-Corvalán 2003, 2014) argue that they are different because the effect of crosslinguistic or interlinguistic influence is quantitative rather than qualitative. For instance, the presence of more overt subjects in the Spanish of English-Spanish bilinguals (Silva-Corvalán 2014) than in monolingual Spanish, or the lower omission of copula *be* in the English of English-Spanish bilinguals (Fernández Fuertes & Liceras 2010; Liceras et al. 2012) would be identified as an instance of crosslinguistic influence. However, the use of an expression such as *dame una mano* in Spanish for "give me a hand" would be an instance of transfer since the Spanish expression is *échame una mano* ("throw me a hand"). We adopt this distinction and follow a quantitative approach to crosslinguistic influence in subsequent sections.

Crosslinguistic influence has been said to be pervasive at the interfaces between internal and external modules of language, such as the syntax-pragmatics interface (i.e. Tsimpli & Sorace 2006). However, many researchers have challenged this view of the so-called Interface Hypothesis both as a *locus* for crosslinguistic influence or for learning difficulty (for an overview of the Interface Hypothesis see Sorace (2011) and commentaries). We should also point out that there are not many studies that use data from the early stages of 2L1 acquisition to test whether crosslinguistic influence plays a relevant role at the interfaces. As we have indicated above, we will discuss crosslinguistic influence as having a facilitating or an interfering effect in 2L1 development and will argue, as in the case of language dominance, that the features and combinations of features that make up the functional and lexical categories of the language pair constitute a valuable tool for both predicting and accounting not only for the type of influence (facilitating or interfering) but also for its directionality (i.e. which language will be the source or *locus* of influence and which one the target of influence).

Language dominance is directly related to whether the outcome of bilingualism consists of a balanced or an unbalanced bilingual. However, this outcome cannot be taken as categorical but rather as a continuum when it comes to comparing individuals. Overall, input and social factors seem to play an important role in the degree of proficiency as measured by monolingual standards achieved by any given bilingual in the minority language (the one that does not have an official status in the country). In the case of the two English-Spanish bilingual brothers whose recordings were analyzed by Silva-Corvalán (2014), at the age of six, the older brother had achieved a higher degree of proficiency than his younger sibling in some specific Spanish structures, a situation that according to this author is to be explained as a result of the greater amount of Spanish input received by the older sibling. Nonetheless, Silva-Corvalán (2014) argues that when compared to monolinguals, these bilinguals' English was not negatively affected by Spanish. On the contrary, the rich morphology of Spanish had a facilitating effect in that the bilinguals acquired the English obligatory subject requirement and the English verb morphology earlier than their monolingual counterparts. Thus, crosslinguistic influence is one of the specific outcomes of 2L1 acquisition that we will discuss in this chapter.

3 The FerFuLice corpus: simultaneous acquisition of English-Spanish by two identical twins

In order to discuss language dominance and crosslinguistic influence, we use spontaneous and experimental data from the simultaneous bilingual acquisition of English and Spanish by two identical twins who were born and grew up in Spain and we compare these data with available data from other bilinguals and monolinguals.

The twins, Simon and Leo, were born in Salamanca (Spain) from an English-speaking mother from the US and a Spanish-speaking father from Spain. The parents have always used the so-called rule of Grammont, the one parent-one language strategy, and so the father always speaks to the children in Spanish and the mother always addresses them in English. According to an extensive and a comprehensive parental questionnaire, this practice was followed from the moment the twins were born. The parents generally speak Spanish with each other, except during the summer when they travel to the United States for approximately two months or when a monolingual English speaker is present. Therefore, this is a case of bilingual English/Spanish first language acquisition in a monolingual-Spanish social context, a type of bilingualism which is referred to in the literature as individual bilingualism (Bhatia & Ritchie 2004).

The spontaneous data from Simon and Leo come from the FerFuLice corpus available through the CHILDES project (MacWhinney 2000). The data cover the age range of 1;01 to 6;11. A total of 178 sessions were recorded on videotape and DVD, of which 117 were in an English context (i.e. with an English interlocutor such as the interviewer or their mother) and 61 in a Spanish context (i.e. with a Spanish interlocutor such as the interviewer or their father). The Spanish recordings were made at intervals of 2 to 3 weeks until age 3;00 (with some interruptions during the summer holidays), and then once a month after that. The English recordings were sometimes made more frequently, but the sessions were usually much shorter and recorded on consecutive days. The children were recorded in naturalistic settings, usually at home, and appeared together in the majority of the sessions. They were mostly engaged in normal play activities with the interlocutor.

As in Fernández Fuertes and Liceras (2010: Table 2), a comparison of the twins' MLUs in both languages with the corresponding MLUs of two age-matched Spanish monolinguals and two English monolinguals yields very similar results[3].

---

3 The MLU (Mean Length of Utterance) is derived from two totals: the total number of utterances and the total number of either morphemes (standard MLU) or words (MLUw) for each

As argued by Hickey (1991) and Miller and Chapman (1981), among many others, MLU has consistently been found to be the most stable measure of comparison between children.

Taking into account the information gathered both in a parental question-naire and in an extensive vocabulary check-list, as well as the corresponding MLUs with age-matched monolingual English and monolingual Spanish children, Fernández Fuertes and Liceras (2010) conclude that the twins' proficiency in English and Spanish is quite balanced between the two languages and relatively equal to their respective monolinguals in both languages.

The experimental data from the twins that we discuss in this chapter come from a code-mixing acceptability judgment task that we describe below. We compare the twins' data to data from other 2L1 bilingual children and adults.

4 Language dominance in bilingual first language acquisition

The notional definition of language dominance that constituted the point of departure for more theoretically grounded research refers to the situation where one of the languages of the bilingual is at a more advanced stage and develops faster than the other, a definition that is, in principle, dependent on measuring the proficiency in each of the languages of the bilingual. For Yip and Matthews (2006) language dominance is a property of the bilingual mind which is assessed by comparing the MLU in the child's two languages. The language with the higher MLU is the dominant language. They argue that the directionality of transfer goes from the language with higher MLU to the language with lower MLU and that there is a correlation between the MLU difference and the pervasiveness of cross-linguistic influence.[4] These authors specifically show that in the English of English-Cantonese bilinguals who are Cantonese-dominant, null objects – which are

---

speaker and in each file/transcript. MLU calculations for the twins were based on word measures (MLUw), while those of the English monolingual children were measured on morphemes (standard MLU). When comparing standard MLU and MLUw values, Malakoff, Mayes, Schottenfeld, and Howell (1999) found that MLU correlates with MLUw at .97 for English, and Aguado (1988) found a correlation of .99 for Spanish (see MacWhinney, 2009, p. 103).

4 Yip and Matthews (2006) use the term syntactic transfer to refer to the type of influence that takes place between the two languages of bilinguals, an influence, they argue, that takes place at the level of competence (p. 101).

illicit in standard English – are used more frequently by those with a larger MLU differential use than by those with a lower MLU differential use.

According to Petersen's (1988) version of the Dominant Language Hypothesis, in an English-Danish bilingual system where the dominant language is Danish, (1) but not (2) may be a code-mixed utterance, whereas, the opposite would be true if English were the dominant language.

(1) **Hendes** dolly
[her dolly]

(2) **Her** duke
[her dolly]

Thus, the dominant language provides the functional category of the switched DP (Determiner Phrase) – Danish in (1) and English in (2).

Liceras, Spradlin, and Fernández Fuertes (2005) and Liceras, Fernández Fuertes, Perales, Pérez-Tattam, and Spradlin (2008) propose a reinterpretation of the concept of language dominance using the theoretical framework provided by the Minimalist Program (Chomsky, 1995, 1998, 1999), and in the spirit of MacSwan (2000). They formulate the Grammatical Features Spell-Out Hypothesis (GFSH) according to which, in the process of activating the features of the two grammars, the child makes choices in terms of the language that will provide the functional vocabulary to a given functional-lexical mixing. These choices are dependent on how these features are 'grammaticized' in the two grammars, namely their degree of 'saliency' and their 'computational value'. This implies that in the case of English-Spanish child acquisition data, mixed utterances such as (3) will prevail over (4) because the Spanish Determiner but not the English Determiner carries a Gender feature.

(3) **El**(masc.) book
[the book]

(4) **The** libro(masc.)
[the book]

Evidence for the GFSH is provided by data produced by Mario (Fantini 1985), Manuela (Deuchar & Quay 2000), Simon and Leo (Liceras et al. 2008), and five children studied by Lindholm and Padilla (1978). In the data from these nine English-Spanish bilingual children, instances of utterances such as the ones in (3) account for almost all cases of mixed Determiner+Noun utterances, as depicted in Table 1, adapted from Liceras et al. (2008).

Table 1: Child bilingual D-N mixings: Spanish/English, French/English and Italian/German.

	Manuela [Deuchar CHILDES]	Mario [Fantini 1985]	Leo [Fernánd. et al. 2002–2005]	Simon [Fernánd. et al. 2002–2005]	5 children [Lindholm & Padilla 1978]	Michael [Swain 1972]	Lisa [Taeschner 1983]	Giulia [Taeschner 1983]
Language pair	Sp / Eng	Sp / Eng	Sp / Eng	Sp / Eng	Sp / Eng	Fre / Eng	It / Ger	It / Ger
Def Art 'the'	1 / –	18 / –	1 / –	3 / –	7 / 2	1 / –	10 / 4	5 / 6
Ind Art 'a/n'	4 / –	16 / –	3 / –	1 / –	5 / 1	2 / –	1 / 6	1 / 8
Dem 'this'	– / 2	2 / –	– / –	– / –	6 / –	– / –	1 / –	8 / 1
Indef. 'another'	11 / –	1 / –	17 / –	– / –	– / –	– / –	– / 5	– / –
Poss. 'my'	– / –	6 / –	1 / –	1 / –	– / –	3 / 2	1 / 1	3 / 2
Total	16 / 2	43 / –	22 / –	5 / –	18 / 3	6 / 2	13 / 16	17 / 17

Child bilinguals systematically choose the Spanish Determiner because they have to specify the features that will make the computational component of the Spanish system work, and this computational component happens to require this type of AGREE operation. In fact, it follows from the GFSH that the free morphemes which encode highly grammaticized features are especially important for the requirements of the computational system and, therefore, for L1 acquisition. This preference for the Determiner which is marked for gender also shows in the case of the French-English bilingual (Swain, 1972) in Table 1 (column 7) since, although there are only eight DPs in total, six have a French Determiner and only two, an English Determiner. The GFSH also predicts that, in a language pair where gender is equally grammaticized in both Determiners, no preference for either Determiner will appear because the bilingual will have to activate both features in the two languages. As Table 1 shows (columns 8 and 9), the code-mixed utterances produced by Lisa and Giulia (Taeschner 1983) support this prediction.

According to Ong and Zhang (2010), the GFSH is also supported by the fact that their English-Mandarin bilinguals overwhelmingly prefer the use of Chinese Determiner + English Noun switches. What these authors argue is that, due to the fact that Mandarin Nouns do not inflect for number, the reported preference is triggered by the lexical category, the English Noun, rather than the functional category. This is so because the English Noun has the added feature [Number]. So as per the GFSH, the preference goes in favor of the language whose features are more relevant for the computational component, which in this case happens to be the English Noun, thus making the Chinese Determiner + English Noun switches the favored option.

Further evidence for the GFSH comes from the DPs produced by the English-German bilinguals in Jorschick, Endesfelder Quick, Glässer, Lieven and Tomasello (2011), since, regardless of the dominance, these children use significantly more mixed DPs with German Determiners and English Nouns than English Determiners which German Nouns, which is expected, given the fact that German Determiners but not English Determiners bear the Gender feature.

In summary, and even though more analyses of naturalistic and experimental data are needed, what the bilingual mixed DPs evidence is that language dominance can be defined in relation to how children activate the formal features of language, which in turn determines how features are represented in the mind of the bilingual.

5 Crosslinguistic influence in bilingual first language acquisition

Even if the two languages are differentiated from the early stages of acquisition, as stated in the Language Differentiation Hypothesis, 2L1 research has been concerned with how the simultaneous development of the two L1s of the bilingual proceeds. In particular, bilinguals' two L1s have been said to develop either autonomously, and, therefore, in a similar way to their monolingual counterparts; or interdependently, and so phenomena such as crosslinguistic influence appear, which make bilingual development different from monolingual development. Some studies comparing bilinguals and monolinguals have found no differences in their developmental paths (e.g. De Houwer 1990; Nicoladis 1994; Paradis & Genesee 1996) and this has been so in several areas of grammar: functional elements such as verb finiteness, negation, and weak and strong pronominal subjects (Paradis & Genesee 1996), root infinitives (Unsworth 2003), pronominal objects (Paradis, Crago & Genesee 2005/2006), subjects and objects (Serratrice 2002; Serratrice, Sorace & Paoli 2004) and, in the case of Spanish, null and overt subjects (Liceras et al. 2012; Liceras, Fernández Fuertes & Pérez Tattam 2008).

Other studies have found differences between monolinguals and bilinguals attributed to crosslinguistic influence, that is, to the transferring of properties from one L1 to the other L1. Crosslinguistic influence has also been attested in different studies (e.g. Döpke 2000; Fernández Fuertes & Liceras 2010; Hulk & Müller 2000; Liceras & Fernández Fuertes 2018; Liceras et al. 2012; Müller 1998; Paradis & Navarro 2003; Yip & Mathews 2000) and in different grammatical areas (e.g. phonological, morphological, and syntactic) as well as in different interfaces (e.g. the syntax-pragmatics and the syntax-lexicon/syntax-semantics).

In summary, the characterization of crosslinguistic influence has been linked to linguistic theory, language dominance or input and there are two factors that have centered most attention in this respect: the effect of crosslinguistic influence (i.e. facilitating or interfering) and the directionality of crosslinguistic influence.

The effect of crosslinguistic influence in 2L1 acquisition

When the properties of one of the L1s (language A) are transferred into the other L1 (language B), in other words, when there is crosslinguistic influence, two possible outcomes appear: delay and acceleration (Paradis & Genesee 1996). This is seen in the attainment of the adult grammar properties as well as in the amount of non-adult-like cases that characterizes child grammars. If delay appears, the influence from language A to language B leads bilinguals to acquire the properties of the adult B grammar later and to produce a higher rate of non-adult-like constructions if compared to their monolingual peers. Crosslinguistic influence, thus, has an interfering effect. If acceleration appears, bilinguals acquire the adult grammar earlier than monolinguals and this would be so because some grammatical properties are acquired earlier in some languages. Therefore, if a property is already acquired in language A, it could be transferred to language B making bilinguals produce the adult structures in language B sooner than would be the norm in monolinguals. Crosslinguistic influence, in this case, has a facilitating effect.

In the case of the copula, it has been shown that Spanish children seldom omit the verb in these constructions (Bel 2001; Sera 1992). However, Becker (2000) showed that English children go over an initial omission stage in which they omit the copula as in (5).

(5) a. I _ (am) in the kitchen   [Nina 2;01]   (Suppes 1974, CHILDES)
    b. Patsy _ (is) a girl   [Peter 2;03]   (L. Bloom 1970, CHILDES)

Becker (2000) argues that, while omission is higher in the case of predicates denoting temporal properties (5a), it is significantly lower in copula predicates denoting permanent properties (5b). In the case of Spanish-English bilinguals, Fernández Fuertes and Liceras (2010) found very low copula omission rates both in the Spanish and in the English production of the children and for both predicate types. The comparative results of these studies appear summarized in Table 2, adapted from Becker's (2004) Table 1 (p. 159) and from Fernández Fuertes and Liceras (2010).

Table 2: Explicit copula in Spanish-English bilinguals and monolinguals.

		Copula with permanent properties	Copula with temporal properties
English monolinguals (Becker 2000)	% of explicit copula [EN]	76.3%	18.8%
Spanish monolinguals (Bel 2001)	% of explicit copula [SP]	99.5%	
Spanish-English bilinguals (Fernández Fuertes & Liceras 2010)	% of explicit copula [EN]	91.2%	88.6%
	% of explicit copula [SP]	96.7%	

In particular, while no differences appear between monolingual and bilingual Spanish (Bel, 2001; Gaulin, 2008) where percentages of overtness are above 95%, bilingual English is different from monolingual English in this particular area of grammar. Given that the adult grammar (i.e. the use of the copula) is acquired earlier in Spanish than in English, Fernández Fuertes and Liceras (2010) explain the low rates of copula omission in the English of these bilinguals as a sign of positive crosslinguistic influence from Spanish into English. That is, bilinguals transfer into English the properties they have already acquired in Spanish and, as a result, less non-adult-like cases are produced and the adult grammar is acquired earlier than in English monolinguals. This facilitating role of Spanish is triggered by the presence of two copulas in Spanish (*ser* and *estar*) and the division of labor they have: *ser* depicts individual-level predicates and *estar* stage-level predicates (as in Carlson 1977; Schmitt & Miller 2007). As opposed to the saliency of Spanish in the use of the two copulas for the two predicate types, in English, both types of predicates are depicted by copula *be*.

In the case of sentential subjects, children acquiring Spanish and English produce cases of subject omission, as in (6), in spite of the fact that null subjects are possible in adult Spanish but not in adult English.

(6) a. (it) Roars   [Simon 2;05]   (FerFuLice corpus)
     b. (yo) Tengo más   [Manuela 1;11] (Deuchar corpus)
         [(I) have more]

The patterns of subject production/omission have been the focus of attention when comparing the monolingual and bilingual acquisition of Spanish and English. If crosslinguistic influence occurs from English into Spanish, this could be reflected in the overproduction of subjects in Spanish; if it goes from Spanish into English, the English of the bilinguals could contain more null subjects than those characterizing the production of English monolinguals. Liceras et al. (2012) and Liceras and Fernández Fuertes (2018) have carried out a comparative analysis of Spanish and English subjects by analyzing the spontaneous production of monolinguals and bilinguals. The results appear in Table 3.

Table 3: Sentential subjects in Spanish-English bilinguals and monolinguals.

Child		Spanish		English	
		null	pronoun	null	pronoun
Simon	[EN/SP]	86.6%	13.4%	18.7%	81.3%
Leo	[EN/SP]	85.8%	14.2%	20.1%	79.9%
María	[SP]	90.9%	16.7%	–	
Naomi	[EN]	–		37.9%	62.1%

Table 3 shows that, in the Spanish spontaneous production, the rate of null *versus* overt pronominal subjects produced by the bilingual children and the monolingual child reflects the implementation of adult Spanish concerning sentential subjects: the preference for null subjects *versus* pronominal ones. The pattern of the monolingual child (María) is very similar to that of the bilingual children which points to the lack of crosslinguistic influence from English into Spanish in the bilinguals' Spanish production.

However, when comparing null and pronominal subjects in the English production of the three children, data show that the monolingual child (Naomi) produces a significantly higher number of non-adult null subjects than the bilinguals. Liceras and Fernández Fuertes (2018) attribute this lower production of null subjects by the two bilinguals to Spanish playing a facilitating role. As in the case of the copula, Spanish has two different realizations of the subject: null, licensed by a rich verbal inflection, and overt. This makes bilingual children realize earlier than monolinguals that the null subject is not an option for English verbs. Therefore, crosslinguistic influence from Spanish into English makes bilinguals reach the adult grammar earlier than monolinguals.

Silva-Corvalán (2014) in her study on the spontaneous production of two Spanish-English bilinguals finds different patterns from those in Liceras and Fernández Fuertes (2018). By analyzing the data longitudinally (from age 1;06 to 5;11), she attested an increase of pragmatically inadequate pronominal subjects in Spanish, which she attributed to crosslinguistic influence from English and, in particular, from the English [subject pronoun + verb] string (pp. 163–4). This influence, which has an interfering effect, is the reflection of Spanish being the non-dominant language as it is the language in which the children receive less input. In the case of the copulas *ser*, *estar* and *be*, no influence from Spanish into English or from English into Spanish is attested as the bilinguals behave similarly to the monolinguals. In fact, the few errors in the children's Spanish copula production are not omission errors (as those reported by Liceras & Fernández Fuertes 2018) but commission errors (e.g. uses of *ser* in *estar*-contexts or the reverse) and are always produced by Brennan, the child who deviates from the Spanish adult target more notably as he has had less exposure to Spanish (pp. 44–45 and 53). Silva-Corvalán argues that crosslinguistic influence is determined by the dominant language and the two siblings in her study were clearly English dominant. Our interpretation of these results when compared to those of the two bilinguals in Liceras and Fernández Fuertes' (2018) study is that there must be a threshold, a minimum competence for crosslinguistic influence to take place and so, while the twins are rather balanced, Brennan's Spanish is quite weak and, therefore, does not trigger influence.

Paradis and Navarro (2003) investigate crosslinguistic influence from English into Spanish in the subject production of a bilingual child exposed to Cuban Spanish. Given the fact that the use of subject pronouns is more abundant in Caribbean Spanish than in other varieties of Spanish, Paradis and Navarro (2003) cannot conclude whether it is this specific type of input or rather crosslinguistic influence that accounts for Manuela's larger production of overt subjects when compared to the monolingual children. In fact, Liceras et al. (2012) and Liceras and Fernández Fuertes (2018) have shown no indication of explicit subject overuse in the production of the two bilingual children they analyze (Table 3 above). Since these children were exposed to peninsular Spanish, it may well be the case that Manuela's overuse of overt subjects be a consequence of the type of input to which she was exposed, rather than of influence from English.

The directionality of crosslinguistic influence in 2L1 acquisition

Crosslinguistic influence between the two L1s of the bilingual can go in the direction of language A to language B or the reverse. As we have indicated above, while some researchers relate the directionality of crosslinguistic influence to dominance so that influence goes from the dominant to the non-dominant language (e.g. Silva-Corvalán 2014), other researchers argue that the nature of grammatical properties can also dictate the directionality of crosslinguistic influence. Namely, if a language presents a lexical-syntactic distinction that is absent in the other language (null and overt subjects or *ser* and *estar* copulas in Spanish), this language may be a good candidate as the source of influence (Liceras et al. 2012). This implies that in the case of Spanish-English bilinguals, crosslinguistic influence will go from Spanish into English and not in the reverse direction, and this would be so regardless of dominance. However, as we indicated above, we believe that for crosslinguistic influence to occur, a certain degree of competence in Spanish, in this case, is necessary. If the level of Spanish is too low, it would behave as an L2 and, in that case, influence will not take place.

Hulk and Müller's (2000) proposal also takes the linguistic specifications of each language as a determinant factor when predicting directionality of influence. These authors propose that two conditions are required for crosslinguistic influence to take place: (i) that the structure in question be located at an interface and (ii) that the language which is influenced contain structures that children may mis-analyze as mirroring those of the influencing language. Specifically, Hulk and Müller (2000) propose that object omission occurs at a high rate in the French of child French-German bilinguals because (i) omission in German is governed at the syntax-pragmatics interface and (ii) because French clitic constructions could be analyzed as instances of object omission by the bilingual child, given that the post-verbal position is empty because the object clitic pronoun is placed before the verb. The conditions proposed by Hulk and Müller (2000) are put to the test by Liceras et al. (2012) as predictors of the directionality of crosslinguistic influence between English and Spanish in the case of sentential subjects and copula constructions. As for subjects, crosslinguistic influence from English into Spanish leading to an overproduction of pronominal subjects in bilingual Spanish is not expected to occur since (i) English pronominal subjects are a pure syntactic phenomenon and are, therefore, not located at an interface; and (ii) as null subjects in Spanish are a robust phenomenon, children would not mis-analyze the Spanish input in terms of the obligatory presence of English pronouns. In fact, as Table 3 above shows, no overproduction of pronominals occurs in the Spanish production of these bilinguals.

If crosslinguistic influence from Spanish into English takes place, it would result in the overproduction of null subjects in English. If so, crosslinguistic influence would have an interfering effect. However, this is not expected either since (i), although pronominal subjects in Spanish are governed at the syntax-pragmatics interface, null subjects, i.e. the transferred property, are a pure syntactic phenomenon; and (ii) it is far from clear that English would provide robust superficial input which could be mis-analyzed as mirroring the Spanish structures where null subjects are licensed, since, in English, null subjects with inflected verbs only occur with coordinated structures. As seen in Table 3 regarding the effect of crosslinguistic influence and as predicted under this view of crosslinguistic influence directionality, no overproduction of null subjects in the English of these bilinguals occurs.

6 Code-mixing

Code-mixing or code-switching has also been investigated as an outcome of 2L1 acquisition. Zentella (1981, 2000) defines code-mixing as alternating languages in unchanged speech situations. Cantone and Müller (2008, p. 811) consider code-mixing (CM) as the ability of a bilingual speaker to use both languages within a discourse (inter-sentential CM, as in 7), or within an utterance (intra-sentential CM, as in 1 to 4 above), according to grammatical and socio-linguistic constraints.

(7)   Sometimes I'll start a sentence in Spanish *y termino en español*

(Poplack 1980)

[sometimes I'll start a sentence in Spanish and I finish in Spanish]

CM constraints have been related to language dominance as discussed in Section 3. Linguistic constraints such as the equivalence constraint (Poplack 1980), the functional head constraint (Belazi et al. 1994) or the matrix language frame (Azuma 1993; Myers-Scotton 1995) share the assumption that CM is constrained by rules different from those of the languages intervening in the mixing, that is, by a grammar of its own (the so-called third grammar); and the fact that they are too general in that, for example, these constraints disallow mixes at boundaries where CM actually happens in the spontaneous production of bilinguals.

MacSwan (1999, 2000), however, proposes that only the grammars of the two languages involved constrain language mixing so that no additional constraints are required. MacSwan (2000: 45), taking the Minimalist Program (MP) as a framework, defines code-switching "as the simple consequence of mixing two lexicons in the course of a derivation" which emphasizes the role of the lexicon (and the features it encodes) when accounting for CM. The MP also guides the analysis carried out by Liceras et al. (2005), Liceras et al. (2008) and Liceras, Fernández Fuertes, and Klassen (2016). These authors carry out an analysis of Spanish-English CM in the spontaneous production of child and adult 2L1 bilinguals as well as in the experimental data of child 2L1 bilinguals. They focus on the specific CM Determiner + Noun, in (1), (2), (3), (4), and as in the examples in (8).

(8) a. los rockets   [Mario 3;08]   (Fantini 1985)
         [the rockets]
     b. el cake   [Manuela 2;02] (Deuchar, CHILDES)
         [the cake]
     c. la rock   [Leo 3;05]   (FerFuLice, CHILDES)
         [the rock]
     d. the vaca   (Lindholm & Padilla 1978)
         [the cow]
     e. the piscina   [Simon 4;04]   (FerFuLice, CHILDES)
         [the swimming-pool]

These authors were concerned with the prevalence of one functional category over the other (Spanish Determiner, as in 8a-8c, or English Determiner, as in 8d and 8e) and, in the case of the Spanish Determiner, with gender agreement (the so-called analogical criterion where the Spanish Determiner agrees with the English Noun as if the English Noun 'inherits' the gender features of the Spanish translation equivalent Noun). Under the analogical criterion (AC; a term initially proposed by Otheguy & Lapidus 2005), a contrast is established between the Spanish Determiner mixes in (9).

(9) a. el$_{masc.}$ book$_{=libro\ (masc.)}$ [+AC]
         [the book]
     b. la$_{fem.}$ book$_{=libro\ (masc.)}$ [-AC]
         [the book]

In (9a) the Spanish masculine Determiner agrees in gender with the English Noun as the English Noun (*book*) bears the corresponding masculine feature of the Spanish translation equivalent (*libro*). In contrast, in (9b) there is a mismatch of gender features between the feminine feature of the Spanish Determiner and the masculine feature that the English Noun inherits from its Spanish translation equivalent. This idea of imposing gender on the English Noun makes it possible that the valuation of gender features in the CM phrase proceeds as in the Spanish monolingual DP.

What Liceras et al. (2005, 2008) show is that, regardless of dominance, as defined by Petersen (1998), Spanish-English 2L1 bilinguals (both children and adults) have a very similar behavior in the spontaneous production of mixed Determiner-Noun sequences. In fact, as shown in Table 4, Spanish Determiners are clearly favored in Determiner+Noun mixes by both child and adult 2L1 bilinguals, and this is so regardless of whether they are rather balanced (as in the FerFuLice corpus) or whether Spanish is their dominant language or not (as in the Deuchar corpus).

Table 4: Code-mixed Det-N sequences: the spontaneous production of 2L1 bilinguals.

		SP Det + EN N	EN Det + SP N
Children	Deuchar (CHILDES)	16	2
	Fantini (1985)	4	–
	FerFuLice (CHILDES)	7	–
	Lindholm & Padilla (1978)	18	3
Adults	Myers-Scotton & Jake (2001)	810	14
	Jake, Myers-Scotton & Gross (2002)	161	0
	Moyer (1993), Moro (2001, 2014)	213	2

To account for these preferences, Liceras et al. (2008) formulate the GFSH (Section 3) and formalize the AC as the Gender Double-Feature Valuation Mechanism in order to capture the strength of linguistic features and, in particular, of gender features that leads to (i) the preference for the functional category which is more grammaticized (i.e. the Spanish Determiner) as it encodes gender features; and (ii) the need to enforce gender agreement between the Spanish Determiner and the English Noun as a linguistic operation rooted in the mind of Spanish dominant Spanish-English bilinguals.

This preference for the Spanish Determiner in production is not seen, however, in the case of the experimental data these authors analyze. In their case, the experimental data are elicited via an acceptability judgment task where participants have to rate a sentence containing CM between Determiner and Noun, as in (10), using a judgment scale with emoticon faces, as in (11). The 2L1 bilingual children tested range between the ages of 6 and 12 years and include the two children in the FerFuLice corpus as well as a group of 2L1 bilingual children with a similar linguistic profile (i.e. they also live in Spain and come from families where each of the parents is a native speaker of one of the two languages and where the one parent-one language strategy of communication is used with the children).

(10) a. El niño está en el plane   Spanish Det, [+AC], MM
        [the child is in the_masc plane_Spanish masc]
     b. El señor está mirando por el window   Spanish Det, [-AC], MF
        [the man is looking through the_masc
        window_Spanish fem]
     c. The man is falling to *the suelo*   English Det, Spanish masc N
        [the man is falling to the
        floor_Spanish masc]

(11)

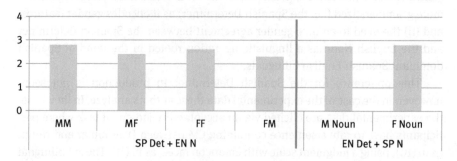

The results of the judgment task (Figure 1) show that the 2L1 children significantly prefer sequences with an English Determiner (the two rightmost columns) over sequences with a Spanish Determiner (remaining columns to the left) ($p=.013$). This is, in a way, to be expected as this CM structure has less processing costs given that no gender valuation operation needs to be implemented as the English Determiner carries no gender features.

Figure 1: Code-mixed Det-N sequences: the experimental judgments of 2L1 bilinguals.

In the case of the Spanish Determiner CM structures, there is a preference for [+AC] options that is almost statistically significant (p=.068). That is, this group of 2L1 bilingual children rate CM in (10a) more favorably than that in (10b). This preference for the matching option seems to suggest that Spanish gender features have a high representational value in the mind of these bilinguals in that they need to implement this valuation procedure between the gender features of the Spanish Determiner and those of the Spanish translation equivalent of the English Noun.

Studies like Liceras et al. (2008, 2016) point to, at least, two issues that have often been discussed in the analysis of CM in 2L1 bilingual acquisition research: the role of language dominance and the social status of CM. With respect to dominance, and given the results presented above, the GFSH captures a view of dominance based on the features encoded in the lexicon of a particular language and on the saliency these features have in this language. Therefore, the dominant language would be the one whose features are most grammaticized because they are the ones that would guide how structures are generated, regardless of whether this particular language is the one in which the bilingual is most proficient or to which he has been more exposed.

The social status of CM has to do with whether CM is part of the speech of the community and, therefore, a common practice, or rather a more *ad hoc* phenomenon. And this is linked to the social context in which the 2L1 bilingual is immersed. As seen in Section 1 above, there are different 2L1 acquisition contexts, so that, while some are more restricted to the family context (as in individual bilingualism), others are part of a broader social context (as in societal bilingualism). Some authors have suggested that the study of CM should be limited to those 2L1 bilinguals who actually use CM on a daily basis, that is, to code-switchers (e.g. Guzzardo Tamargo, Valdés Kroff & Dussias 2016; Valdés Kroff, Dussias, Gerfen, Perrotti & Bajo 2016).[5] However, potentially all 2L1 bilinguals can code-switch and have intuitions about code-switched structures.[6] Besides, as shown in

---

5 These authors specifically argue that bilinguals who code-switch at the societal level may produce code-switches that differ from those produced and processed by other bilinguals (i.e. non-code-switchers) (e.g. Beatty-Martínez & Dussias 2017; Guzzardo Tamargo et al. 2016; Valdés Kroff 2016; Valdés Kroff et al. 2016). Although the populations in these studies do not involve children in Spain, as it is our case, their Spanish-English bilinguals mostly prefer Spanish-masculine Determiner – English Noun CM structures. And this seems to be so for both US east coast bilinguals (who arguably may now be more English dominant) but also for Spanish dominant Puerto Ricans.
6 The information that is obtained on the representation of language in the mind of the bilingual and on language competence through the analysis of experimental data complements that

Table 4, children who are immersed in an individual bilingualism context (Spain in the case of the FerFuLice corpus, or the UK in the case of the Deuchar corpus), also produce instances of CM. Furthermore, and in the case of experimental data, what is being tested is the internal knowledge speakers have of their two grammars and how these grammars interact. The fact that the judgments, as shown in Figure 1, are around the mid value 2 could be accounted for in this respect: these speakers are not used to code-switching. However, as the statistical analyses show, these speakers do not treat all CM in (10) in the same way: unlike in production, in the grammaticality judgment task they prefer English Det mixes where no gender agreement features are involved because processing this DP is less costly. However, if gender features appear (i.e. in Spanish Det mixes), they show a clear preference for the enforcement of the gender agreement mechanism, that is, for the implementation of the AC.

7 Conclusions and future directions

In this chapter, we have provided an analysis of data from two English-Spanish 2L1 bilinguals growing up in Spain as compared to data from other bilinguals and monolinguals. We have focused on two core issues that are specific to 2L1 acquisition: language dominance and crosslinguistic influence. Our analysis has pointed to how language properties shape the directionality and the effect of crosslinguistic influence. In particular, Spanish lexical specialization explains that, in the early stages of English-Spanish 2L1 acquisition, Spanish be the language that constitutes the *locus* of influence and that influence has a facilitating effect. This is reflected in how the adult grammatical requirement in both copula constructions and sentential subjects emerges earlier in the spontaneous production of these English-Spanish bilinguals as compared to that of English and Spanish monolinguals. Differences with other bilinguals (e.g. Paradis & Navarro 2003) could rather be attributed to input differences or a rather weak command of one of the two languages (Silva-Corvalán 2014) and not so much to negative influence from Spanish into English or to lack of crosslinguistic influence.

Language properties and, in particular, Spanish highly grammaticized features, are also behind the CM preferences that appear in the spontaneous and experimental data of these bilingual children as well as in that of other bilingual

---

obtained from naturalistic data. That is, experimental data allow us to gather different and complementary information.

children and adults. As captured under the GFSH and the Gender Double-Feature Valuation Mechanism, the strength of Spanish gender features makes these bilinguals prefer the Spanish Determiner in switched DPs and enforce gender agreement between the Spanish Determiner and the Spanish translation equivalent of the (ungendered) English Noun. Although a contrast is seen in spontaneous *versus* acceptability judgment data, the strength of Spanish gender features is seen not only in the preference for the Spanish Determiner (spontaneous data) but also in the preference for the [+AC] Spanish Determiner (judgment data; examples 10a *versus* 10b).

While many future directions may be taken to investigate the outcomes of 2L1 acquisition, we would like to mention four that are relevant to the outcomes that we have discussed. First, both the *locus* and directionality of crosslinguistic influence as well as language dominance should be investigated with other language pairs where the semantic values (i.e. *be versus ser/estar*) take different realizations. Second, it would be important to carry out analyses of both experimental and spontaneous data from other language pairs to determine whether constructs such as the GFSH or the Analogical Criterion hold across the board and whether other constructs have to be proposed to deal with alternative scenarios. For instance, what is the spontaneous output and what are the preferences when mixing a language with a three gender value DP and a language without grammatical gender or with a two gender value DP (German vs. English or Spanish as in Klassen 2016)? Third, in order to complement the results obtained from the analysis of spontaneous data and off-line experimental data, the outputs and preferences of 2L1 representation and processing should be investigated using on-line tasks, eye-tracking, ERPs or neuroimaging (as in Dussias, Valdés Kroff, Guzzardo Tamargo & Gerfen 2013). Fourth, language dominance, crosslinguistic influence and code-switching should be investigated in both contexts of 2L1 individual bilingualism and 2L1 societal bilingualism.

Acknowledgements: This research has been funded by the Castile and León Regional Government Education Division (Spain) and FEDER [VA009P17] and by the Distinguished University Professor Fund of the University of Ottawa (Canada).

References

Azuma, S. 1993. The frame-content hypothesis in speech production: evidence from intrasentential code-switching. *Linguistics* 31. 1071–1093.

Baker, C. 2011. *Foundations of bilingual education*. Bristol: Multilingual Matters.

Beatty-Martínez, A. L. & P. E. Dussias. 2017. Bilingual experience shapes language processing: evidence from codeswitching. *Journal of Memory and Language* 95. 173–189.

Becker, M. 2000. *The development of the copula in child English: The lightness of Be*. Los Angeles: University of California doctoral dissertation.

Becker, M. 2004. Copula omission is a grammatical reflex. *Language Acquisition* 12(2). 157–167.

Bel, A. 2001 *Teoria lingüística i adquisició del llenguatge. Anàlisi comparada dels trets morfològics emcatalà i en castellà*. Barcelona: Institut d'Estudis Catalans.

Belazi, H, E. Rubin & A. J. Toribio. 1994. Code-switching and X-bar theory: The functional head constraint. *Linguistic Inquiry* 25. 221–237.

Bhatia, T. J. & W. C. Ritchie. 2004. *The handbook of bilingualism*. Oxford: Blackwell.

Bhatia, T. J. & W. C. Ritchie. 2012. *The handbook of bilingualism and multilingualism*. Oxford: Wiley-Blackwell.

Burkholder, M. 2018. Language mixing in the Nominal Phrase: Implications of a Distributed Morphology perspective. Languages 3(2).10. Special Issue Romance Languages at the Forefront of Language Acquisition Research (volume 1), edited by J. M. Liceras & R. Fernandez Fuertes. doi:10.3390/languages3020010

Cantone, K. F. & N. Müller. 2008. Un nase or una nase? What gender marking within switched DPs reveals about the architecture of the bilingual language faculty. *Lingua* 118. 810–826.

Carlson, G. 1977. *Reference to kinds in English*. Amherst: University of Massachusetts doctoral dissertation.

Chomsky, N. 1995. *The minimalist program*. Cambridge, MA: MIT Press.

Chomsky, N. 1998. Minimalist inquiries: the framework. *MIT Working Papers in Linguistics 15*. Also in R. Martin, D. Michaels & J. Uriagereka (eds.), *Step by step: essays on minimalist syntax in honor or Howard Lasnik* (2000). Cambridge, MA: MIT Press.

De Houwer, A. 1990. *The acquisition of two languages from birth: A case study*. Cambridge: Cambridge University Press.

De Houwer, A. 2009. *Bilingual first language acquisition*. Clevendon: Multilingual Matters.

Deuchar, M. & S. Quay. 2000. *Bilingual acquisition: theoretical implications of a case study*. Oxford: Oxford University Press.

Döpke, S. 2000. Generation of and retraction from crosslinguistically motivated structures in bilingual first language acquisition. *Bilingualism: Language and Cognition* 3(3). 209–226.

Dussias, P. E., J. R. Valdés Kroff, R. E. Guzzardo Tamargo & C. Gerfen. 2013. When gender and looking go hand in hand. Grammatical gender processing in L2 Spanish. *Studies in Second Language Acquisition* 35. 353–387.

Fantini, A. E. 1985. *Language acquisition of a bilingual child: a sociolinguistic perspective (to age ten)*. Clevedon: Multilingual Matters.

Fernández Fuertes, R. & J. M. Liceras. 2010. Copula omission in the English developing grammar of English/Spanish bilingual children. *International Journal of Bilingual Education and Bilingualism* 13(5). 525–551.

Gaulin, R. 2008. Examination of copula omission within the data of Spanish-English twin infants, Leo and Simon: The effects of transfer. University of Ottawa MA research paper.

Genesee, F. 1989. Early bilingual development: one language or two? *Journal of Child Language* 6. 161–179.

Genesee, F. 2003. Rethinking bilingual acquisition. In J. M. de Waele (ed.), *Bilingualism: Challenges and directions for future research*, 158–182. Clevedon: Multilingual Matters.

Genesee, F., E. Nicoladis & J. Paradis. 1995. Language differentiation in early bilingual development. *Journal of Child Language* 22(3). 611–631.

Grosjean, F. 1982. *Life with two languages: an introduction to bilingualism*. Cambridge, MA: Harvard University Press.

Grosjean, F. 1985. The bilingual as a competent but specific speaker-hearer. *Journal of Multilingual and Multicultural Development* 6. 467–477. Also in M. Cruz-Ferreira (ed.), *Multilingual norms*, 19–31. Frankfurt am Main: Peter Lang.

Grosjean, F. 2008. *Studying bilinguals*. Oxford: Oxford University Press.

Guzzardo Tamargo, R. E., J. R. Valdés Kroff & P. E. Dussias. 2016. Using code-switching as a tool to study the link between production and comprehension. *Journal of Memory and Language* 89. 138–161.

Hulk, A. and N. Müller. 2000. Bilingual first language acquisition at the interface between syntax and pragmatics. *Bilingualism: Language and Cognition* 3(3). 227–244.

Jake, J. L., C. Myers-Scotton & S. Gross. 2002. Making a minimalist approach to codeswitching work: Adding the matrix language. *Bilingualism: Language and Cognition* 5(1). 69–91.

Jessner, U. 2008. A DST dynamic system theory. Modern of multilingualism and the role of metalinguistic awareness. *The Modern Language Journal* 92(2). 270–283.

Jorschick, L., A. Endesfelder Quick, D. Glässer, E Lieven & M. Tomasello. 2011. German–English-speaking children's mixed NPs with 'correct' agreement. *Bilingualism: Language and Cognition* 14(2). 173–183.

Klassen, R. 2016. The representation of asymmetric grammatical gender systems in the bilingual mental lexicon. *Probus* 28(1). 9–28.

Köppe, R. & J. Meisel. 1995. Code-switching in bilingual first language acquisition. In L. Milroy and P. Muysken (eds.), *One speaker, two languages*, 276–301. Cambridge: Cambridge University Press.

Lanza, E. 1997. *Language mixing in infant bilingualism: a sociolinguistic perspective*. Oxford: Oxford University Press.

Liceras, J. M. & R. Fernández Fuertes. 2018. Subject omission/production in child bilingual English and child bilingual Spanish: The view from linguistic theory. *Probus* 29(1).

Liceras, J. M., R. Fernández Fuertes & A. Alba de la Fuente. 2012. Overt subjects and copula omission in the Spanish and the English grammar of English-Spanish bilinguals: On the locus and directionality of interlinguistic influence. *First Language* 32(1–2). 88–115.

Liceras, J. M., R. Fernández Fuertes & R. Klassen. 2016. Language dominance and language nativeness: the view from English-Spanish codeswitching. In R. E. Guzzardo Tamargo, C. M. Mazak & M. C. Parafita Couto (eds.), *Spanish-English codeswitching in the Caribbean and the U.S.*, 107–138. Amsterdam: John Benjamins.

Liceras, J. M. R. Fernández Fuertes, S. Perales, R. Pérez-Tattam & K. T. Spradlin. 2008. Gender and gender agreement in bilingual native and non-native grammars: a view from child and adult functional-lexical mixings. *Lingua* 118. 827–851.

Liceras, J. M., R. Fernández Fuertes & R. Pérez-Tattam. 2008. Null and overt subjects in the developing grammars (L1 English/L1 Spanish) of two bilingual twins. In C. Pérez-Vidal, M. Juan-Garau & A. Bel (eds.), *A portrait of the young in the new multilingual Spain*, 111–134. Bristol: Multilingual Matters.

Liceras, J. M., K. T. Spradlin & R. Fernández Fuertes. 2005. Bilingual early functional-lexical mixing and the activation of formal features. *International Journal of Bilingualism* 9(2). 227–251.

Lindholm, K. J. & A. M. Padilla. 1978. Language mixing in bilingual children. *Journal of Child Language* 5. 327–335.

Malakoff, M.E., L. C. Mayes, R. Schottenfeld & S. Howell. 1999. Language production in 24-month-old inner-city children of cocaine-and-other-drug-using mothers. *Journal of Applied Developmental Psychology* 20. 159–180.

Meisel, J. M. 2008. Child second language acquisition or successive first language acquisition? In B. Haznedar and E. Gavruseva (eds.), *Current trends in child second language acquisition: a generative perspective*, 55–80. Amsterdam: John Benjamins.

Meisel, J. M. 2011. *First and second language acquisition*. New York: Cambridge University Press.

MacSwan, J. 1999. *A minimalist approach to intrasentential code switching*. New York: Garland.

MacSwan, J. 2000. The architecture of the bilingual language faculty: evidence from intrasentential code switching. *Bilingualism: Language and Cognition*. 3 (1). 37–54.

MacSwan J. (ed.). 2014. *Grammatical theory and bilingual codeswitching*. Cambridge, MA: MIT Press.

MacWhinney, B. 2000. *The CHILDES project: tools for analyzing talk*. 3rd edn.. Mahwah, NJ: Lawrence Erlbaum Associates.

Moro, M. 2001. The semantic interpretation and syntactic distribution of determiner phrases in Spanish/English codeswitching. Paper presented at ISB3, Briston, UK.

Moro, M. 2014. The semantic interpretation and syntactic distribution of determiner phrases in Spanish-English codeswitching. In J. MacSwan (ed.), *Grammatical theory and bilingual codeswitching*, 213–226. Cambridge, MA: MIT Press.

Moyer, M. 1993. *Analysis of code-switching in Gibraltar*. Bellaterra: Universidad Autónoma de Barcelona doctoral dissertation.

Myers-Scotton, C. 2005. Supporting a Differential Access Hypothesis. In J. Kroll and A. de Groot (eds.), *Handbook of bilingualism, psycholinguistic approaches*, 326–348. New York: Oxford University Press.

Myers-Scotton, C. & J. L. Jake. 2001. Explaining aspects of code-switching and their implications. In J. L. Nicol (ed.) *One mind, two languages: bilingual language processing*, 84–116. Malden, MA: Blackwell.

Müller, N. 1998. Transfer in bilingual first language acquisition. *Bilingualism: Language and Cognition* 1(3). 151–172.

Nicoladis, E. 1994. *Code-mixing in young bilingual children*. Montreal: McGill University doctoral dissertation.

Nicoladis, E. 2002. The cues that children use in acquiring adjectival phrases and compound nouns: Evidence from bilingual children. *Brain and Language* 81. 635–648.

Nicoladis, E. & G. Secco. 1998. The role of translation equivalents in a bilingual family's code-switching. In A. Greenhill, M. Hughes, H. Littlefield & H. Walsh (eds.), *Proceedings of the 22nd annual Boston University Conference on Language Development*, 576–585. Somerville, MA: Cascadilla Press.

Nicoladis, E. & F. Genesee. 1998. Parental discourse and code-mixing in bilingual children. *International Journal of Bilingualism* 2. 85–99.

Ong, K. K. W. & L. J. Zhang. 2010. Metalinguistic filters within the bilingual language faculty: A study of young English-Chinese bilinguals. *Journal of Psycholinguistic Research* 39(3). 243–272.

Otheguy, R. & N. Lapidus. 2005. Matización de la teoría de la simplificación en las lenguas en contacto: el concepto de la adaptación en el español de Nueva York. In L. Ortiz-López and M. Lacorte (eds.), *Contactos y contextos lingüísticos: el español en Estados Unidos y en* contacto con otras lenguas, 143–160. Madrid and Frankfurt: Editorial Iberoamericana / Vervuert Verlag.

Paradis, J. & S. Navarro. 2003. Subject realization and crosslinguistic interference in the bilingual acquisition of Spanish and English. *Journal of Child Language* 30. 1–23.

Paradis, J. & F. Genesee. 1996. Syntactic acquisition in bilingual children: Autonomous or interdependent? *Studies in Second Language Acquisition* 18(1). 1–25.

Paradis, J, M. Crago & F. Genesee. 2005/2006. Domain-general versus domain-specific accounts of Specific Language Impairment: Evidence from bilingual children's acquisition of object pronouns. *Language Acquisition* 13(1). 33–62.

Petersen, J. 1988. Word-internal code-switching constraints in a bilingual child's grammar. *Linguistics* 26. 479–493.

Poplack, S. 1980. Sometimes I'll start a sentence in Spanish y termino en español: Toward a typology of code-switching. *Linguistics* 18. 581–618.

Redlinger, W. E. & T. Park. 1980. Language mixing in young bilinguals. *Journal of Child Language* 7. 337–352.

Sera, M. D. 1992. To be or to be: Use and acquisition of the Spanish copulas. *Journal of Memory and Languages* 31. 408–427.

Serratrice, L. 2002. Overt subjects in English: evidence for the marking of person in an English-Italian bilingual child. *Journal of Child Language* 29. 327–355.

Serratrice, L., A. Sorace & S. Paoli. 2004. Crosslinguistic influence at the syntax-pragmatics interface: Subjects and objects in English-Italian bilingual and monolingual acquisition. *Bilingualism: Language and Cognition* 7(3). 183–205.

Schmitt, C. & K. Miller. 2007. Making discourse-dependent decisions: The case of the copulas ser and estar in Spanish. *Lingua* 117. 1907–1929.

Silva-Corvalán, C. 2003. Linguistic consequences of reduced input in bilingual first language acquisition. In S. Montrul and F. Ordoñez (eds.) *Linguistic theory and language development in Hispanic languages*. 375–397. Somerville, MA: Cascadilla Press

Silva-Corvalán, C. 2014. *Bilingual language acquisition: Spanish and English in the first six years*. Cambridge: Cambridge University Press.

Sorace, A. 2011. Pinning down the concept of "interface" in bilingualism. *Linguistic Approaches to Bilingualism* 1(1). 1–33.

Swain, M. 1972. *Bilingualism as a first language*. Irvine: University of California at Irvine doctoral dissertation.

Taeschner, T. 1983. *The sun is feminine: a study on language acquisition in bilingual children*. New York: Springer Verlag.

Toribio, A. J. 2001. On the emergence of bilingual code-switching competence. *Bilingualism: Language and Cognition* 4 (3). 203–231.

Tsimpli, I. M. & A. Sorace. 2006. Differentiating interfaces: L2 performance in syntax-semantics and syntax-discourse phenomena. In D. Bamman, T. Magnitskaia & C. Zaller (eds.), *Proceedings of the 30th annual Boston University Conference on Language Development, BUCLD 30*, 653–664. Somerville, MA: Cascadilla Press.

Unsworth, S. 2003. Testing Hulk & Müller (2000) on crosslinguistic influence: Root infinitives in a bilingual German/English child. *Bilingualism: Language and Cognition* 6(2). 143–158.

Vihman, M. 1985. A developmental perspective on code-switching conversations between a pair of bilingual siblings. *TESOL Quarterly* 19(2). 371–373.

Volterra, V. & T Taeschner. 1978. The acquisition and development of language by bilingual children. *Journal of Child Language* 5. 311–326.

Valdés Kroff, J. R. 2016. Mixed NPs in Spanish-English bilingual speech: using a corpus-based approach to inform models of sentence processing. In R. E. Guzzardo Tamargo, C. Mazak & M. C. Parafita Couto (eds.), *Spanish-English code-switching in the Caribbean and the US*, 281–300. Amsterdam: John Benjamins.

Valdés Kroff, J. R., P. E. Dussias, C. Gerfen, L. Perrotti & M. T. Bajo. 2017. Experience with code-switching modulates the use of grammatical gender during sentence processing. *Linguistic Approaches to Bilingualism 7.* 163–198.

Wapole, C. 2000. The bilingual child: One system or two? In E. V. Clark (ed.), *The Proceedings of the 30th Annual Child Language Research Forum*, 187–194. Stanford: CSLI.

Yip, V. & S. Matthews. 2000. Syntactic transfer in a Cantonese-English bilingual child. *Bilingualism: language and cognition* 3(3). 193–208.

Yip, V. & S. Matthews. 2007. *The bilingual child: early development and language contact.* Cambridge: Cambridge University Press.

Zentella, A. C. 1981. *Hablamos los dos. We speak both: Growing up bilingual in el Barrio.* Philadelphia: University of Pennsylvania doctoral dissertation.

Zentella, A. C. 2000. Puerto Ricans in the United States: Confronting the linguistic repercussions of colonialism. In S. L. MacKay and S. L. C. Wong (eds.), *New immigrants in the United States*, 137–164. Cambridge: Cambridge University Press.

Francisco Dubert-García and Juan Carlos Acuña-Fariña

Restructuring and complexification of inflectional morphology under linguistic contact: The case of a Galician dialect

Abstract: Galician has been in contact with Spanish since the very origins of both languages. Galician and Spanish are strongly structurally, genetically and typologically related. As the intensity of the contact has been growing and the number of bilingual speakers has been steadily increasing along the 20th century, more and more grammatical Spanish features entered into Galician. In this study, we analyse how the borrowing of Spanish morphological patterns that hypercharacterize the expression of various morphosyntactic features of some verbs causes a restructuring in the grammar of an urban variety of Galician mainly spoken by bilinguals. The incorporation of those Spanish borrowings also seems to provoke an increase in the complexity of the grammar of this Galician variety. We reflect on whether what seems to be a complexification from the point of view of an isolated grammar may be considered a simplification from the point of view of a bilingual mind/speaker.

1 Introduction

Galician is a Romance language spoken in the Northwest of the Iberian Peninsula. It is commonly assumed that Galician and Portuguese resulted from the split of an old unitary medieval language, today known as Galician-Portuguese. From its very beginning, Galician has been in contact with Spanish, conforming a case of intense and old inter-community bilingualism. This contact has influenced the internal history of Galician and partially explains the separation of Galician and Portuguese (Mariño 2008; Monteagudo 1999; Dubert & Galves 2016; Dubert-García 2017). For example:

Note: This research was supported by grants PSI2015-65116-P and FFI2015-65208-P from the Spanish Government and grants GRC2015/006 and ED431C_2017/34 by the Autonomous Galician Government/ERDF. We owe many observations made in the text to Ana Iglesias, Xulio Sousa, Paul O'Neill, Iván Tamaredo, two anonymous reviewers and the editors, to whom we are grateful.

Francisco Dubert-García, Instituto da Lingua Galega / Universidade de Santiago de Compostela
Juan Carlos Acuña-Fariña, Universidade de Santiago de Compostela

https://doi.org/10.1515/9781501509988-008

- Galician and Spanish lack phonemic voiced fricatives and nasal vowels (present in Medieval Galician and preserved in Portuguese); Galician and Spanish share voiced non-lateral palatals replacing an old palatal lateral (preserved in European Portuguese); Galician and Spanish developed a devoiced dental fricative (lacking in Portuguese).
- Galician and Spanish share the form of some morphemes like -ble in amable 'kind' (Portuguese -vel, amável) or -ción in admiración 'admiration' (Portuguese -ção, admiração)
- Galician and Spanish substituted the Presents of Indicative and of Subjunctive for the Future of Subjunctive (preserved in Portuguese).

In this study, we will adopt the view by Thomason (2003: 688) that contact between languages "is a source of linguistic change whenever a change occurs that would have been unlikely, or at least less likely, to occur outside a specific contact situation". These changes are externally motivated, in that they are guided by social, not structural considerations (Hickey 2012: 388). Although extended bilingualism is not a necessary condition to produce linguistic changes due to contact (Hock 1991: 493), the more widespread bilingualism is in a community, the more the possibilities of change due to contact exists. By bilingualism we understand here individual bilingualism, the ability by one person to use two languages with similar (not necessarily equal) proficiency for different purposes.

We will also adopt the view by Matras (2009, 2010) that from the *perspective of the individual multilingual speaker*, language contact is about "the challenge of employing *a repertoire of communicative resources* [...] in such a way that it will comply with the expectations of audiences and interlocutors in various interaction settings" (2009: 38, emphasis added). In this view, multilingual speakers have a single *multilingual repertoire*, not two or more linguistic repertoires; and they must maintain strict demarcation boundaries among subsets of their linguistic repertoire to be able to communicate in different monolingual settings.

One of our goals is to study linguistic change and its consequences by showing how the influence of Spanish has restructured the Galician dialect spoken in Santiago de Compostela. In order to do that, we shall analyse the results of various morphological changes that modified the roots of some verbs (oír 'to hear', traer 'to bring' and caer 'to fall'; salir 'to go out' and valer 'to be good at/for'; poder 'to be able to/can' and haber 'to have'; verbs ending in the suffix –ecer like obedecer 'to obey'), whose forms have become similar to the corresponding Spanish ones; those modifications rearranged those verbs in different morpholexical classes.

The other goal we have is to show that although the morphological borrowings taken from Spanish have produced a complexification in the abstract system of Galician grammar, a resulting related simplification has also taken place. In addition to the dynamics imposed by linguistic change, language shift and the various explicative phenomena covered in social network theory (Newman et al. 2006; Carrington & Scott 2011; Kadushin 2012), changes provoked by language contact may also be contemplated from the complexity vs simplification of the grammar of the recipient languages (Trudgill 2011; Thomason 2003). This *complexification* (or lack of it, but we will use 'complexification' in what follows to cover both directions of change) may simply occur as a result of the addition of features transferred from one language to another (Trudgill 2010: 301).[1] For analysing this complexification various approaches have been proposed, a prominent one being a distinction between *absolute* vs *relative* complexity (Miestamo 2008; Kusters 2008). Absolute complexity is a function of the number of elements conforming a *system* or the length of the description of its working; thus, a system including two allomorphs in complementary distribution for expressing Plural is more complex than a system including only one morph, since the first contains more units than the second and its description is longer. Relative, speaker-oriented complexity, is related to the difficulties that a concrete speaker has for using a language; Miestamo (2008: 25) calls this complexity *difficulty* or *cost* ("how difficult a phenomenon is to process (encode/decode) or learn"). Kusters (2008) defends the view that relative complexity offers the best approximation to the study of linguistic complexity, in line with the invocation of efficiency and computational principles in Hawkins (1994, 2004). In this contribution, we will not be too concerned with the specificities of the complexity literature but will rather be interested only in the basic debate whether language contact (a major theme for us here) brings about either a more complex (Nichols 1992: 193) or a less complex (e.g. Kusters 2008) *system*. Importantly, we *will* be concerned with whether that debate is framed from the perspective of the abstract *system of a grammar* or, alternatively, from the perspective of the mind of actual speakers (a different kind of *system*).[2]

---

1 The term *complexity* is usually employed as a generic or neutral term to refer to the complexity of a system of grammar (the number of elements it contains, of connections among elements, etc. See the *Introduction* of Miestamo et al. 2008). *Complexification* implies an increase in the complexity of the system, and *simplification* a reduction thereof.
2 Part of the reason for not wishing to become involved here with the technicalities of the complexity literature is that the very concept of relative complexity has in our opinion never been defined with precision: it usually covers processing and/or learning difficulties and almost everything that may be relevant from the standpoint of the speaker/hearer. The distinction

In our discussion, we will adopt a usage based exemplar model (Bybee 1985, 1988, 2001; Langacker 2000), a non-derivative framework in which frequent complex words are stored in the lexicon, even if they are regularly formed and have a predictable meaning. Nevertheless, complex words stored in the lexicon have an internal structure emerging from the lexical connections that words sharing similarities of form and meaning establish among them. The lexical connections (that emerge through the reinforcement of the common features inherent in multiple experiences) produce the *schemata* that give structure to the stored words. Thus, *schemata* are "the commonality that emerges from distinct structures when one abstracts away from their points of difference by portraying them with lesser precision and specificity" (Langaker 2000: 3). Schemata, inherent in the stored words, are used to create, by analogy, infrequent complex words that are not stored.

We would like to stress the fact that our goal is not to write a study on contemporary linguistic variation from a sociolinguistic, Labovian, point of view, but to compare two varieties which are different according to the intensity of the morphological interference they have gone through.

In this article, lexemes and morphosyntactic features are written in small capitals (e.g. CANTAR 'to sing'; 1SG 'first person singular'); word-forms, unless they are phonetically transcribed, are written in italics (*cantar* 'to sing'). The citation forms of the Galician verbs are the word forms of the infinitives (written in small capitals); the citation forms of the Latin verbs are the word forms of the 1SG. IND.PRS (written in small capitals).

All abbreviations for the morphosyntactic features are in accordance with the Leipzig Glossing Rules[3]: FUT future, COND conditional, PST past, PFV perfective, IPFV imperfective, IND indicative, SBJV subjunctive, INF infinitive, 1 1st person,

---

between representational and processing difficulty is probably better captured in the distinction between *systemic* vs *structural* complexity (Dahl 2004: 40–45). *Systemic complexity* refers to the complexity of the grammatical rules (or constructions, templates, patterns etc.), whereas *structural complexity* refers to the complexity of the structures that are the result of those rules. This distinction complements the absolute vs relative complexity fork. Thus, for instance, we can talk about *absolute systemic complexity* (e.g. the number of rules that are necessary to explain the verbal morphology of a language) and about *absolute structural complexity* (e.g. the number of phonemes/morphemes that the verbal forms of a language may have). Likewise, we can also talk about *relative systemic complexity* and *relative structural complexity* to refer to the domains just mentioned above but from the perspective of the speaker (representational difficulties vs processing costs).

3 https://www.eva.mpg.de/lingua/pdf/Glossing-Rules.pdf

2 2nd person, 3 3rd person, sg singular, pl plural. The asterisk (*) represents a reconstructed etymon, not documented in Latin (*pōneo 'I put').

In §2 the source of our data will be presented; §3 contains a description of the linguistic community of Santiago in terms of social networks; §4 analyses cases of morphological borrowing; in §5 we discuss the data and in §6 we offer a few concluding remarks.

2 The case study: the Galician of Santiago de Compostela

The Galician dialects of Santiago were studied by Dubert-García (1999) in an exploratory survey that tried to discover their basic features. The data were gathered between 1991 and 1998 mostly through semi-directed conversations, although direct questions were needed to obtain grammatical structures difficult to obtain in spontaneous settings. This was the first time that a survey on the Galician dialects included an urban community and data taken from young people, university graduates, white-collar workers, and bilingual speakers of Galician and Spanish.

Dubert-García (1999) used 35 informants with different social backgrounds. 16 of them claimed to speak both Galician and Spanish depending on the language of their interlocutors; all of them lived or worked in the city. 4 of these 16 also declared that Spanish was the language learned at home and that they had learned Galician with their friends or at school, while, conversely, the other 12 pointed out that Galician was the language learned at home and that they had learned Spanish with friends or at school. The other 19 informants lived in the rural parishes surrounding the city; they were peasants or blue collar workers, and declared that they had Galician as their mother tongue (most of them were monolinguals in Galician); these last 19 people could be considered as the prototypical informants of classical linguistic geography (Chambers & Trudgill 1998: 29–30).

The data collected by Dubert-García will be complemented with those other gathered by the authors of the *Atlas Lingüístico Galego* (*ALGa*) among 1974–1977. In the survey network of the *ALGa*, Santiago was represented by point C35, Sar, which in the mid-1970s was a periurban neighbourhood of the city (see map in the Appendix).

In his survey, Dubert-García (1999) discovered a huge and surprising range of dialectal variation across the territories administrated by the municipality of Santiago. These territories, despite containing a city, were characterized by a complicated lattice of numerous isoglosses. Dubert-García (1999: 237–239) considered that, at least in the past, the urban Galician spoken in Santiago did not have a great influence on the surrounding rural dialects, which were different in phonological and morphological features. After analysing his data, Dubert-García (1999: 236) also concluded that, roughly speaking, two *models* of language coexist in the municipality of Santiago: an *urban* and a *rural Galician*. The varieties are different not only in the features they present, but even in the way their speakers treat the linguistic variables: e.g., rural speakers overtly use phonological features that urban speakers condemn.[4] One of the features distinguishing both varieties is the presence of more Spanish morphological borrowings in the variety spoken in the city. Some of these borrowings are the object of this work.

3 Santiago, a bilingual city

To explain why there exists more Spanish morphological borrowing in the urban Galician of Santiago, we need a short sketch of the sociolinguistic landscape and of the linguistic history of the territory where the data were collected. We will try to show that the degree of contact between Galician and Spanish is different in the rural and urban parts of the municipality of Santiago de Compostela because the degree of contact is higher in the city than in rural areas.

Seat of the University of Santiago de Compostela, capital of the Community of Galicia, and see of the Archdiocese of Santiago, Santiago de Compostela is a city with nearly 100 000 inhabitants, a hub of a complex of hospitals servicing areas well beyond the municipality boundaries, as well as a commercial centre attending to a large geographic area. A large rural area, divided in parishes (autonomous religious and social entities), surrounds the city.

The growth of Santiago is very recent and came about through a migratory phenomenon that carried people from the countryside to the city; this process was accompanied by the parallel urbanization of the rural areas of Santiago. These phenomena surely had important consequences both in the original Galician dialect of the city and in the speech of the immigrants.[5]

---

4 This is the case of features like the *seseo* (the lack of [θ], whose lexical incidence is occupied by [s]: [faser] instead of [faθer] 'to do'), or the *gheada* (the lack of [g], whose lexical incidence is occupied by [h]: [hato] instead of [gato] 'cat').

5 Unfortunately, these consequences are yet to be studied. Santiago seems to be an ideal place to develop surveys like those of Bortoni-Ricardo (1985), García Mouton / Molina Martos (2009), Martín Butragueño (2004), and Molina Martos (2006)

Until the middle of the 20th century, the rural parishes of Santiago had an agrarian way of life (Torres Luna & Lois González 1995; López Iglesias 2016). In this rural world, social networks have strong ties among their members: relatives, acquaintances and workmates tend to be the same people. This organization contributes to the preservation of little autonomous speech communities and hinders the exchange of linguistic innovations (Milroy 1992; Valcárcel Riveiro 2001; Chambers 2009; Kusters 2008). In the decade of 1950s, the municipality of Santiago "demonstrated the impossibility to reach significant growth rates", since it appeared marginalized "as an administrative capital and lacked industrial tradition" (Torres Luna & Lois González 1995: 733, our translation). Dubert-García (1999: 237–239) attributes to those facts the high degree of dialectal variation that he still found in the rural and periurban territories of Santiago in the 1990s. However, from the 1950s to the 1970s Santiago witnessed

> The dismantling of the traditional country society, most plainly evidenced by the intense migratory process that, from the fifties to the middle of the seventies, leaves the interior and rural regions hardly without any young population (Torres Luna & Lois González 1995: 733, our translation).

From the 1950s onwards, the city of Santiago underwent a spectacular development: the growth of the University, the network of hospitals, the city's status as the capital of Galicia, the creation of industrial parks and malls, transformed the city and increased its population. The municipality had 35 710 inhabitants in 1900, 61 852 in 1950, and 93 695 in 1981. The city had 15 386 inhabitants in 1900 (43,1% of the total population), while it had 61 480 in 1981 (65,6% of the total population). The creation of jobs in the city and the waning agricultural economy made the rural inhabitants turn their sights to the city as a place for living, leisure and shopping. From the beginning of the 1950's onwards, the sharp contrast rural vs urban is difficult to maintain, as is the opposition countryside vs city. What is found is a complex continuum between some more densely inhabited human settlements and others with a more diffused population (Valcárcel Riveiro 2001: 196). In fact, what has been occurring in Santiago for the past 60 years is a process of urbanization.[6]

---

6 "The term *urbanization* is used in the Social Sciences to refer to three different complementary processes. First, it reflects the phenomenon whereby population concentrates around a series of principal centres or privileged spaces. Second, it refers to the location of industry and other economic and non-agricultural activities in cities and their peripheries. Finally, it expresses the way in which the urban ways of life diffuse throughout the territory to society as a whole" (Torres Luna / Lois González 1995: 732).

The diffusion of the distinction countryside vs city was closely related to a shift from Galician to Spanish. In urban communities, social networks have weaker ties, since relatives, workmates and acquaintances may be different people coming from different origins (Milroy 1992; Valcárcel Riveiro 2001; Chambers 2009; Kusters 2008). In these cases, speakers may easily introduce innovations (often via borrowings) in their language because they may take features they hear from the members of other groups; this social structure increases the chances of linguistic change and dialectal levelling (the loss of dialectal differences through the selection and spreading of some variants). Interaction among individuals with weaker ties may produce accommodation phenomena (Trudgill 1986: 1–38). More mobile individuals, who tend to occupy a marginal position to some cohesive group, usually carry information across social boundaries and diffuse innovations of various kinds (Milroy 1992: 180–181).

In comparison with the surrounding rural areas, the city of Santiago has been bearing a larger weight of Spanish as a "roof tongue", that is, the preferred communication language (Muljačić 1991): in Galicia, the middle classes of the cities (craftsmen, shopkeepers...) are Spanish speakers and the popular working classes (labourer, peons...) are typically bilingual (Valcárcel 2001: 194). Table 1 contains data about the mother tongue in the municipality of Santiago at the beginning of the nineties (*MSG 1992-1*: 31). As can be seen, Galician tends to be the mother tongue of older people, originally from the countryside, and residing in the periurban area; Spanish tends to be the mother tongue of younger people born in the urban environment; even those who declare they acquired both languages in their childhood are generally urban people. Thus, we see that Spanish has a strong presence as the mother tongue in the people with an urban origin.

Table 2 contains data of the language which is most usually spoken in Santiago (*MSG 1992-2*; unfortunately, the authors of the survey did not correlate the origins of the speakers with their usual language, but we have data about the correlation between the mother tongue and the usual language); it shows that the differences in the current use of the two languages also correlate with age and residential environment; while the older population usually tends to use Galician, younger people tend to use Spanish. We also see that most speakers are bilingual independently of their mother tongue and those data are slightly favourable to Spanish.[7]

---

7 There exist data closer to our days (*MSG 2004-1, MSG 2004-2*), but we prefer to use those data of the nineties because they are contemporary to the linguistic data gathered by Dubert-García (1999). The data of *MSG 2004* show that, for example, in 2004 the index of Galician as the mother tongue in Santiago diminished: it was 35,1% (including "only Galician" and "more Galician"); regarding usual language, 20,2% answered "only Spanish"; 37,2%, "more Spanish"; 28,7%,

Table 1: Mother tongue in Santiago de Compostela[a].

	Galician	Spanish	Both	Other
AGE:				
16–25	25,3%	53,6%	20,7%	0,4%
26–40	43,5%	39,0%	15,6%	1,9%
41–65	66,2%	22,4%	10,6%	0,8%
+65	76,3%	14,1%	8,3%	1,3%
ORIGIN:				
Urban	28,8%	50,7%	20,5%	
Periurban	86,9%	5,2%	8,0%	
Villages	31,0%	52,1%	16,9%	
Rural 1	67,1%	19,2%	12,3%	1,4%
Rural 2	79,1%	9,9%	11,0%	
Out of Galicia	4,9%	76,7%	6,8%	11,7%
RESIDENTIAL ENVIRONMENT:				
Urban	40,3%	41,8%	16,8%	1,1%
Periurban	80,2%	11,7%	6,9%	1,2%
TOTAL	51,9%	33,0%	14,0%	1,1%

[a] *Origin* refers to the kind of settlement (rural, periurban, urban) where the informant was born. *Periurban* settlements are areas surrounding the cities and having a great dependency on them. Rural-1 settlements have less than 2000 inhabitants, streets, squares, sewage systems, banks, etc.; Rural-2 settlements also have less than 2000 inhabitants, but are disperse, without an urban appearance (*MSG 1992-1*: 18).

The bilingual status of the urban population and the relative linguistic weakness of the urban networks affected the urban Galician dialects. In fact, Dubert-García (1999) has shown that the Spanish borrowings are producing dialectal levelling across all the dialects of the municipality (e.g. the Spanish borrowing *hermano* 'brother' eliminates the dialectal variation between *irmán* and *irmao*, both present in the rural dialects). In turn, the Galician substrate has created a specific Spanish dialect in Galicia that incorporated Galician features, depending on the social background of the speakers (Álvarez Cáccamo 1989; Dubert 2002; Monteagudo & Santamarina 1993; Rojo 2004). Prominent among these features, for instance, are the use of the Galician

---

"more Galician"; 13,2% "only Galician". Those data show a decrease in the presence of Galician in the municipality. Anyway, in the *MSG 2004* survey, informants older than 54 years were excluded from the sample.

Table 2: Usual language in Santiago.

	Only Spanish	More Spanish	More Galician	Only Galician
AGE:				
16–25	16,5%	48,5%	20,3%	14,8%
26–40	13,2%	32,5%	33,9%	20,4%
41–65	7,7%	18,6%	33,8%	39,9%
+65	7,7%	11,5%	33,3%	47,4%
RESIDENTIAL ENVIRONMENT:				
Urban	14,8%	33,9%	32,1%	19,2%
Periurban	2,7%	14,4%	28,1%	54,2%
MOTHER TONGUE:				
Galician		6,0%	40,6%	53,3%
Spanish	32,0%	54,1%	12.3%	1,6%
Both	1,2%	49,7%	41,0%	8,1%
Other	46,2%	30,8%	7,7%	15,4%
TOTAL:	11,3%	28,3%	31,0%	29,5%

phonology and intonation patterns (Fernández Rei 2016), the use of simple past forms to refer to events coded in standard Spanish via the present perfect (*Me lastimé ahora mismo* 'I've got hurt just right now', instead of *Me he lastimado ahora mismo*), or the use of originally Galician morphological features (*dea* GIVE:1SG.SBJV.PRS, instead of *dé*) (Rojo 2004). The Galician borrowings into the Spanish spoken in Galicia made this language closer to Galician in general, which, in turn, might have helped to introduce Spanish borrowings into Galician (see below). The situation is that Santiago´s urban Galician has borrowed from Spanish not only words, but also elements of the morphology and syntax.

4 Inflectional borrowing in some Galician verbs in Santiago

The urban Galician dialects of Santiago de Compostela have taken more borrowings from Spanish than the rural ones, a fact that allows us to distinguish both varieties. In Galician linguistics, these items are usually known as *castelanismos* 'castilianisms' (since the common name Galician given to Spanish is *castellano* 'Castilian' in Spanish and dialectal Galician, or *castelán* in standard Galician).

These borrowings can be classified in two kinds, both present in the data gathered by Dubert-García (1999): *matter borrowing*, i.e., "the borrowing of concrete phonological matter" like words, affixes, roots, clitics...; and *pattern borrowing*, i.e., "the borrowing of functional and semantic morphological patterns" by which "a R[ecipient] L[anguage] rearranges its own inherited morphological structure in such a way that it becomes structurally closer to the S[ource] L[anguage]" (Gardani, Arkadiev &Amiridze 2015: 3).

A little sketch of Galician verbal morphology

As shown in Table 3, the prototypical word-form of a Galician regular verb presents a *root* (simple, like *mat-* 'to kill'; or complex, like *remat-* 'to finish off, to conclude') followed by a *thematic vowel*, a vowel that indicates the conjugation or inflectional class of the verb and that is located between the root and the inflectional endings. The root plus a thematic vowel make up a *theme*, the part of the word-form to which the inflectional endings are added to form the word-form. Finally, the prototypical inflectional ending is formed by two suffixes: a tense, aspect, and mood suffix and an agreement suffix (Álvarez, Regueira & Monteagudo 1986; Álvarez & Xove 2002; Freixeiro Mato 2000; Santamarina 1974; Villalva 2000).

Table 3: Morphological structure of *cantabamos* 'we used to sing'.

Word-form			
Theme		Inflectional ending	
Root	Thematic vowel	Tense, Aspect, Mood	Number, Person
cant	a	ba	mos

Each Galician verb must belong to one inflectional class or conjugation, marked by the thematic vowel: /a/ for the 1st conjugation, *cantar* 'to sing'; /e/ for the 2nd, *bater* 'to beat'; and /i/ for the 3rd, *partir* 'to split'. This is the same template that Spanish has. Some verbs belonging to the 2nd and 3rd conjugations share similar irregularities that allow us to group them in *morpholexical classes*, that is, groups of verbs with a special morphological behaviour: thus, the verbs OÍR 'to hear' and CAER 'to fall' present a special root ending in a semivowel /j/ in the 1SG of the Indicative Present (*oi-o* and *cai-o*) and in all the Subjunctive Present (*oi-a, cai-a*; § 4.3), despite the fact that they belong to different conjugations. These shared irregularities between different verbs make it possible to identify morphological formatives and patterns, and to show the inner organization and structure of the verbal paradigms.

Borrowing in the FUT word-forms of the verbs POÑER, TER, VIR, VALER and SAÍR

The Galician verbs POÑER 'to put', TER 'to have', VIR 'to come', VALER 'to be good at/ for', SAÍR 'to go out' are, in different degrees, irregular. The first three, strongly irregular, are historically related and share many family resemblances: their word-forms result from the palatalization of Lat. /VnjV/ (Lat. *těneo* > Gal. *teño* 'I have') or the dropping of an intervocalic Lat. /n/ (Lat. *těnes* > Gal. *tes* 'you have') (Ferreiro 1995).

As for VALER (< Lat. VALEO 'to be strong') and SAÍR (< Lat. SALIO 'to jump'), these verbs have had different historical developments in the standard variety,[8] where both belong to different morpholexical classes; while VALER retained its intervocalic Lat. /l/, SAÍR lost it. In (1a) we present the standard conjugation of the FUT and in (1b) that of the COND:

1)	'to put'	'to have'	'to come'	'to be good to/at'	'to go out'
a)	POÑER:FUT	TER:FUT	VIR:FUT	VALER:FUT	SAÍR:FUT
1SG	poñ-e-re-i	t-e-re-i	v-i-re-i	val-e-re-i	sa-i-re-i
2SG	poñ-e-rá-s	t-e-rá-s	v-i-rá-s	val-e-rá-s	sa-i-rá-s
3SG	poñ-e-rá	t-e-rá	v-i-rá	val-e-rá	sa-i-rá
1PL	poñ-e-re-mos	t-e-re-mos	v-i-re-mos	val-e-re-mos	sa-i-re-mos
2PL	poñ-e-re-des	t-e-re-des	v-i-re-des	val-e-re-des	sa-i-re-des
3PL	poñ-e-rá-n	t-e-rá-n	v-i-rá-n	val-e-rá-n	sa-i-rá-n
b)	POÑER:COND	TER:COND	VIR:COND	VALER:COND	SAÍR:COND
1SG	poñ-e-ría	t-e-ría	v-i-ría	val-e-ría	sa-i-ría
2SG	poñ-e-ría-s	t-e-ría-s	v-i-ría-s	val-e-ría-s	sa-i-ría-s
3SG	poñ-e-ría	t-e-ría	v-i-ría	val-e-ría	sa-i-ría
1PL	poñ-e-ria-mos	t-e-ria-mos	v-i-ria-mos	val-e-ria-mos	sa-i-ria-mos
2PL	poñ-e-ria-des	t-e-ria-des	v-i-ria-des	val-e-ria-des	sa-i-ria-des
3PL	poñ-e-ría-n	t-e-ría-n	v-i-ría-n	val-e-ría-n	sa-i-ría-n

---

[8] It is important not to lose sight of the fact that standard Galician is the result of a contemporary process of language planning by which some dialectal variants were conventionally selected among the pool of forms collected in the dialects; it was conceived on a purist orientation, in such a way that it avoids the castilianisms common in the dialects; it is also, fundamentally, a written variety. Standard Galician was elaborated in 1982 (Ramallo & Rei-Doval 2015).

The conventional, structuralist, morphological analysis of the FUT and the COND in current Galician linguistics is as follows:

(2)	R	TV	TAM(FUT)	Agr(2PL)		R	TV	TAM(COND)	Agr(2PL)
	poñ-	-e-	-re-	-des		poñ-	-e-	-ria-	-des
	t-	-e-	-re-	-des		t-	-e-	-ria-	-des
	v-	-i-	-re-	-des		v-	-i-	-ria-	-des
	val-	-e-	-re-	-des		val-	-e-	-ria-	-des
	sa-	-i-	-re-	-des		sa-	-i-	-ria-	-des

It should be noted that Galician and Spanish share all the endings of these verbal word-forms, except for the 1SG.FUT, Galician -[ej] (*cantarei*), Spanish -[e] (*cantaré*); and the 2PL, Galician -[des] (*cantaredes*), Spanish -[js] (*cantaréis*); the word-forms corresponding to the 1PL.COND and 2PL.COND are stressed on the penultimate syllable in Galician (*can.ta.ri.á.mos* 'we would sing') and on the antepenultimate syllable in Spanish (*can.ta.rí.a.mos*).

However, in most Galician dialects, SAÍR 'to go out' has word-forms preserving the Lat. /l/. Thus, depending on the dialect, SALIR belongs to different morpholexical classes (*ALGa*, maps from 161 to 174); *salir* is precisely the form found in Santiago. In (3) we present all the word-forms of the FUT and COND of POÑER, TER, VIR, SALIR, and VALER registered by Dubert-García (1999: 171–172):

3)	Santiago's rural Galician		Santiago's urban Galician	
	FUT	COND	FUT	COND
POÑER	*poñerei*	*poñería*	not found[9]	*pondría*
TER	*terei*	*tería*	*tendrei, tendrá, tendrán*	*tendría, tendríamos*
VIR	*virei*	*viría*	not found	*vendrían*
VALER	*valerei*	*valería*	*valdrei*	*valdrían*
SALIR	*salirei*	*saliría*	*saldrei, saldrán*[10]	not found

---

9 A reviewer suggested that the authors might search for the forms not found in current urban Galician of Santiago. We prefer to use only the forms effectively registered by Dubert-García (19999) in order to avoid the mixing of new and old data. The forms lacking can be easily registered in spontaneous conversations with Galician speakers from Santiago. In fact, those forms can even be found in the literary language: e.g., the corpus *TILG* registers 6 tokens of *pondrei*, 59 of *poñerei* and 83 of *porei*; 4 tokens of *saldría*, 6 of *saliría* and 100 of *sairía* (07/20/2017). Forms like *pondrei* can be found in the web: http://asmelloresrecetasengalego.blogspot.com.es/, https://ocioloxia.wordpress.com/2007/07/19/novecento/ (07/20/2017).

10 The form *saldrei* was also collected in Santiago (C35) in the *ALGa*, map 168.

Those forms are found in the speech of informants XX1a, 003, 002a, 002f, XX2g, 004a, all bilinguals with Galician as the language learned at home, and in the speech of 002b and 002c, bilinguals who had Spanish as their mother tongue. As shown in (3), in the rural Galician of Santiago POÑER, TER, VIR, VALER, and SALIR, the FUT/COND word-forms have the same internal morphological structure as any other regular verb: [R-TV-TAM-Agr]; in urban Galician, however, we find word-forms following the template [R-/d/-TAM-Agr], i.e., lacking the thematic vowel, introducing an interfix /d/ between the roots and the endings. In (4) we analyse the urban Galician forms of Santiago according to (1) and (2) and present the corresponding Spanish forms. We also include the INF word-forms in both languages:

4)	Santiago's urban Galician [R-/d/-TAM-Agr]	Spanish
POÑER:COND.1/3SG	pon-d-ría (INF poñ-e-r)	pondría (INF poner)
TER:COND.1/3SG	ten-d-ría (INF t-e-r)	tendría (INF tener)
TER:COND.1PL	ten-d-ría-mos (INF t-e-r)	tendríamos (INF tener)
VIR:COND.3PL	ven-d-ría-n (INF v-i-r)	vendrían (INF venir)
VALER:COND.3PL	val-d-ría-n (INF val-e-r)	valdrían (INF valer)
TER:COND.1SG	ten-d-re-i (INF t-e-r)	tendré (INF tener)
TER:COND.3SG	ten-d-rá (INF t-e-r)	tendrá (INF tener)
TER:COND.3PL	ten-d-rá-n (INF t-e-r)	tendrán (INF tener)
VALER:FUT.1SG	val-d-re-i (INF val-e-r)	valdré (INF valer)
SALIR:FUT.1SG	sal-d-re-i (INF sal-i-r)	saldré (INF salir)
SALIR:FUT.3PL	sal-d-rá-n (INF sal-i-r)	saldrán (INF salir)

While in Spanish the INF and the FUT/COND share the same root in the five verbs (pon-, ten-, ven-, sal-, val-), in urban Galician this only occurs in the case of SALIR and VALER (sal-, val-), since in POÑER, TER and VIR, the INF has different roots from the FUT/COND (INF: POÑER poñ-, TER t-, VIR v-; FUT/COND POÑER pon-, TER ten-, VIR ven-). The urban forms with /d/ and without a thematic vowel are to be considered Spanish borrowings.[11]

---

11 For the history of those word-forms in Spanish, see Penny (2002) and Lloyd (1987). In their evolution to Old Spanish, the Vulgar Latin forms lost the thematic vowel and inserted an epenthetic /d/: *tener+é 'I will have' > tenré > tendré. For their history in Galician, see Varela Barreiro (1998). The contemporary rural Galician forms of the kind terei are late-medieval analogical reconstructions. In their evolution to Old Galician, the Vulgar Latin word-forms also lost their thematic vowel, *tener+ei 'I will have' > tenrei, however, no epenthetic transitional /d/ was inserted between the consonants, but there were produced phonological assimilations (terrei, nowadays

Although the urban Galician of Santiago has taken the roots, the interfix /d/ and the lack of the thematic vowel from Spanish, the TAM and Agr suffixes are still those characteristic of Galician: the 1SG.FUT *tend-rei, sald-rei* in the urban Galician end in the same way as the rural Galician *te-rei, sali-rei.*

Dubert-García (1999: 170–171) has also detected other FUT/COND word-forms in the urban Galician of Santiago that lack the expected thematic vowel: in PODER 'to be able', *podría* 1/3SG.COND, *podrían* 3PL.COND, instead of *podería, poderían* (found in the rural dialects of Santiago and in standard Galician); in HABER 'to have', *habrá* 3SG.FUT, *habría* 1/3SG.COND in the urban speech, instead of the expected *haberá, habería* (found in the rural dialects and in standard Galician).[12] Again, we find the lack of the thematic vowel in the corresponding Spanish cognate word-forms, *podría, podrían, habrá, habría, sabr*é. What is interesting is that the regular verbs of the urban Galician variety preserve their thematic vowel in this morphophonemic context if their Spanish cognates also preserve them: Gal. *deberían* 'they should', Gal. *beberei* 'I will drink', cf. Spanish *deberían, beber*é. In a way, then, both the omissions (loss of the thematic vowel) and the selective preservations seem to speak to the same underlying cause: the influence of Spanish.

To sum up, in the urban Galician of Santiago we find that:

(a) In POÑER, TER, VIR, SALIR, VALER, PODER and HABER, the thematic vowel may be absent in FUT/COND; this seems to result from the replication of a Spanish morphological pattern ([R-TAM-Agr], without TV), i.e., a case of pattern borrowing.

(b) In POÑER, TER, VIR, SALIR, and VALER, an interfix /d/ is found between the root and the TAM suffix; this seems to be a case of matter borrowing.

(c) In POÑER, TER and VIR we find a different root in the FUT/COND than that in the INF word-forms; again, this seems a case of matter borrowing too.

All these urban formatives and patterns are the result of different interferences from Spanish. By comparing Tables 4 and 5, it is easy to see how different irregularities are introduced into the Galician urban grammar and some regularity is in fact lost: verbs that had a regular morphology, at least in the COND/FUT

---

lost) or the triumphant analogical reconstructions based on the infinitival root (*terei*). The word-forms *poñer, poñerei, poñería* of POÑER are even more recent analogical innovations based on the root *poñ-* of the 1SG.IND.PRS and all the SBJV.PRS (Ferreiro 1995). A reviewer observes that these innovations of Galician illustrate a process of simplification. Thus, since the Spanish borrowings of the kind *tendría, pondría* have recently eliminated the Galician analogical forms of the kind *tería, poñería*, contact has resulted in the reintroduction of irregularities.

12 In *ALGa*, map 349, we can find *sabrei* and *saberei* 'I will know' in C35 (Santiago).

Table 4: Exponence of FUT/COND in the rural Galician of Santiago.

DEBER, BEBER, HABER, PODER, POÑER, TER, VIR, VALER, SALIR
R-TV-TAM-Agr // R(FUT/COND) = R(INF) Regular exponence
debería, habería, valería, viría

Table 5: Exponence of FUT/COND in the urban Galician of Santiago.

Regular exponence	Lacking a thematic vowel (pattern borrowing)		
		interfix /d/ (matter borrowing)	
		Infinitival root	Special root
DEBER, BEBER	HABER, PODER	VALER, SALIR	POÑER, TER, VIR
debería	*habría*	*valdría*	*vendría*

word-forms, are now integrated in four different morpholexical classes. All these changes involve the generation of lexical exceptions to regular morphological exponence.

Borrowing in the L-pattern context of OÍR, CAER, TRAER, SALIR and VALER

In standard Galician, the verbs OÍR 'to hear' (< Lat. AUDIO), CAER 'to fall' (< Lat. CADO), TRAER 'to bring' (< Lat. TRAHO) and SAÍR 'to go out' (< Lat. SALIO 'to jump') form a morpholexical subclass since they share the same irregularity in the root corresponding to the 1SG.IND.PRS and all the SBJV.PRS, although they belong to different conjugations: CAER and TRAER belong to the 2nd conjugation and OÍR and SAÍR to the 3rd. All these verbs present a palatal semivowel between the last vowel of their roots and the inflectional endings. The distribution of this /j/ behaves in what Maiden (2005, 2016) calls an L-pattern. In (4a) we offer CAER 'to fall' as a model of the conjugation of all the members of this morpholexical class; the roots with the /j/ (spelt <i>) are underlined.

4)	a)		IND.PRS	SBJV.PRS	b)	IND.PRS	SBJV.PRS
		1SG	*cai-o*	*cai-a*		*vall-o*	*vall-a*
		2SG	*ca-es*	*cai-as*		*val-es*	*vall-as*
		3SG	*ca-e*	*cai-a*	.	*val-e*	*vall-a*

1PL	*ca-emos*	*cai-amos*	*val-emos*	*vall-amos*
2PL	*ca-edes*	*cai-ades*	*val-edes*	*vall-ades*
3PL	*ca-en*	*cai-an*	*val-en*	*vall-an*

In standard Galician, VALER 'to be good at/for' belongs to another morpholexical subclass, since it has one root ending in a palatal consonant[13] according to the L-pattern, in the 1SG.IND.PRS and in the SBJV.PRS, and another root ending in a lateral alveolar elsewhere (4b).

In the rural Galician of Santiago (5a), we find different groupings: in one subclass we find OÍR, CAER, and TRAER, with the semivowel /j/ in the L-pattern, as in (4a); and in another subclass, we find VALER and SALIR, which preserve the intervocalic -/l/-, with the alternation between a palatal (spelt <ll>) in the L-pattern and a lateral alveolar (spelt <l>) elsewhere (5b):

5) Santiago's rural Galician
a) Subclass: insertion of /j/
    OÍR: *oi-o, oi-a*; but *o-es, o-ímos*
    CAER: *cai-o, cai-a*; but *ca-es, ca-emos*
    TRAER: *trai-o, trai-a*, but *tra-es, tra-emos*
b) Subclass: palatal/alveolar alternation
    VALER: *vall-o, vall-a*, but *val-es, val-emos*
    SALIR: *sall-o, sall-a*, but *sal-es, sal-imos*

Nevertheless, in the urban Galician dialects, as illustrated in (6), we find a feature which seems to be Spanish in origin: the presence of a velar interfix (g)[14] at the right of the root, also following the L-pattern.[15] In these urban dialects, OÍR, CAER, TRAER, SALIR, and VALER belong to this subclass. Again, inside this subclass, OÍR, CAER, and TRAER also present the semivowel /j/ (spelt <i>) at the left of (g) in the L-pattern:

---

13 In conservative dialects, the L-Pattern root ends in a lateral palatal, /baʎ/-; in innovative dialects, it ends in a palatal stop, /baɟ/-; both segments are spelt with <ll>, *vall-*. The presence of the palatal stop is known as *yeísmo* or *delateralization*.

14 We use the notation (g) in order to show that what we see is a phonologic sociolinguistic variable, with three realizations: /g/, /x/ and /h/.

15 For the origins of these velar consonants in Spanish, see Penny (2002) and Lloyd (1987). For the origins of the traditional Galician forms, see Ferreiro (1995). Mariño Paz (2003: 223) has found forms of the kind of *valga* in journalistic texts written in Santiago de Compostela in 1836.

6) Santiago's urban Galician
a) OÍR: _oig-o, oig-a_, but _o-es, o-ímos_
   CAER: _caig-o, caig-a_, but _ca-es, ca-emos_
   TRAER: _traig-o, traig-a_, but _tra-es, tra-emos_
b) SALIR: _salg-o, salg-a_, but _sal-es, sal-imos_
   VALER: _valg-o, valg-a_, but _val-es, val-emos_[16]

All these cases are surely matter borrowings, and what has been taken was the entire Spanish roots _oig-, caig-, traig-, salg-_ and _valg-_; the distribution of these forms in Spanish is in accordance with the morphomic L-pattern.

What we see now is that the two subclasses of (5) are imperfectly reduced to one in (6). The presence of (g) reinforces the L-pattern in OÍR, CAER, and TRAER; and its use in the five verbs implies the presence of new matter without new functions, since (g) only reinforces a pre-existing L-pattern that is marked enough in the rural Galician of Santiago. From this point of view, the adjunction of (g) is also a case of hyper-characterization of 1SG.IND.PRS and of SBJV.PRS. Note that the remaining word forms of the paradigms of OÍR, CAER, and TRAER preserve their Galician form: Galician _oes_ 'you hear', _oe_ '(s)he hears', _oísemos_ 'we heard-SBJV' vs Spanish _oyes, oye, oyésemos_.

If we now compare the form and distribution of the roots of SALIR in the urban and rural Galician of Santiago, as illustrated in (7), we can see again how the conjugation of this verb has become more systemically complex under the influence of Spanish:

7) Rural Galician of Santiago
   root _sall-_, L-pattern: e.g., 1SG.IND.PRS _sallo_ and SBJV.PRS _salla, sallas, sallamos_
   root _sal-_, elsewhere: e.g., 3SG.IND.PRS _sale_, 1SG.FUT _salirei_, 1SG.COND _saliría_
   Santiago's urban Galician
   root _salg-_, L-pattern: e.g., 1SG.IND.PRS _salgo_ and SBJV.PRS _salga, salgas, salgamos_
   root _sald-_, FUT/COND: e.g., 1SG.FUT _saldrei_, 1SG.COND _saldría_
   root _sal-_, elsewhere: e.g., 3SG.IND.PRS _sale_, 1SG.PST.PFV _salín_, 1SG.PST.IPFV _salía_

Obviously, the same is true for VALER. We can compare this situation with the data taken from the dialect of the first author, the Galician of Muros (A Coruña), which presents _sal-_ and _val-_ as the only roots all across the conjugations of SALIR and VALER, respectively: _salo_ in SALIR:1SG.IND.PRS, _sala_ in SALIR:1SG.SBJV.PRS, _salirei_

---

16 In the _ALGa_ we could find _salgo_ (map 161), _salga_ (170), _valgo_ (121), _valga_ (133), _oigo_ (294) and _traigo_ (380).

in SALIR:1SG.FUT; *valo* in VALER:1SG.IND.PRS, *vala* in VALER:1SG.SBJV.PRS, *valerei* in VALER:1SG.FUT. Similar forms were gathered by Dubert-García (1999) in the west-ernmost rural dialects of Santiago (see the distribution of the forms *salo/sala, sallo/salla, salgo/salga* all across the Galician speaking territory in the maps 161, 170 and 171 of the *ALGa*; see also Map 1 in the appendix). We notice a progression from the greatest regularity / predictability in Muros to the least regularity / pre-dictability in the urban dialect of Santiago.

Additionally, contact with Spanish has also produced a reorganization of the morpholexical subclasses of some other verbs of the 2nd and 3rd conjugations in urban Galician. For example, in two conservative rural speakers from Santi-ago (Y12c and Y13a) Dubert-García (1999: 188–193) found that the verbs TRAER 'to bring', CAER 'to fall', OÍR 'to hear', ROER 'to gnaw', and MOER 'to mill' behave in the way reflected in (5a); VALER and SALIR behave in the way of (5b); and CONOCER 'to know' (perhaps a loanword eliminating the Galician form *coñecer*) and PARECER 'to seem' are fully regular (unaffected by any L-pattern):

Table 6: Morpholexical classes in the rural Galician of Santiago (Y12c, Y13a).

L-Pattern		Regulars
Insertion of /j/	Palatal/alveolar alternation	PARECER (*parezo/pareza*)
TRAER (*traio/traia*)	SALIR (*sallo/salla*)	CONOCER (*conozo/conoza*)
CAER (*caio/caia*)	VALER (*vallo/valla*)	
OÍR (*oio/oia*)		
ROER (*roio/roia*)		
MOER (*moio/moia*)		

In two young urban bilingual speakers from Santiago (XX1a and 003), however, Dubert-García (1999) has found that the frequent verbs TRAER 'to bring', CAER 'to fall', and OÍR 'to hear' have passed to the morpholexical class of (6a), *traigo/ traiga, caigo/caiga, oigo/oiga*, while the infrequent verbs ROER 'to gnaw' and MOER 'to mill' have lost their /j/ in the L-pattern and have become regular (a typical phe-nomenon that links frequency of use and idiosyncrasy; Bybee 1985), *roo/roa* (not *roio/roia*), *moo/moa* (not *moio/moia*); the verbs CONOCER 'to know' and PARECER 'to seem' have been transferred to the L-pattern under the Spanish model, and now introduce an interfix /k/ (spelt <c>) between the old root and the inflectional endings, like their Spanish cognates do: *conozco/conozca, parezco/parezca* (Table 6). Thus, in the Galician variety of the bilingual urban speakers XX1a and 003, now TRAER, CAER, OÍR, SALIR, VALER, PARECER, and CONOCER group together under the L-pattern, while ROER and MOER have escaped the L-pattern and have become regular.

5 Discussion

We have seen how the reviewed phenomena of contact have restructured the grammar of the urban Galician varieties in a setting of extended bilingualism (the presence in the community of a great number of people speaking Galician and Spanish). We intend now to reflect (a) on the factors that could have helped in the introduction of the borrowings, and (b) on the consequences of the introduction of the borrowing in terms of the possible complexification of the Galician grammar.

With respect to the facilitative factors that helped the introduction of the morphological borrowings we may point out the strong structural similarities between Galician and Spanish. In fact, the basic morphological skeleton of the verbal word-forms in Galician is identical to that of Spanish: [R-TV-TAM-Agr]. Many differences between both languages tend to be only phonological, the (sequences of) phonemes constituting the morphemes: the 1PL.SBJV.PST.IPFV word-form of COMER 'to eat' in Galician is *com-é-se-mos*, with a TV /e/; in Spanish, it is *com-ié-se-mos*, with a TV /je/. Under a usage based exemplar model (Bybee 1985, 1988, 2001; Langacker 2000), it makes sense to say that the Spanish borrowing *tendrei* 'I will have' has emerged from the merge of an inflectional Galician schema like that of (8a), which links inflectional endings to morphosyntactic representations, with another Spanish schema that links the verbal lexeme TER, the properties FUT and COND with the Spanish root /ten/, followed by the interfix /d/, without a thematic vowel (8b), creating the form *tendrei* (8c):

8) a) FUT   1SG   b)   TER:FUT/COND   c)   TER:1SG.FUT
      /'re/   /j/   /tend/   /ten'drej/

In a schema like (8a), FUT may be linked to /'re/ in *cantarei*, (cf. *cantaremos* 'we will sing', *cantaredes* 'you-PL will sing'); 1SG to /j/ in *cantarei* (cf. *cantei* 'I sang', *dei* 'I gave', *hei* 'I have'); and IND.FUT.1SG to /'rej/ (Dubert-García 2014). Speakers extract schemata such as those thanks to the frequency of their types in language use (Bybee 2001): e.g., all the Galician IND.FUT.1SG verbal word-forms end in /'rej/.

Schemata emerge and are also strengthened by high token frequency. This is important in irregular forms, which are usually very frequent in discourse. Speakers may also detect that some of these frequent items share commonalities. Spanish irregular forms like *tendré*, *vendré*, *saldré*, *salgo*, *valgo*, *oigo*, *caigo* are surely stored. Throughout the lexical connections that these forms establish among them (and with other regular ones), its structures emerge at different levels of abstraction (as shown in Tables 4–7). In the Spanish forms like *saldré*, *valdré*,

Table 7: Morpholexical classes in the urban Galician of Santiago (XX1, 003).

L-Pattern (Subclass: insertion of velar)		Regulars
Insertion of /g/	Insertion of /k/	ROER (*roo/roa*)
TRAER (*traigo/traiga*)	PARECER (*parezco/parezca*)	MOER (*moo/moa*)
CAER (*caigo/caiga*)	CONOCER (*conozco/conozca*)	
OÍR (*oigo/oiga*)		
———		
SALIR (*salgo/salga*)		
VALER (*valgo/valga*)		

tendré, pondré, vendré, the 1SG.IND.FUT properties may associate with different phonological features (e.g., the position of stress, the presence of the /d/, etc.). Those associations produce possible schemata like that of (8b) that speakers may use to produce the innovative, borrowed, Galician forms like *sald-rei, vald-rei, tend-rei, pond-rei, vend-rei.*

A reviewer argues that, since only certain lexical items are affected, we face a problem of lexical storing and not of productive, compositional, morphology. It is important, however, to bear in mind that these few stored items present regular endings and are related among them by their similarities, producing lexical connections; besides, their roots are in complementary distribution with other roots (*val-e-s,* but *vald-rías* and *valg-o*). Thus, although stored as individual lexical items in the lexicon, irregular word forms like *saldrei, valdrei, tendrei, pondrei, vendrei* are complex and have internal morphological structure.

In its turn, the strong linguistic similarities between Spanish and Galician could have made it easier for speakers to fall into lapses during the linguistic processing of their multilingual repertoire. This has to do with the degree to which speakers are able to exercise control over the mental organisation of their linguistic repertoire. In fact, as is often noted (Matras 2009: 219), very often those phenomena that stand out as diachronic changes in the repertory of structures that we define as the (system of the) grammar of a language are often the end result of old lapses on the part of speakers in exercising such control. In fact, in the present case, the consolidation and conventionalization of the results of those old lapses led to the recategorization as Galician of forms, patterns and schemata formerly classified as Spanish by the speakers; in the multilingual repertory of the contemporary speakers, those forms are, nowadays, utilizable to create discourse categorized as Spanish and discourse categorized as Galician.

These facts also raise the question of the possible complexification or simplification of the Galician grammar because of the linguistic changes due to borrowing. Resolving this question is not an easy task. The changes detected in the verbs analysed in this study seem to be a counterexample to the tendency predicted by Trudgill (2011), according to whom long-term co-territorial contact does not produce increases in the irregularity or in the redundancy of the grammar (via hyper-characterization, in the sense of Malkiel 1957–58, of the exponence of morphosyntactic properties) but rather the opposite, simplification, understood as the regularization of irregularities, an increase in lexical and morphological transparency and loss of redundancy (see also Mühlhäusler 1977; Thomason & Kaufman 1988; Trudgill 2009). In fact, the result of contact in urban Galician seems to be more absolute complexity, since more irregularities -exceptional behaviour- are introduced into the Galician system: e.g. the absence of the regular thematic vowel preceding the inflectional endings (*vald-rei, hab-rei* instead of *val-e-rei, hab-e-rei*) and the root changes depending on tense and mood (*vald-rei* instead of *val-e-rei*). More irregular forms entail an increase in absolute systemic complexity. We understand complexity here as a minimal inference that cannot be avoided if we compare Tables 4 and 5 or the data in (7). In fact, one morpholexical (Table 4) class was split in four (Table 5). All these changes involve the generation of lexical exceptions to regular morphological exponence, so that their result implies an increase in the overall complexity of the system of grammar, rather than the reverse (Nichols 1992; Trudgill 2011).

If, however, we contemplate these changes from the perspective of the actual language users, their representational and encoding challenges, then the very opposite might be true: in the actual multilectal morphological repertory of these speakers (which comprises all of the Galician morphology and all of the Spanish morphology in virtue of their being bilinguals) there are now in fact fewer and more similar forms. The *costs* or *difficulties* inherent to the processing of a more complex linguistic system in one language are in fact compensated by a simplification of the overall multilingual repertoire of the bilingual speakers. Consider the *Minimize Forms* principle of Hawkins (2004: 38), defined as follows:

> The human processor prefers to minimize the formal complexity of each linguistic form F (its phoneme, morpheme, word, or phrasal units) and the number of forms with unique conventionalized property assignments, thereby assigning more properties to fewer forms. These minimizations apply in proportion to the ease with which a given property P can be assigned in processing to a given F.

Impressionistically at least, it seems clear that Minimize Forms applies here. It is also true that, as noted by Levinson (2000), the minimizations that Hawkins talks about often also result in greater ambiguity and in the need to have recourse to greater use of inferential processing, that is, the kind of global, strategic, extralinguistic processing that enriches interpretations when the form of the message is underspecified. This, however, does not seem to be the present case. From the perspective of the actual language user, the minimization in question here boils down to a reduction in the number of forms that may do the same functional job. Given that both forms are in fact quite similar, the representational move taken by these speakers makes perfect usage-based sense. Of course, this begs the question why such moves are not more radical in view of their apparent utility. We suspect that little understood principles of 'language preservation' are at play, for otherwise languages like Galician would have succumbed under the pressure exercised by Spanish long ago. But indeed it is evident that such pressure exists, for the phenomenon we are analysing here is simply one of many that conform to a well-established pattern: the loss of features of Galician and the replacement of such features for the corresponding Spanish ones. A prominent case is, for example, the loss of phonemic contrasts in the domain of the mid vowels: traditional Galician has a vowel system with 4 heights, /i, e, ɛ, a, ɔ, o, u/, but mid vowels are merging in the speech of many speakers who have Spanish as their mother tongue; this brings about a system of 3 heights instead, /i, e, a, o, u/ (Vidal Figueiroa 1997).

We are therefore led to conclude that the increase in irregularity and redundancy in the urban dialects of Galician is possible due to the structural similarity between Galician and (Galician) Spanish; and, perhaps, also to the relative simplification of linguistic processing that it entails.

6 Concluding remarks

In this study, we have tried to show how very particular areas of the Galician system of verbal inflectional morphology have changed as a result of contact with (borrowing from) Spanish in the city of Santiago de Compostela and its surroundings.

We have shown how the introduction of those morphological borrowings have restructured the Galician system of grammar and have even increased its absolute complexity by augmenting morphological irregularity.

On the cognitive side, it has been argued that the extension of these morphological borrowings might have started as lapses due to the difficulty in processing a multilingual repertory that is largely very similar, a fact that invites a kind of 'ironing out' of the small differences. In this sense, the 'ironing out' seems to have been driven by processing considerations such as the (relative) need to reduce the number of forms that ultimately do the same functional job.

The reviewed facts show that borrowing is a complex multifaceted, process that must be explained from social, linguistic, and cognitive perspectives. They also show the explicative power of relative, language's user-oriented complexity.

References

ALGa = Santamarina, Antón, Rosario Álvarez Blanco, Francisco Fernández Rei, Manuel González González. 1990. *Atlas Lingüístico Galego. Volume I: Morfoloxía verbal.* A Coruña: Fundación Barrié.

Álvarez Cáccamo, C. 1989. Variaçom lingüística e o factor social na Galiza. *Hispanic Linguistics* 2:2. 253–298

Álvarez, Rosario & Xosé Xove. 2002. *Gramática da lingua galega.* Vigo: Galaxia.

Álvarez, Rosario, Luís Xosé Regueira & Henrique Monteagudo. 1986. *Gramática galega.* Vigo: Galaxia.

Bortoni-Ricardo, S. M. 1985. *The urbanisation of rural dialect speakers: a sociolinguistic study in Brazil.* Cambridge: Cambridge University Press.

Bybee, Joan. 1985. *Morphology.* Amsterdam: John Benjamins.

Bybee, Joan. 1988. Morphology as lexical organization. In M. Hammond & M. Noonan (eds.), *Theoretical morphology,* 119–41. San Diego, Academic Press.

Bybee, Joan. 2001. *Phonology and language use.* Cambridge: Cambridge University Press.

Carrington, Peter J. & John Scott. 2011. *The Sage handbook of social network analysis.* CA: Sage.

Chambers, J. K. 2009. *Sociolinguistic theory. Revised edition.* Oxford: Wiley-Blackwell.

Chambers, J. K. & P. Trudgill. 1998. *Dialectology.* Cambridge: Cambridge University Press.

Dubert-García, Francisco. 1999. *Aspectos do galego de Santiago de Compostela.* Santiago de Compostela: Universidade de Santiago de Compostela.

Dubert-García, Francisco. 2014. *Splinter* morphologique et analogie dans les dialectes galiciens et portugais. In *Morphologie flexionnelle et dialectologie romane: typologie(s) et modélisation(s)*, *Mémoires de la Société de Linguistique de Paris*, 22, 69–87. Louvain: Peeters.

Dubert-García, Francisco. 2017. Sobre a *Gallaecia Magna* e as relacións históricas e xeolingüísticas entre galego, portugués e asturiano. *Estudis romànics* 39. 43–69.

Dubert, Francisco & Charlotte Galves. 2016. Galician and Portuguese. In Adam Ledgeway & Martin Maiden (eds.), *The Oxford guide to the Romance languages*, 411–446. Oxford: Oxford University Press.

Elisa Fernández Rei. 2016. Dialectal, historical and sociolinguistic aspects of Galician intonation. *Dialectologia. Special Issue VI.* 147–169.

Ferreiro, Manuel. 1995. *Gramática histórica galega.* Santiago de Compostela: Laiovento.

Freixeiro Mato, Xosé Ramón. 2000. *Gramática da lingua galega. II. Morfosintaxe.* Vigo: A Nosa Terra.

García Mouton, Pilar & Isabel Molina Martos. 2009. Trabajos sociodialectales en la Comunidad de Madrid. *Revista de Filología Española LXXXIX*, 1.°.175–186.

Gardani, Francesco, Peter Arkadiev & Nino Amiridze. 2015. Borrowed morphology: an overview. In Francesco Gardani, Peter Arkadiev & Nino Amiridze (eds.), *Borrowed morphology*, 1–26. Berlin: De Gruyter Mouton.

Hawkins, John A. 1994. *A performance theory of order and constituency.* Cambridge: Cambridge University Press.

Hawkins, John A. 2004. *Efficiency and complexity in grammars.* Oxford: Oxford University Press.

Hickey, Raymond. 2012. Internally and externally motivated language change. In Juan Manuel Hernández-Campoy & Juan Camilo Conde-Silvestre (eds.), *The handbook of historical sociolinguistics*, 387–407. Malden: Wiley-Blackwell.

Hock, Hans Heinrich. 1991. *Principles of historical linguistics*. Berlin, New York: Mouton de Gruyter.
Kadushin, Charles. 2012. *Understanding social networks: Theories, concepts, and findings*. Oxford: Oxford University Press.
Kusters, Wouter. 2008. Complexity in linguistic theory, language learning and language change. In Matti Miestamo, Kaius Sinnemäki & Fred Karlsson (eds.), *Language complexity. Typology, contact, change*, 3–22. Amsterdam/Philadelphia: John Benjamins.
Langacker, R.W. 2000. A dynamic usage-based model. In M. Barlow & S. Kemmer (eds.), *Usage based models of language*, 1–63. Standford, CSLI.
Levinson, Stephen C. 2000. *Presumptive meanings: The theory of generalized conversational implicature*. Cambridge, MA: MIT Press
López Iglesias, Edelmiro. 2016. Do atraso ao progreso económico de Galiza? Un proceso histórico á espera dun relato. In Isidro Dubert (ed.), *Historia das historias de Galicia*, 329–356. Xerais: Vigo.
Lloyd, Paul M. 1989. *From Latin to Spanish. Vol. 1: Historical phonology and morphology of the Spanish Language*. American Philosophical Society.
Maiden, Martin. 2005. Morphological autonomy and diachrony. In Geert Booij & Jaap van Marle (eds.), *Yearbook of morphology 2004*, 137–175. Dordrecht: Springer.
Maiden, Martin. 2016. Morphomes. In Adam Ledgeway & Martin Maiden (eds.), *The Oxford guide to Romance languages*, 708–721. Oxford: Oxford University Press.
Malkiel, Y. 1957–58. Diachronic hypercharacterization in Romance. *Archivum Linguisticum* 9(2): 79–113; 10(1): 1–36.
Mariño Paz, Ramón. 2003. *O idioma Galego no limiar da súa renacenza*. A Coruña: Área de Filoloxías Galega e Portuguesa, Departamento de Galego-Portugués, Francés e Lingüística.
Mariño Paz, Ramón. 2008. *Historia de la lengua gallega*. Muenchen: Lincom.
Martín Butragueño, Pedro. 2004. El contacto de dialectos como motor del cambio lingüístico. In Pedro Martín Butragueño (ed.), *Cambio lingüístico. Métodos y problemas*, 81–144. Mexico: El Colegio de México.
Matras, Yaron. 2009. *Language contact*. Cambridge: Cambridge University Press.
Matras, Yaron. 2010. Contact, convergence, and typology. In Raymond Hickey (ed.), *The handbook of language contact*, 66–85. Oxford: Wiley-Blackwell.
Miestamo, Matti. 2008. Grammatical complexity in a cross linguistic perspective. In Matti Miestamo, Kaius Sinnemäki, Fred Karlsson (eds.), *Language complexity. Typology, contact, change*, 23–41. Amsterdam/Philadelphia: John Benjamins.
Milroy, James. 1992. *Linguistic variation and change*. Oxford: Blackwell.
Molina Martos, Isabel. 2006. Innovación y difusión del cambio lingüístico en Madrid. *Revista de Filología Española* LXXXVI, 1., 127–149.
Mondorf, Britta. 2009. More support for more-support: the role of processing constraints on the choice between synthetic and analytic comparative forms. *Studies in Language Variation* 4. Amsterdam: John Benjamins.
Monteagudo, H. 1999. *Historia social da lingua galega*. Vigo: Galaxia.
Monteagudo, H. & A. Santamarina. 1993. Galician and Castilian in contact: historical, social and linguistic aspects. In R. Possner & J. N. Green (eds.), *Bilingualism and linguistic conflict in Romance*, 117–173. Trends in Romance linguistics and philology 5: Berlin: Mouton de Gruyter.
MSG 1992-1 = Fernández Rodríguez, Mauro A. & Modesto A. Rodríguez Neira (coords.). 1994. *Lingua inicial e competencia lingüística en Galicia*. A Coruña: Real Academia Galega.

MSG 1992-2 = Fernández Rodríguez, Mauro A. & Modesto A. Rodríguez Neira (coords.). 1995. *Usos lingüísticos en Galicia. Compendio do II volume do Mapa sociolingüístico de Galicia*. A Coruña: Real Academia Galega.

MSG 2004-1 = González González, Manuel (dir.). 2007. *Mapa sociolingüístico de Galicia 2004. Vol. 1: Lingua inicial e competencia lingüística en Galicia*A Coruña: Real Academia Galega.

MSG 2004-2 = González González, Manuel (dir.). 2008. *Mapa sociolingüístico de Galicia 2004. Vol. 2: Usos lingüísticos en Galicia*. A Coruña: Real Academia Galega

Mühlhäusler, Peter. 1977. *Pidginisation and simplification of language*. Canberra: Pacific Linguistics.

Muljačić, Žarko. 1991. Per un approccio relativistico al rapporto: lingua nazionale dialetti. In Giovan Battista Pellegrini (ed.), *XVIII Congresso di studi dialettali italiani "Fra dialetto e lingua nazionale: realtà e prospettive"*, 247259. Padova: Unipress.

Newman, Mark, Albert-László Barabási & Duncan J. Watts. 2006. *The structure and dynamics of networks* (Princeton Studies in Complexity). Oxford: Princeton University Press.

Nichols, Johanna. 1992. *Linguistic diversity in space and time*. Chicago: Chicago University Press

Penny, Ralph. 2002. *A history of the Spanish language*. Cambridge: Cambridge University Press.

Ramallo, Fernando & Gabriel Rei-Doval. 2015. The standardization of Galician. *Sociolinguistica* 29. 61–81.

Rohdenburg, Günter. 1996. Cognitive complexity and increased grammatical explicitness in English. *Cognitive Linguistics* 7(2). 149–182.

Rojo, Guillermo. 2004. El español de Galicia. In Rafael Cano (coord.), *Historia de la lengua española*, 1087–1101. Barcelona: Ariel.

Santamarina, Antonio. 1974. *El verbo gallego*. Santiago de Compostela: Universidade de Santiago de Compostela.

Thomason, Sarah Grey. 2003. Contact as a source of linguistic change. In Richard D. Janda & Brian D. Joseph (eds.), *The handbook of historical linguistics*, 687–712. Oxford: Blackwell.

Thomason, Sarah Grey & Terrence Kaufman. 1988. *Language contact, creolization, and genetic linguistics*. Berkeley: University of California Press.

TILG = Santamarina, Antón (coord.). *Tesouro informatizado da lingua galega*. Santiago de Compostela: Instituto da Lingua Galega. http://ilg.usc.es/TILG/ (accessed 07/20/2017).

Torres Luna, María Pilar de & Rubén Lois González. 1995. Claves para la interpretación del mundo urbano gallego. *Anales de Geografía de la Universidad Complutense* 15. 731–740.

Trudgill, Peter. 1986. *Dialects in contact*. Oxford: Blackwell.

Trudgill, Peter. 2009. Sociolinguistic typology and complexification. In Geoffrey Sampson, David Gil & Peter Trudgill (eds.), *Language complexity as an evolving variable*, 98–109. Oxford: Oxford University Press.

Trudgill, Peter. 2010. Contact and sociolinguistic typology. In Raymond Hickey (eds.), *The handbook of language contact*, 299–319. Oxford: Willey-Blackwell.

Trudgill, Peter. 2011. *Sociolinguistic typology*. Oxford: Oxford Universtity Press.

Valcárcel Riveiro, Carlos. 2001. Llengua, desenvolupament urbà i diversificació socioespacial a la Galícia atlàntica: breu repàs de la situació des de la geolingüística. *Treballs de la Societat Catalana de Geografia* 51. 189–201.

Varela Barreiro, Xavier. 1998. *Verrá*: os futuros irregulares con vibrante múltiple na *Lírica profana*. In Xosé Luís Couceiro Pérez & Lydia Fontoira (eds.), *Martín Codax, Mendiño, Johán de Cangas*, 175–188. Santiago de Compostela: Universidade de Santiago de Compostela.

Vidal Figueiroa, T. 1997. Estructuras fonéticas de tres dialectos de Vigo. *Verba* 24. 313332.

Villalva, A. 2000. *Estruturas morfológicas: unidades e hierarquias nas palavras do português*. Lisboa: Fundação Calouste Gulbenkian.

Appendix

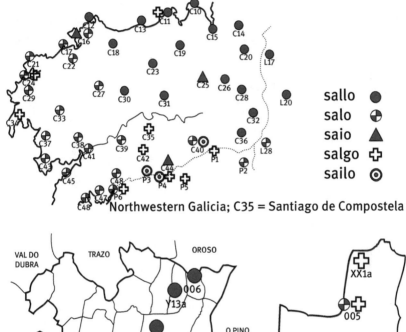

Map 1: Distribution of the word-forms corresponding to the 1SG.IND.PRS of SALIR 'to go out' in North-western Galicia and in Santiago de Compostela.
Sources: *ALGa* and Dubert-García (1999).

Index

https://doi.org/10.1515/9781501509988-009